W9-AGB-996

Praise for

Business Ethics and the Natural Environment

"With business's renewed focus on sustainable growth, Newton's hopeful book comes at the right time, providing us theoretically sound, eloquently presented, and practically wise frameworks and conclusions."

Dennis J. Moberg, Santa Clara University, and President, Society for Business Ethics

"This excellent book perfectly balances philosophical and case study analysis to help students explore within today's political and legal framework the responsibilities of business and of individuals to the natural environment."

Mark Sagoff, University of Maryland

"This is an important book by one of the leading scholars in the fields of business ethics and environmental ethics. For too long has business ignored the reality that the economy is but a subsystem within the wider biosphere; Lisa Newton addresses these overlapping fields thoughtfully and perceptively."

Joseph Des Jardins, College of St Benedict

"Lisa Newton has written the perfect text for philosophy courses in applied ethics, environmental studies courses featuring ethics, and business ethics courses including environmental as well as social concerns – theoretically robust and case specific."

Baird Callicott, University of North Texas

Foundations of Business Ethics

Series editors: W. Michael Hoffman and Robert E. Frederick

Written by an assembly of the most distinguished figures in business ethics, the Foundations of Business Ethics series aims to explain and assess the fundamental issues that motivate interest in each of the main subjects of contemporary research. In addition to a general introduction to business ethics, individual volumes cover key ethical issues in management, marketing, finance, accounting, and computing. The volumes, which are complementary yet complete in themselves, allow instructors maximum flexibility in the design and presentation of course materials without sacrificing either depth of coverage or the discipline-based focus of many business courses. The volumes can be used separately or in combination with anthologies and case studies, depending on the needs and interests of the instructors and students.

Series List:

Business Ethics and the Natural Environment

Lisa H. Newton

Blackwell
Publishing

BLACKWELL PUBLISHING
350 Main Street, Malden, MA 02148-5020, USA
108 Cowley Road, Oxford OX4 1JF, UK
550 Swanston Street, Carlton, Victoria 3053, Australia

First published 2005 by Blackwell Publishing Ltd

Library of Congress Cataloging-in-Publication Data

Newton, Lisa H., 1939–
Business ethics and the natural environment / Lisa H. Newton.
  p.   cm. — (Foundations of business ethics ; 6)
Includes bibliographical references and index.
ISBN-13: 978-1-4051-1662-6 (hardcover : alk. paper)
ISBN-10: 1-4051-1662-5 (hardcover : alk. paper)
ISBN-13: 978-1-4051-1663-3 (pbk. : alk. paper)
ISBN-10: 1-4051-1663-3 (pbk. : alk. paper)
1. Industrial management—Environmental aspects.   2. Social
responsibility of business.   3. Environmental protection—Moral
and ethical aspects.   I. Title.   II. Series.
HD30.255.N49 2005
174′.4—dc22
2004024668

A catalogue record for this title is available from the British Library.

Typeset in 10.5/12.5pt Plantin
by Integra Software Services Pvt. Ltd, Pondicherry, India
Printed and bound in the United Kingdom
by MPG, Bodmin, Cornwall

The publisher's policy is to use permanent paper from mills that operate
a sustainable forestry policy, and which has been manufactured from
pulp processed using acid-free and elementary chlorine-free practices.
Furthermore, the publisher ensures that the text paper and cover board
used have met acceptable environmental accreditation standards.

For further information on
Blackwell Publishing, visit our website:
www.blackwellpublishing.com

Conts

Preface

❧ WHY I WROTE THIS BOOK ❧

First, of course, there are the urgent practical, social, and moral problems. Things are not going well for the world. There is war, there is terror, and there is political instability. But the world has always had war, terror, and political instability; all these we have known since our youth. In addition to all these, underlying and exacerbating them, there is also an increasing sense that the natural environment of the globe is under terrible pressure, and this fear is quite new, no more than half a century old. There are new logging ventures in equatorial Africa, which enrich corrupt elites while slicing roads through forests recently untouched, making paths for the poachers who think nothing of killing the last wild gorillas, chimpanzees, and white rhinoceros. New governments in South America are pressing for economic development, which may come only at the expense of the Amazonian rainforest, home to half the species on earth. The Arctic National Wildlife Reserve may be invaded to acquire new reserves of oil. They say the great fisheries off New England are fished out. There are graphs that show that the earth is getting warmer, probably because of all the new carbon we are putting in the air through burning fossil fuels. If it gets much warmer we may lose some island nations, and the people of the Seychelles are very upset at that. They say the great coral reefs are bleaching, beginning to die. Hunters may take the last whales from the ocean, the last tigers from the forests, and eventually the last wild elephants from the African plains. We do not seem to be able to get a real handle on the problems. As stated, they seem real and objective enough, and no matter how serious or otherwise they turn out to be, they should be addressed and brought under control. Yet every statement of the problems (including in this paragraph), let alone every proposed solution, seems politically tinged, part of some political agenda, therefore safely ignored by those of the opposite political persuasion, and no one seems to know how to break through that perception.

We need methods to sort out the problems and the passionately held positions on the problems. One reason to write this book, then, is to analyze the conflicts that bedevil us in our daily lives, and see if formulations, and sensible courses of action, can be found that will dissolve the dilemmas and allow us to proceed peacefully. It is no accident that almost any environmental dilemma can be described, if we like, as a confrontation between business interests and the interests of the land itself. The familiar scenario pits economic interests – profits, jobs, economic development, shareholder wealth – against environmental values – preservation of unspoiled wilderness, the health of wild species, the protection of the waterways from chemical pollution, the public health in the very long term. The result of this scenario is the polarization of the people best qualified to solve environmental problems, the scientifically knowledgeable environmentalists and the corporate managers who work most directly with the natural environment, into opposed and often non-communicating camps. Since every dispute that occupies the American mind ends up in politics and in the courts, the opposition plays it out as a political campaign issue and it becomes mired in litigation. But both the political and the courtroom settings are essentially adversarial, such that no matter what the short-range resolution (the election, the verdict), the parties are left as adversaries, and cannot work together to preserve both sets of values. In short, we have set up our environmental problems, in the context of our accustomed institutional solutions, in such a way that we cannot solve them.

Why does this conflict seem inevitable? Consider Figure 1, a variant of the old Venn diagram of our baby logic days. Each circle represents a sphere of activity and constituents – "stakeholders" – and therefore each circle contains a strong norm of protection.

The "Economics" circle is the familiar world of business and economics: the norm is to increase the long-term welfare of all by making correct economic decisions (decisions that maximize efficiency) within the context of the free market. In this circle, there is a strong presumption in favor of allowing the market to govern itself – to decide, on the basis of what people are willing to pay, what should be for sale, at what price, at what quality and quantity, and under what conditions of manufacture and merchandising. Government is useful

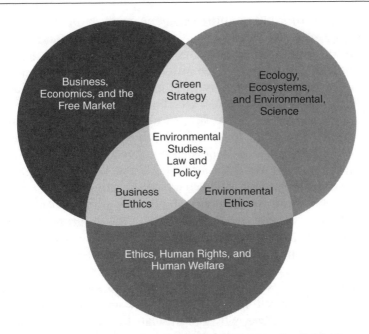

Figure 1   Environmental studies, law and policy: How the fields discussed in this book are related to each other.

only to protect property rights and enforce contracts. Naturally available products, the products of nature, are governed by property rights, and are the property of the owner to dispose of as may be most advantageous for that owner. There is a strong presumption against the government, or any other body, limiting the free use of natural products or of private property in land.

The "Ethics" circle is the realm of human rights and claims: the norm is to protect present human welfare (health, employment, education – fulfillment generally) and above all human rights – life, liberty, dignity, and property. Ordinarily, this norm opposes the economic norm, as unions oppose management, Occupational Safety and Health Administration (OSHA) opposes industry, and strong limits are placed on what may be bought and sold. There is no inherent economic reason, after all, not to permit the sale of humans as slaves; it was, in fact, common practice for at least 5,000 years of our history. There is no economic reason not to let the market select the degree of safety in the workplace for the factory worker or in the automobile for the customer. Nor is there any inherent economic reason to restrict (by time, age, or audience) the sale of cigarettes, alcohol, cocaine, marijuana, heroin, or human organs. There is a market; let the market speak. In the end, economic reasoning holds, we will all be better off. We have laws precisely in order to tell the corporation when it may not employ exclusively economic reasoning. These laws are controversial, and constantly subject to adjustment; neither the economic nor the ethical absolutes are accepted without question. The argument for a free market in all the commodities noted above (except live humans) has not fallen on deaf ears; the debate continues. The very existence of the debate shows that we acknowledge two different normative spheres here, and are willing to allow their competing claims to battle it out in the political and legal arenas.

The "Ecology" or Environment circle is the realm of the natural world: the norm is to protect the natural world wherever and whenever possible, preserving what is there, restoring what has been lost, and always ready to act on certain priorities – endangered species, pollution of air, water, or soil, wilderness and wildlife areas, rainforests, deserts, and oceans. This circle has an ideal all its own – the absence of the human footprint. As we will note in what follows, it is possible for humans to live in the world leaving no footprint. We did it for 50,000 years, as foragers; only since the onset of agriculture, maybe 10,000 years ago, have we had the capacity to degrade the environment. There are ways we can still live in intact ecosystems, but it would take a radical restructuring of our lifestyles and expectations. This possibility, as dealing more with personal than corporate life, will not be explored in this book (but see my *Ethics and Sustainability*).[1] The Ecologic norm limits the normative claims of both Economics and Ethics, in that it continually restricts economic enterprise that violates species or wetlands or air quality, and continually limits human freedom to travel, build on their own property, and dispose of all their trash as they see fit.

The three circles, then, are strong norms that pull in logically independent and often incompatible directions. For 30 years we have been working out the implications of the overlap of Economics and Ethics, the field we now call "Business Ethics." Chapter 2 will explore that interface. The second overlap, between Ethics and Ecology, is much more recently explored, and we have no consensus on its dimensions. Chapter 3 categorizes the attempts at stating the nature of the interface. The third overlap, between Economics and Environment, is the most recent and the most charged with tension. Can business be Green? Can it increase shareholder wealth while protecting the natural environment? The answer, recently, has been yes, it can, and Chapter 5 on Green Business Strategies organizes some of the attempts to do that.

The second major reason for writing this book, then, besides the practical problems posed by inappropriate and frustrating oppositions, is the enormous theoretical enjoyment of sorting out the intersections of three normative systems that are logically independent of each other, and pull in three different directions, but are not essentially contradictory; common ground can be found, although the search may be difficult.

There is a theoretical point worth noting, although we will not have the space to explore it in this book: if we attempt to occupy any one of those spheres exclusively, we lose the individual in a total system that excludes central areas of human activity. Let me say that again: each sphere, if not tempered and balanced by the others, entails choices, policies, and human life that are not adequate to fulfill human potential. That goes for the Environmental sphere: if every choice and policy we make must first rule out the possibility of a human footprint, even in the short run, nothing great will ever be accomplished, and most of human creativity – music, art, literature, all lasting monuments to human thought – become impossible. Note also that there are those among us who would be willing to make that sacrifice for the sake of preserving the environment.

That limitation, interestingly, is just as powerful in the Ethics sphere, exclusive attention to which preserves human life and welfare at some level, but prevents human flourishing by depriving humans of essential areas of mental, physical, and spiritual expansion. By reducing nature to commodities to be used only for the benefit of humans, the Ethics sphere cuts off a realm of valuing and communication that humans have traditionally found to be very valuable. By insisting that human welfare and satisfactions, measured in many terms beyond the Economic, always supersede efficiency, the Ethics imperative locks the Economy into comfortable traditions, prescribed rights and entitlements, long-term relationships, and family loyalties. (That is not what is intended, but that is what happens.) Set aside for a moment the fact that the society that chooses the Ethics sphere exclusively for its criteria of the worth of policy and laws (and many have) will find itself overwhelmed by neighboring societies that have made different choices (the usual outcome). Even within itself, the society loses the excitement and, again, creativity that the pursuit of new opportunity affords. If it does nothing else, the free market teaches us to seek out and explore new opportunities; if the result of the search is a better way of living for all, the search is justified.

The same limitation also goes for the Economic sphere: where markets and efficiency and competition decide everything, not only is everything commodified and for sale (including you and me), but the human virtues and dispositions that have preserved us for the entirety of evolutionary time – virtues of altruism, loyalty, solidarity, compassion, humility, and the pursuit of honor – are rapidly deselected in the drive toward efficiency. There is one step from the deselection of those virtues to the disappearance of the business virtues – honesty, promise-keeping, and abstention from the use of force to obtain what you want. Unlike the norms of the Environmental and social spheres, which will stifle human creativity but will succeed in defending nature or the human community, the norms of the Economic sphere are eventually self-defeating. The Economic sphere depends entirely upon resources that have always been freely available from the natural world, and will disappear when they do. It also depends upon the social disposition of the citizens, as workers and as customers, to be honest, law-abiding, and prompt to pay their debts. Let those disappear and the market will cease to operate the next day.

The reservations attached to each of the three spheres, or orienta-tions, really apply only in the (hypothetical) case where one orientation has absolute primacy in the society, the other two having no place at all. The complex society familiar to us incorporates a continual balancing process among the spheres, constantly correcting trends to emphasize one of them by calling attention to the others, the balancing carried on by normal political processes or by the directions of a central government.

"Environmental Studies," as it is called, attempts to analyze that balancing act, with an eye to understanding it better; to spot the points where decision making is irrational or shortsighted; and to suggest directions for more rational arrangements of the balances. This book, then, is an essay in environmental studies, as much as an essay in business ethics. It is primarily a work in philosophy, as is appropriate, setting the fundamental assumptions of the market against those of the environmentalist to see where they may join and reinforce each other, not only where they may stand against each other. We will take seriously the claims of all sides that whatever "compromises" may have been agreed to in the past are no longer relevant in the changed global conditions of the present. Beyond that we hope to provide guidance through the complex fields of business management impacted by concerns for the state of the natural environment – law, strategy, and dealing with the new puzzles of global reach and the new influence of the NGOs, the nongovernmental organizations (or CSOs, civil society organizations, as we shall call them).

The clichés are all true. The pace of change is accelerating. We have to think globally now, in every kind of business. The quality of the natural environment is deteriorating on many worrisome fronts. Technological progress can help as well as harm the natural environment. This book is an attempt to stitch these truths together in a way that will make the paths of business a little clearer in the challenging days ahead. We hope it will be useful.

❧ NOTES ❧

1. Lisa H. Newton, *Ethics and Sustainability: Sustainable Development and the Moral Life*, Upper Saddle River, NJ: Prentice-Hall, 2003.

Acknowledgments

No work of this size – in my case, no work of any size – gets done without tons of help from others. In general, I am grateful to innumerable students and colleagues who in various settings have thrown entirely justified tomatoes at portions of this work, most of which have been aired elsewhere in preliminary form in professional colloquia, book chapters, and journal articles, inspiring me to make improvements. (Self-plagiarism is ethically permitted, isn't it?) In particular I am grateful to my family for putting up with the distraction, my two wonderful graduate readers, Michele Hoffman and Jennifer Blackmon, my series editor, Robert Frederick, and the Blackwell reviewers, one of whom (anonymous) I think I disagree with, and the other of whom, John Nolt of the University of Tennessee at Knoxville, gave the book the kind of careful reading it desperately needed, saving me from some very embarrassing errors and making the work stronger from beginning to end. The errors that remain, despite everyone's best efforts, are my responsibility alone.

Introduction

The heart of the problem is that every human endeavor that is properly called "economic" has an impact on the natural world that is probably damaging. It is not just that we do not always know what to do about that; it is that we do not know how to think about it – we do not know what is more valuable than what, nor where our duties lie, nor in which direction to pursue human happiness (see Chapter 1). In every other field of business ethics, we can ordinarily find a route of compromise, a way to thread through the entirely healthy motivations of self-interest and the equally important need to provide for the common good (see Chapter 2). We are, after all, negotiating among humans with similar interests. But the natural environment changes the equation. Those most dedicated to its preservation assert for it primarily a right to be left alone – to be taken out of the human world, protected from human contact, and removed from all human uses. There is an ultimate position (see Chapter 3) from which all human activity of any kind is seen as a violation of right and irreconcilable with the ultimate safety of life (other than human).

Yet the natural environment has always been our home, and the only source of everything we have needed to live. Only now, in the last 50 years, has it become clear that some human activity is devastating to the environment, and therefore to our own future. With that realization, we have had to acknowledge restrictions on our uses of the environment (see Chapter 4), and arrive at new ways of doing business that reconcile the needs of the natural world with the desires of humans for a good life (see Chapter 5), in the US and elsewhere (see Chapter 6). Possibly more importantly, we have to learn new ways of thinking, to reconceive our relationship with the natural world and with those who step forward to represent its interests when it itself is mute (see Chapter 7), into approaches that will inform doing business in the future. This book is primarily about the thinking, as is all philosophy, and secondarily about the doing; we hope to chart the directions that will make it possible to achieve environmental sustainability in business (see Chapter 8).

There is a way for human beings to live completely sustainably on this earth, in a way that leaves no "environmental footprint" at all, and we did it for millions of years, or at least tens of thousands (depending on how you set the borders of "we humans"). The life that is totally environmentally sustainable (that is, can be carried on *indefinitely* without compromising its biological support system at all) is called "foraging," or "hunting/gathering." This is the way every species except the human species lives – whatever nature has provided in the way of edibles, the creatures find and consume, usually according to patterns very stable over time.[1] It is not clear how many people the earth could sustain in this manner; possibly one-tenth of one percent of the number currently living on the earth, or six million souls.[2] The yield of human food per acre in the wild is not large, and if several human groups foraged in the same territory, there could come a time when there would not be enough for all, and the weaker groups would be crowded out, or driven off, and would starve. That is the way it happens with every species other than the human. Eventually, had we remained foragers, the human population would have spread into all viable zones in numbers that could be sustained, and the population would have leveled off at about six million. The story of human life, development, existence, and eventual extinction, would have followed the pattern of every other species – or at least, the pattern that every other species would have followed had not human beings intervened.

That is not the way the story went, as it turned out; about 10,000 years ago, in several parts of the world independently, groups of humans turned from semi-sedentary foraging to the active manipulation of the natural seeding, growth, and harvest of plant materials that we call agriculture. (About the same time, humans turned from following wild herds of ungulates to herding them, domesticating and breeding the most tractable varieties to form the core of the shepherd cultures found in, for instance, the Bible.) From the development of agriculture to the present time, the story of human activity has, unavoidably under available technologies, been one of destruction of the natural world. Even the earliest agriculture, in the Fertile Crescent in the ninth millennium BC, slowly destroyed its soil: once the forests were destroyed, the rainfall lessened, irrigation was required, and overirrigation waterlogged and then salinized the soil. By the time crop yields began to fall precipitously as the salt content in the soil rose, the population was so high that it was politically impossible to allow overused fields to lie fallow for a period of years, to allow the water table to drop and the soil clean itself. The result was that the Fertile Crescent became the Iraqi desert now daily on all of our television screens.[3]

Virtually all industry after that Neolithic agriculture accelerated the destruction. As agriculture became the organized management of large farms for the feeding of an empire, in Roman times, increasingly large swaths of the ancient world – notably the entire North African coastal area, which used to be the breadbasket of the empire – were turned from forest to field to desert.[4] Mining the earth for metals deposited poisonous slag for miles around the mines, creating toxic wastelands that ended fertility. Where intensive agriculture or deforestation stripped the soil, free-ranging herds made sure that new growth had no chance to replenish it. The patterns set for the growth and decline of civilizations in Mesopotamia – village agriculture, transformed to mass agriculture supporting an urban elite and its armies in major cities, extended to increasingly distant areas and collapsing into warfare with depleted soil and hungry people, finally collapsing into scattered tiny villages as the cities starve (sometimes helped along by revolution or plague) and the captains and the kings depart – were repeated in the Indus and Yangtze valleys, and millennia later by the Maya in the New World.[5] Only Egypt managed to maintain its original agricultural system intact into the twentieth century (until the building of the Aswan Dam) by continuing to use the natural flooding of the Nile as its source of fertility.

The pace of destruction picked up in the seventeenth and eighteenth centuries with the increased rationalization and the beginnings of industrialization of agriculture. It picked up again with the industrial revolution of the eighteenth and nineteenth centuries, when the imperative of efficiency was first articulated and applied mercilessly to the entire process of crafting the goods we need for everyday life. (Karl Marx [see Chapter 2] gleefully noted the demise of crafts – shoemaking, leatherworking, woodcarving, and ironwork – with histories measured in millennia, in the course of a few decades of industrialization.) The factories incorporated all the environmentally insensitive practices of the crafts – disposing of waste products out the back door, gathering raw materials with no thought to replacement – which had done very little harm while each craftsman's shop was small, but did a great deal of harm with an increase of volume 10- and 50-fold. (We may note in passing, that the most dangerous wastes of our time, organochlorines and radioactive materials, only emerged after the factory system was established.)

We may think of progress as the increasing pace of the release of carbon into the atmosphere, or of the consumption of the products of photosynthesis, for they amount to the same thing. Left to itself (i.e. without humans) nature took vast amounts of carbon from the air in the form of carbon dioxide, through photosynthesis. Photosynthesis uses the energy of the sun to transform carbon dioxide and water into the sugars and starches of which plants are mainly made, releasing oxygen in the process. When plants or animals died, or forests caught fire, carbon would be returned to the atmosphere; but on the whole the story was of slow accumulation of carbon on the earth. Over the course of the pre-human millennia, carbon had been stored in rich fern forests, which were crushed in the upheavals of the earth to form, deep below the surface, enormous deposits of coal and oil (and the occasional diamond) – carbon in its pure, most condensed form. The buried forests were replaced by new ones over several cycles; the last forests were standing when humans set out to occupy the earth and subdue it. As foragers, humans lived off the merest interest of the carbon deposits – just the yearly growth, and not all of the growth at that, of just a few types of plants. Clearing and burning the forests to make room for agriculture was the first significant inroad into the earth's principal of carbon; and the forests could recover even from that if left alone long enough. But the wholesale destruction of the forests, especially for wood fuel for cooking and heating (especially charcoal), slowly denuded the earth of its principal, its carbon storehouses. This depletion occurred first only in the developed world. By the first quarter of the nineteenth century, Connecticut (for instance) was nearly bald, on its way to becoming one more of the world's deserts. Most of its woods had been harvested, partly for building, but especially for fuel to heat the factories and homes in the winter. (It took eight cords of wood to heat a New England farmhouse for the winter, and that is a good many trees.) More was lost to charcoal burning – the preparation of fuel that burns clear and hot for smelting and other industries. It is ironic, given the campaigns of a later generation of environmentalists to "split wood, not atoms," that burning wood brought this area of the world to its worst environmental crisis yet. Where the forests were gone, the cows grazed so no new ones could grow, and cows, sheep, horses, and oxen grazed all natural cover down to the bare earth.

Fossil fuels saved the environment in Europe and North America. Their highly concentrated carbon, carbon savings salted away in vaults under the earth for millennia, replaced both the raw wood that had been used for ordinary fuel and the charcoal that had been required for the fires of industry. Now humans were using not only the interest of yearly photosynthesis (as in foraging), not only the present principal (in the forests and fields of the earth), but the most ancient carbon savings – the products of photosynthesis 250–300 million years ago. All the carbon that had been removed from the atmosphere at that time is returned to it every time we use electricity generated by burning oil or coal, every time we start the car, and every time the furnace, linked to the thermostat, roars into action. No wonder we are creating a crisis of global warming.

The industrial revolution did not create, but completed, the long evolution of the objectification of the natural world. Nature, which had been a terrifying swarm of deities at one time, a partner in human endeavor for 10,000 years, became at best a simple warehouse of "raw materials," "resources," ripe for exploitation, and at worst a cowering adversary ripe for destruction. The century that gave us "science," as the method that turns everything into value-neutral objects, finally reduced all approaches to nature to a simple utilitarianism (sometimes called "positivism"), which completed the depersonalization of nature.

We are talking about doing and thinking. The doing is reasonably clear: for the entirety of human existence, we have degraded the natural environment, generally unintentionally. But the orientation toward nature that has both resulted from and enabled this destruction is more serious. We see the relation between business and the environment as necessarily adversarial, not just in individual cases (see Chapter 4 and Case 4: Pacific Lumber and the Law), but inherently and conceptually. Prosperity and business success generally require economic growth, but as far as we can tell the preservation of the natural environment requires an end to growth and indeed, the rolling back of economic enterprise, with all the consequent loss of jobs, investment, and the standard of living to which we have become accustomed. This is a very new thought. As recently as 1906 – less than a century ago, following upon 10,000 years of steady campaign, William James still found his "moral equivalent to war" in the recruitment of youth to "an army enlisted against *Nature*" to fight a battle he found at once glorious in its virtues and superbly practical in its results.[6]

So we have some wars of our own to fight. Chapters 4 through 9 will cover aspects of the current practical problems faced by American businesses in dealing with the complexities of the natural environment in America and elsewhere, assembling case examples and urging the adoption of effective practices. Chapters 1 through 3 will address the conceptual issues, the effort to rethink the natural environment from being a storehouse of resources to being the natural body in which we all, with our children to the seventh and the seventieth generations, must live.

In this rethinking, we will adhere to the following principles:

1   **Respect objectivity** (and eschew ideology).   This matter is too serious to define easy sides, adopt one and despise the other, and use all information to back up the choice. If the environment is irreparably damaged, and becomes unable to sustain life, there will be no winners, only losers.
2   **Respect the science**.   We have no time, and no right, to dismiss the evidence of the best science in the name of some preferred policy. What the human mind has done, the human mind can remedy, but we must respect that mind.
3   **Respect economic efficiency**.   A perpetual temptation of the environmentalists is the retreat to some romantic pre-industrial time, when the Bottom Line and the cash nexus were powerless to overthrow the ancient traditions of respect for nature. That age, if it ever existed, is not possible to recreate now, and societies that attempt to do so will be left in the dust by the societies that adopt all the efficiencies discovered in the last two centuries.
4   **Respect values based on duty, virtue, and the pursuit of happiness**.   This is also no time to attempt to abandon ethics, a perpetual temptation of the anti-environmentalists. Economic efficiency is a value, but it is not the only value, and part of the problem addressed in this book is to show how the central ethical principles may be squared with business practice on the one hand and environmental requirements on the other.
5   **Reserve some respect for contrarian values derived from tradition, identity, and the democratic process**.   The best course of action for people is not always the one that they would choose for themselves. In this book we will meet

many people – New England fishermen, West Coast loggers, traditional farmers in the developing world – who argue, against economic efficiency and sometimes their own best interests, that their lifestyles, bound up with their identity as communities, are sufficiently important that they, too, must be weighed in the equation. We cannot continue inefficient industries that destroy the environment, and we must hear the voices of the members of communities that have grown up around them.

⊕ WHAT THIS BOOK IS, AND IS NOT ⊕

The temptation to write a novel – with a sweeping, intricately connected, plot line that reveals only on the last page what was embedded in the first – lurks deep within each of us. In my case, I have decided to let it lurk. This is a text directed to students, graduate and undergraduate, studying philosophy, business ethics, management, environmental management and strategy, contemporary challenges for business, or any number of other courses. Their backgrounds vary, their needs and the needs of the program need fit no preconceived pattern. From my own experience of teaching graduate and undergraduate students these fields under these circumstances, I know that not all instructors will use the whole book in the order in which it is printed. They may (indeed, are invited to) tailor the choice of chapters and order to their own syllabi.

Accordingly, I have written each chapter to be a self-contained elementary introduction to its subject matter – ethics; business ethics; environmental philosophy and terminology; environmental law, regulation and policy; "Green strategies" for business; global implications; the political and economic role of the civil society organizations (CSOs) (or nongovernmental organizations [NGOs], the private voluntary organizations of "civil society"); and a summary chapter of new directions and lasting problems. In some of these fields (ethics, business ethics) I have worked for many years, and look forward to sharing my experience; in others (law, civil society) I am a dedicated student sharing, I trust, my enthusiasm. None of these introductory chapters should be taken as a replacement for a proper course in its subject.

As this text is not the comprehensive authoritative tome on any of its subjects, so it is not a series of groundbreaking scholarly treatises.

Much of the material contained in this book has seen the light elsewhere in my published articles; I have found it unnecessary to encumber most of this space with the scholarly apparatus of citations and careful literature review more appropriate to the journals. School is hard enough without the textbook writer showing off in front of the students for the benefit of colleagues. The content of this book is not a fully constructed house, but a floor on which the student may build his or her own conception of the interface between the economic activity we know as "business" and the natural environment from which we arose.

NOTES

1. Sometimes, as with leaf-cutter ants, there are strange pathways to the finding and consumption.
2. That number is based on Clive Ponting's estimate that the four million people on earth 10,000 years ago had to turn from foraging to agriculture because of population pressures; foraging could no longer support a growing population. It is not clear that all possible human habitats had been explored at that time, so the extra two million is added to the estimate. See Clive Ponting, *A Green History of the World: The Environment and the Collapse of Great Civilizations*, New York: Penguin Books, 1993. See Chapter 2 generally, p. 42 in particular. Biocentric egalitarians ("deep ecologists") who take strict sustainability to be the goal of the environmental movement have pronounced the current human population "excessive," and have called for a "significant decrease," without committing themselves to foraging as a way of life. See collections in *Radical Environmentalism*, ed. Peter C. List, Belmont, CA: Wadsworth, 1993: Arne Naess, "Identification as a Source of Deep Ecological Attitudes," pp. 24–37, and Bill Devall and George Sessions, "Deep Ecology," pp. 38–46, esp. p. 42. To the best of my knowledge, specific "sustainable" numbers have not been advanced by the theorists of Deep Ecology.

   One more note on those numbers: within historical time, we have observed only a very small number of foragers – certain groups of African Bushmen comprise the last examples. The Yanomami of Amazonia, as described by Napoleon Chagnon, kept gardens to supplement their foraging, and were semi-settled; the American Indians, when we reached these shores, had developed several forms of agriculture as well as organized big-game hunting. Big-game hunting is not environmentally sustainable; by historical time, the ancestors of the American Indians had already hunted to extinction all the large mammals in North America except the bison.

3. Clive Ponting, op. cit., pp. 70–73.
4. Ibid., p. 77.
5. Ibid., pp. 82–83.
6. William James, "The Moral Equivalent of War," address delivered at Stanford University in 1906.

chapter one

Ethics: Terms and Forms of Reasoning

WHY STUDY ETHICS?

Consider the cases that open the Appendix to this chapter. Note the change in structure from case to case: in the first case, you know "the right thing" to do and how to do it, but you really do not want to do it because of the terrible consequences for your interests; in the second, you know what should be done, but you are not sure just what means will best accomplish your ends; in the third, you really do not know what is right, because your values are in conflict (if you are really clear on the right thing to do here, given only the facts as presented, write me immediately, because no one I know around here has the right answer!); and in the fourth, you probably have strong opinions on the matter, but in dealing with those equally convinced on the other side, you have this uneasy feeling that there may be no right answer at all.

With luck, you will never encounter cases like those above, but we cannot count on that kind of luck. The dilemmas illustrate a few of the reasons why you should want to study ethics:

1 Your reactions to the cases above might be clear, and not wrong, but they might not be adequate to the complexity of the cases. The human mind has a strong (and saving!) orientation to simplicity – to speed to a conclusion and put the issue to rest. But that is not always the best idea. (Recall the ancient saying: "For every complex problem, there is a solution that is simple, neat, and *wrong*.") Ethics will help you handle complexity.

2 Ethical principles sometimes conflict. We will spend a whole section on why this has to be true. When they do, no simple appeal to "principle" will solve the problem. When you know

two things that contradict each other, you have to have some methods of analysis to see where the conflict lies and where the solution might come from.

3   The applications of principles change, slowly but surely. What was ethically acceptable practice, with regard to the natural environment, at one point in American history, is no longer so. Early in the twentieth century, factories were constructed beside rivers *so that* they could empty their waste products there at no cost, and the neighbors approved, or at least did not object. Now, the slightest accidental spills into the waterway will result in the neighbors – some of them the sons and daughters of the original residents – up in arms, an enforcement action planned, and if the spill is really large, maybe a separate chapter in a muckraking environmental studies book.

4   If you are in business, you probably hold several sets of moral codes that have little to do with each other: one to govern the work of your department, one to govern your life at home, and one to inform your life as a citizen. But somewhere along the line, you have to become one person, not several. What is *your* essential code? How do you resolve your different, and occasionally conflicting, roles in this life? Ethics will help you sort this out.

5   Often you have to make decisions in your working life that have serious ethical implications. In the crisis of the moment, it is easy to forget centrally important aspects of the situation and the decision that has to be made. It is always a good idea to have a checklist of essential moral considerations that must enter into the decision. In the Appendix to this chapter we will provide three such decision procedures or checklists, acronymed (ADAPT, ORDER, DEAL) to help you remember them. Using them will not necessarily give you the right answer – only you can do that – but will at least make sure that you have not forgotten some huge category of moral claim that others will expect you to take into account.[1]

PHILOSOPHICAL ETHICS: DEFENDING JUDGMENTS

Ethics, in its origins and in its current location in the curriculum, is a branch of philosophy. Philosophy is primarily the study of discourse – a particularly thorough examination of the ways that we talk about things, the judgments we make, and the categories and conceptual orders we put upon our experience. It helps us to interpret that experience for ourselves and to find the handles that will let us operate effectively in the world as we experience it. Ethics is a systematic study of morality and human conduct that attempts to extract from our moral codes and traditions our most basic beliefs, the concepts on which all morality ultimately rests. Doing ethics, then, is first of all talking *about* talking about morality – figuring out how we state moral judgments, how we justify them if we are challenged, what kinds of reasons weigh significantly in the discussion, and how we shall know, if ever we will, when we have reached a demonstrably true conclusion.

The vocabulary of ethics

Any text on ethical theory has to open with the observation that of all matters in ethics, the meanings of the terms have caused the most acrimony and dispute. Since the earliest of the Socratic dialogues, we have argued about the meanings of key terms like "morals," "ethics," "virtue," "piety," "justice," and the others, all the others. Given the limited purposes of this text, I will simply stipulate at this point how I intend to use the key terms of ethics, observing only that my usage is not bizarre. More than that no philosopher will claim. In what follows you may expect the following words to be used in general in these ways:

- *Morals or Morality*: **Rules** and *prima facie* **duties** that govern our behavior as persons to persons.
  Examples
    Do not hurt people (gentleness, compassion)
    Do not tell lies (veracity, fidelity)
    Do not take more than your fair share (fairness)
  A note on morals: all you really need to know you probably learned in kindergarten. The rules and duties are easy to know and to remember – but very hard to follow consistently.
- *Values*: **States of affairs** that are desired by and for people and that we want to increase; ends, goals.
  Examples
    Health (as opposed to sickness)
    Wealth (as opposed to poverty)

Happiness in general

Freedom, justice, respect for human rights

- *Virtues*: **Conditions of people** that are desirable both for the people themselves and for the good functioning of the society.
  Examples

  Wisdom (vs ignorance, irrationality)

  Courage (vs weakness, unreliability)

  Self-control (vs greed, violence, indulgence)

  Justice (vs egoism, favoritism, deviousness)
- *Ethics*: Properly speaking, the study of morals, duties, values, and virtues, to find:

  Their theoretical links and relationships

  How they work together (or do not) in practice

  Other understandings of the term ethics:

  1 More generally, the whole field of morals, moral rules, duties, values, and virtues – the whole study of our attempts to order human conduct toward the right and the good.
  2 More specifically, a **professional ethic** is a particular code of rules and understandings worked out by the members of a profession to govern their own practice.

- *Ethical principles*: Very general conceptual schemes that sum up a range of morals, values, and virtues, from which moral imperatives can be derived.

Moral commitments and the discipline of ethics

In ordinary daily conversation we make no distinction between the notions of "morality" and "ethics," "moral obligations" and "ethical duties," and "moral codes" and "codes of ethics." But in philosophy we may distinguish "morals" from "ethics," according to the level of analysis intended. "Morality" governs conduct, tells us to follow the rules, and calls our attention to the fundamental commitments with which we order our lives. Morality tells us not to steal; one tempted to steal is morally bound not to steal, and one who habitually succumbs to that temptation is an immoral person. "Ethics" is primarily an academic discipline; it has to do with forms of reasoning rather than conduct, it reflects on, compares, and analyzes rules, and it traces the logical connections between fundamental principles and the moral commitments that guide us. Ethics derives the principle of respect for the property of others from which we further derive the rule that we should not take the property of others without authorization; ethics describes the conditions under which the principle fails to apply or can be overridden. We can live moral lives without knowing ethics, but we cannot discuss the morality of our lives, defend it, and put it into historical context, without the intellectual tools to do so. Ethics provides those tools.

Morality is a precondition for ethics, in two ways. First, morality, as a shorthand way of referring to all our transactions with each other, is the subject matter of ethics, just as our transactions with the physical world form the subject matter of science. Second, ethics is an activity, and any activity requires certain moral commitments of those who take part in it. We cannot do anything well without moral commitments to excellence, or anything for any length of time without the moral virtue of perseverance. The doing of ethics also has moral commitments appropriate to it. These commitments, to reason and to impartiality, or to the moral point of view, can rightly be demanded of any person who would take ethics seriously.

In any troubling case, we have first of all an obligation to think about it, to examine all the options available to us. We must not simply act on prejudice, or on impulse, just because we have the power to do so. We call this obligation the commitment to **reason**. The commitment to **reason** entails a willingness to subject one's moral judgments to critical scrutiny by oneself, and to submit them for public scrutiny by others; further, to change those judgments, and modify the commitments that led to them, if they turn out (upon reflection) not to be the best available. This commitment rules out several approaches to moral decision making, including several versions of **intuitionism** (a refusal to engage in reasoning about moral judgment at all, on grounds that apprehension of moral truth is a simple perception, not open to critical analysis), and all varieties of **dogmatism** (an insistence that all moral disagreements are resolved by some preferred set of rules or doctrines; that inside that set there is nothing that can be questioned, and that outside that set there is nothing of any moral worth). Second, we have an obligation to examine the options from an objective standpoint, a standpoint that everyone could adopt, without partiality. We want to take everyone who has a stake in the outcome ("stakeholders," we will call them) into account. Since this consideration for other persons is the foundation of morality, we call this perspective **impartiality**, or as Kurt Baier called it in a book of that name, **the moral point of view**. The commitment to **the moral point of view** entails a willingness to give equal consideration to the rights, interests, and choices of all who are party to the situation in question. This commitment to impartial judgment has one essential role in the study of ethics: once we have decided that all persons are to count equally in the calculations, that each is to count as one and as no more than one, we have the unit we need to evaluate the expected benefit and harm to come from the choices before us, to weigh the burdens placed and the rights honored. We also know that if anyone's wants, needs, votes, or choices are to be taken seriously and weighed in the final balance, then everyone's wants etc. of that type must be weighed in equally; that is, if anyone is to be accorded respect and moral consideration, then all must be. We can derive most of the moral imperatives that we will be using from this single commitment.

By way of example, the familiar **Golden Rule**, that we ought to treat others as we would have them treat us, is a fine preliminary statement of those commitments. With regard to anything we plan to do that will affect others, we ought not just to go ahead without reflection; we ought to ask, how would we like it if someone did this to us? That consideration is perfectly adequate as a satisfaction of the moral commitments that precede ethics. In general it may be said that if we will not agree to submit our decisions to reason, and to attempt to see the situation from the point of view of all who are caught up in it, it will be impossible for us to do ethics.

The principles of ethics

Ethics is ordinarily about human beings, and for purposes of this chapter, all ethical reasoning is anthropocentric, centering on the rights, duties, and interests of human beings. (In Chapter 3 we will consider biocentric, life-centered, ethics, as part of environmental philosophy.) The values that we have appealed to quite uncritically in the preceding stories – values of food for the hungry, of fair treatment, of neighborhood peace, and respect for rights – are not arbitrary or merely conventional. We can discover their foundations in the life of the human being, and derive them from fundamental aspects of human nature. The human being and human nature are endlessly complex, of course; yet the human being is universally recognizable to others of the species, and their preferences are very generally predictable. So if we avoid the complexities of the outer limits of human potentiality, it should be possible to say enough about the fundamentals of human morality just from the easily discoverable truths about the human being. In the course of the discussion, we will make some initial attempts to foreshadow the major ethical orientations which philosophers have, through our history, adopted as reflective of these most basic moral principles.

Then what are human beings about? Given the normative premise that moral principles must be appropriate to human life if they are to govern human life, three basic, simple, readily observable facts about human beings determine the structure of our moral obligations:

People are embodied

People are animals. They have bodies. They are matter; they exist in time and space and are subject to physical laws. These bodies are organic processes, requiring regular sustenance internally, and suffering all manner of slings and arrows of violent change externally. They experience pain, deprivation, and danger. They are prone to periodic failure unpredictably and to ultimate failure inevitably; they are mortal.

Then, people have needs that must be satisfied if they are to survive. They need at least food, water, and protection from the elements and natural enemies. That means that they must control the physical environment to make from it the means to those ends. Failure to do so will lead quickly to pain and suffering. These are inevitable in any case; in this way we are reminded of our mortality.

The first and immediate implication for ethics is that, if we have any reason to care about human beings, then the relief of that suffering and the satisfaction of those needs should be our first concern. In philosophical terms, human need and vulnerability to harm give rise to duties of *compassion* (for suffering), *non-maleficence* (avoiding harm), and more generally, *beneficence*: working to satisfy human need, maximize human happiness, and optimize human interests in all respects.

In general, the moral reasoning that takes help and harm to human beings as the primary determinant of the rightness of action is called "utilitarianism," following John Stuart Mill's description of that reasoning (Mill, 1859).

People are social

Social animals regularly live in large groups of their own kind (i.e. in groups containing several to many active adults); individuals raised apart from such groups are, and exhibit behavior that is, abnormal for the species. Whatever problems, therefore, that people have with their physical environment, they will have to solve in groups. They will soon discover that this necessity produces a new set of problems; they must cope with a social environment as well as the physical one. That social environment produces two further needs: for a social structure to coordinate social efforts, and for a means of communication adequate to the complex task of such coordination. The need for communication is fulfilled by the evolution of language.

The implication for ethics is that, given that there are so many of us, we must take account of each other in all our actions. We come saddled by nature with obligations, to the group in general and to other members of the group in particular, that we cannot escape or evade. Normal people (not psychopaths) seem to know this without being told. By nature human beings try, most of the time, to do good and avoid evil, in advance of knowing just what counts as good or evil. The attempt to do good, to others as to oneself, involves the adoption of "the moral point of view," or a stance of impartiality with regard to the distribution of benefits and burdens. *Fairness*, or *justice*, demands that we subject our actions to rule, and that the rule be the same for all who are similarly situated. What will make an act "right," ultimately, is not just that it serves individual happiness but that it serves the whole community; people are equal, and since *equality* is itself a value (derived from "equal dignity") the society must deal with them equally unless good reason is given for differential treatment.

A philosopher who has made justice central to his theory of society is John Rawls. Rawls points out that the duty of justice may require us to favor just those persons who would *not* succeed in getting their claims recognized if personal power, or even majority benefit, were to determine the distribution (Rawls, 1970).

People are rational

Normal adult human beings are able to consider abstract concepts, use language, and think in terms of categories, classes, and rules. Since Immanuel Kant, we have recognized three categories of thought that characterize the way human beings deal with the objects and events of the world. These are *time* (*when* did something happen? in the past, the present, the future; and *how long* did it take? duration); *space* (*where* is some object? or *how far* away is it? location, bulk, distance); and *causation* (*how* did something happen? what brought it about? antecedents, agencies, powers, consequences). "Rationality," of course, in our ordinary discourse, means a good deal more than the basic ability to think in terms of when, where, and how. Ordinarily we use the word to distinguish calm and dispassionate decision making from "emotional" or disorganized decision making; we use it to distinguish people capable of making good decisions from people who are not. But for our purposes here, we need go no further with the word. The creature that is "rational" will think, on occasion, in *general* terms, about classes and laws, extending over time, space, and possibility, while the creature that is "not rational" will think, if at all, only about *particular* (individual) objects or events.

Since people are rational, they can make *rational choices*. When people think about action they think in terms of classes of acts as well as individual acts. For instance, if my neighbor has a particularly attractive camera, and I desire to take it from him, and am currently making plans to do so, I shall make my plans based on what I already know about all cases of people taking things from other people. And I can contemplate not only those past acts of taking, and the present plan to take that camera, but all cases that will ever be of taking, especially of cameras – future acts as well as past and present acts. But in that case I am thinking of action not yet taken, of action therefore undetermined, for which real alternatives exist. Since people can conceive of alternatives, they can choose among them – having thought over the circumstances, and deliberated on the outcomes, they can decide what to do. Put another way: I do not *have* to take that camera, if I have not yet done it. People are *free*, as we say, or *autonomous moral agents*. But then they can also realize that they could have done differently – I did not have to take the camera, and given my neighbor's understandable grief and anger at its loss, maybe I *should* not have. That is, I can feel *guilt* and *remorse* and assume *responsibility* for having chosen as I did.

As far as we know, we are alone among the animals in possession of this ability. Since people can conceive of classes of acts for which alternatives exist, they can make *laws* to govern acts in the future, specifying that the citizens (or whoever may be bound by the law) *ought* to act one way rather than another. No one, for instance, ought to take things that do not belong to them, and such takings, henceforth to be called "theft," shall be collectively punished. (Incidentally, theft and even murder were made public crimes only in order to prevent private vengeance, or self-help, and the bloody feuds that often followed.) General obligations can be formulated and articulated for a whole society. Collectively (acting in their groups), people make collective choices, especially choices of rules, rather than relying on instinct; and they are then collectively responsible for those choices and individually responsible for abiding by them.

Rationality's implication for ethics is that, as freedom of choice is the characteristic that sets humans apart from the other animals, if we have any duty to respect human beings at all, it is this *choice* that we must respect. Persons are categorically different from the things of the physical world. They have *dignity, inherent worth*, rather than mere price or dollar value; they are bearers of *rights* and subjects of *duties* rather than mere means to our ends or obstacles to our purposes. Our duty of *respect for persons*, or respect for persons as autonomous beings, requires that we allow others to be free, to make their own choices and live their own lives; especially, we are required not to do anything to them without their consent.

Just as utilitarianism makes human happiness central to ethics, and the Rawlsian account of fairness makes justice central, a complete theoretical account of ethics can follow from the value of human autonomy. The philosopher most identified with the centrality of autonomy and moral agency to ethical theory is Immanuel Kant (Kant, 1785).

The human condition

In summary: By the section "People are rational," humans have minds, or as the philosophers call it, a rational nature; and by "People are embodied," humans have an apparently limitless capacity for physical and psychological suffering. Rationality and suffering are not found together anywhere else; possibly the angels have the first, and surely all beasts possess the second, but only human beings appear to be able to reflect upon their own suffering and contemplate the suffering of others of their kind, and that sets them apart from all creation. By virtue of rationality, human persons possess *dignity* and command respect. Ultimately, that respect entails the willingness to let other people make their own choices, develop their own moral nature, and live their lives in freedom. By virtue of that abysmal capacity for suffering, the human condition cries out for compassion and compels attention to human *well-being* and the relief of pain. And by "People are social," this condition is shared; we are enjoined not only to serve human need and respect human rights, but to establish *justice* by constructing a political and legal structure which will distribute fairly the burdens and benefits of life on this earth in the society of humans. These most general concepts: *human welfare, human justice*, and *human dignity* – are the source and criteria for evaluation of every moral system authored by human beings.

The same concepts are the source of every moral dilemma. Attention to human welfare requires us to use the maximization of human happiness (for the greatest number of individuals) as our criterion of right action. Attention to the needs of groups, and of social living, requires us to set fairness for all above benefit for some as our criterion. Yet duty can require that we set aside both the feelings of the groups and the happiness of the individual in the name of respect for human dignity. To protect the welfare of many it is often necessary to limit the liberty of the individual (the liberty to operate dangerous or noisy vehicles without a license, for instance). On the small scale as well as the large, to respect the liberty of persons is not always to further their best interests, when they choose against those interests (for instance, by taking addictive drugs or by spending themselves into debt). To maintain a rough equality among persons, it is often necessary to put unequal demands on the interests of some of them (by progressive taxation, for example). To preserve the community, it is sometimes necessary to sacrifice the interests of the few – but that course seems to discount the worth of the few, and so to violate justice.

The basic imperatives

Such conflict is fundamental to ethics, and is the major reason why ethics is famous as the discipline that has no clear answers. The human being is a complex creature, and when we extract human values from that complexity, we find them logically independent at the least, and often in opposition. There are, by tradition, two ways to formulate the opposition (see "The vocabulary of ethics," above):

1 **As a conflict of values.** A value is a desired state, which we try, in our dealings, to advance or enhance or promote. The concepts so far discussed can be treated as values that are difficult to pursue simultaneously – the happiest society, the fairest or most equal society, the most free society or the lifestyle incorporating the most freedom.

2 **As a conflict of imperatives**. An imperative prescribes a duty to do or to forbear. It is occasionally more useful to see ethical conflict as a conflict of injunctions or prescriptions telling us what to do in any given situation. We are told – by the law and the prophets, by our religion, by our parents, by our employers, by the civil law – that we must respect the rights of others, be fair to everyone, and serve each other's needs. Sometimes it is not possible to do everything at once.

Over against every clear value, there is another value, which sometimes conflicts. Over against every clear imperative, there is a contrary imperative, equally clear, which sometimes applies. Ethics is the discipline that derives these values and imperatives, works out the consequences of our efforts to protect them, and musters what light it can to show us the possible reconciliations and the necessary compromises that attend their application in practice.

The terms "principle," "imperative," and "value" are sometimes used interchangeably. We will attempt, in the course of this book, to use "concept" to mean the principle in the form of a definition, as above; "value" as a desired end-state, to be achieved or enhanced; "imperative" as a prescription of duty. Morality is sometimes best understood as a system of imperatives, and generally imperatives are cited as the basis for the conclusions of applied ethics. The three concepts described above – **welfare, justice, and dignity** – correspond to three imperatives for human conduct.

1 **Centering on welfare**: *Do no harm, and where possible do good* – Because we must live, and because we can suffer, we must value life and happiness – safety, protection from harm, absence of pain, hunger or suffering of any kind, enjoyment, and pleasure. That is, we have an obligation to help and protect each other, to relieve suffering, and to choose each action, or rule of action, according to the amount of pain it will relieve or happiness it will provide. This general duty we may call *beneficence*, or *concern for welfare*.

This imperative is often broken down into four logically related but different prescriptions:

(a) **Do no harm** (the duty of *non-maleficence*) – In the pattern of duties to do good and to avoid harm, this duty is the negative, individual, and immediate part.

(For instance, no matter how much fun it would be, do not blow up the bridge.)

(b) **Prevent harm** wherever possible (the duty of *prudence*, or *stewardship*) – This duty generalizes the one before, enjoining us to attempt to keep agencies besides ourselves from doing harm. (If the bridge is near collapse, act to shore it up and keep people off it until it is fixed.)

(c) **Remedy harm** wherever possible (the duty of *compassion* or *charity*) – This duty is the proactive equivalent of the two before, enjoining concern for suffering and positive efforts to relieve it. (If the bridge has collapsed, pull the people out of the water, even if you do not know them and have no other obligations to them.)

(d) **Do good**, provide benefit, wherever possible. (Build better bridges.)

Note that in this pattern of duties, the duty of non-maleficence takes moral priority (i.e. if you can provide benefit to many people, only at the cost of doing harm to a few, there is a presumption *against* doing whatever would result in the benefit and harm). The second two follow from the same presumption, and the last comes into play only when the others are taken care of. The priority of non-maleficence can, of course, be overridden, as when the state takes my property to build a road, doing harm to me in order to do good for many; but it can only do so on proper authority, with at least an attempt to provide compensation, and on presentation of compelling reasons.

2 **Centering on justice**: *Observe the requirements of fair dealing* – Because we must live together, we must adhere to rules of equal treatment, justice, fairness, and rule of law (equality before the law), trust and trustworthiness, and honesty in word and deed. Then we have an obligation to acknowledge our membership in, and dependence on, the human community and the community in which we live – to contribute to its life; obey its laws, customs, and policies; to be honest in all our dealings with our fellows; and above all to hold ourselves accountable to them for our actions, especially as they affect others. This duty we may call the duty of *justice*.

This duty also has recognizable sub-imperatives, which follow from it logically:

(a) **Obey the law** and the codes of your profession. All are equally bound by these general prescriptions, and it is not fair to make an exception of yourself. Also, as possible: take responsibility for enforcement.

(b) **Treat all groups alike**: do not condition treatment of persons on their membership in a favored group. This is the duty of *non-discrimination*, or provision of *equal opportunity*.

(c) **Act affirmatively** to remedy the results of past injustices; wherever possible, seek out the least advantaged and the previously excluded for occupation of preferred posts.

(d) **Recognize merit**: treat people as they deserve to be treated based on what they have done or merited. Included in this general duty is the more personal duty of *gratitude*.

3 **Centering on dignity**: *Respect persons (as autonomous beings)*: Because we aspire to the full potential of humanity, we must value freedom. We take liberty, autonomy, and rationality to be ideals, and value them in others as much as we prize our own. The human enterprise is an endless quest to become better, wiser, and more loving people, and we must cultivate people and institutions that will protect that quest. We have an obligation to respect the choices of others, to allow them the space to live their lives, to the end, the way they see fit. For ourselves, we have the obligation to realize our own potential, not only to discern for ourselves the moral course of action, and to take responsibility for the moral choices we make, but to extend our knowledge and the scope of our reason to become as fully as possible the autonomous persons we are capable of being. This duty we may call the duty of *respect for persons*.

Again, more specific duties can be derived from respect:

(a) **Tell the truth**: the duty of *veracity* or *truth-telling* is primarily derived from the duty to enhance autonomy by making rational decision possible. No person can act rationally if denied the truth. From this duty we derive the requirement of *informed consent* in the health care professions, and the duty of *full disclosure* in law and business.

(b) **Celebrate differences**, whether individual or cultural. Create a positive atmosphere for the developing of idiosyncratic lifestyles that fulfill individual needs and preferences – as long as they violate no one else's rights.

Clearly none of these imperatives is optional. We cannot choose not to have bodies. We cannot choose not to need each other, and although we may sometimes wish we could, we cannot choose not to choose, not to be free. And these imperatives are logically independent one from another. They can conflict. Most ethical dilemmas follow from that fact.

A summary of sorts: The need for clarity

No one form of reasoning is inherently superior to the other. We may use them all, and usually, in the course of a discussion involving ethics, we do. But *it is important to note the differences among them*, for if we do not, we condemn ourselves to talk past each other and frustrate our dialogue. For example, at a dinner party some years ago, I came across a heated debate on the problem of educating inner-city black teenagers. One side of the debate was arguing that the black people had been treated so badly in the past, and had been denied such basic amenities and encouragement, that it was *unjust* to expect them to measure up to middle-class educational expectations. The other side, made up of schoolteachers, was arguing that education provided the only *decent prospects for the future*, and indeed, the only way out of the ghetto for these youngsters, and unless they got their act together and got motivated somehow to finish school, the next generation would be just as disadvantaged and ill-treated as the present one.

Were these two groups really arguing against each other? No. Each could easily have conceded the other's point (and sometimes did) while maintaining its own. Rather, they were arguing *past* each other, one arguing consequentially (toward the future, bleak or somewhat brighter, depending on the means, especially educational means, adopted now), and the other deontologically (from justice). Both, by the way, were making excellent points. You might want to warm up your minds at this point by joining that debate; but please, do a better job than they did at keeping straight what kind of argument you are using.

✿ CASE 1: NEW ENGLAND FISHERIES ✿

Once upon a golden time, an enormous fleet of fishing schooners sailed from Gloucester to the rich fishing area of Georges Bank, off Cape Cod. The fleet would anchor for periods ranging about a week (they had only salt, no ice, to preserve the fish they caught), set out long lines of hooks from dories, haul in the fish, and race for the shore, to be the first to market. The fisherman's occupation was dangerous beyond any standard we would accept today, hard work, rain-or-shine uncomfortable, but a proud way of life to the New England towns that supported the fleet. Rudyard Kipling celebrated that fleet in his magnificent novel, *Captains Courageous*, which enshrined the Gloucester fishermen forever in our national mythologies. That may have been a bad idea.

By the end of the twentieth century, the industry was in very bad trouble. Consider the progression:

1900   All fishing was done on fishing lines from sailing schooners or, close to shore, smaller boats. Yearly catch in metric tons in the North Atlantic: 2.6 million, of which one-third were cod, halibut, and tuna. (These figures include the cod fishery of Georges Bank, and also of the surrounding North Atlantic.)

1950   The steam engine replaced sails, providing power to drag huge trawls. The yearly catch grew to 7.3 million metric tons, of which 40 percent were large fish.

1975   The diesel engine displaces steam engine, allowing for larger boats and faster travel to distant waters. A yearly catch of 15.1 million metric tons of fish brought in, of which 30 percent were large commercial species.

1999   By now we have supertrawlers, that can drag nets up to a quarter mile wide. But the catch was only 12.4 million metric tons, of which 31 percent were the large table fish. By now, the population of large fish in the Atlantic has dwindled to 15 percent of what it was in 1900.

Those figures do not capture how steep the decline was at the end of the twentieth century. Think of it this way: the catch in the Northeast of the most popular commercial species was worth over $150 million as late as 1991, then fell to $130 million the next year, and to less than $116 million in 1993. Cod, mainstay of the Gloucester fishery, was worth $75 million in 1991, but fell to $45 million in 1993. What happened? Too many fishers chasing too few fish; between 1970 and 1990, the world fishing fleet doubled, from 13.5 million gross registered tons to 25.5 million.

The collapse of the Atlantic fisheries is a premier example of first-level environmental crises: viewing the relevant portion of the natural environment *only as an economic resource and as nothing else* (more nuanced views of nature will join us in subsequent chapters), how could we, as fishers or those who depend on fishers for our food, allow this to happen? Could we have been entirely ignorant of the processes that were destroying the primary livelihood of the Captains Courageous enshrined by Rudyard Kipling and all the New England families and towns that depended on them?

It all makes sense if we separate out the strands of natural processes and human incentives that govern the fishing trade. The natural process is simplicity itself. As long as there are enough adult fish to breed, adequate breeding grounds for the eggs to hatch and the fingerlings to grow, and an adequate supply of nutrients for food, there will be fish. The nutrients are supplied by the peculiar physical features of the Bank: shallow water in rapid motion brings nutrients from the bottom to the sunlit top. It is an ideal place for growing large numbers of fish. There is no natural reason for the decline of the fish stocks.

But the technology adopted by the fishing industry is not compatible with the preservation of the fishery. The Gloucester fishermen with their long lines and guesswork methods of locating fish could have fished the waters indefinitely, for while they depleted the adult stocks, their take was limited and they were doing nothing to damage the reproduction. The times have changed; sonar and precise navigational gear make sure that no fish can find a place to hide from the fishers. As soon as the new power-driven larger boats started dragging trawls across the bottom, several troublesome effects became evident: first, obviously, many more fish were caught. (That was *why* they used the new trawl nets.) Second, all manner of sea life was gathered in the net, hauled to the deck of the boat and dumped. Afterwards, the "bycatch," the unwanted fish or other creatures brought up from the bottom – including juveniles of the commercial species too small to keep – would be thrown back in the water, dead. This measureless slaughter, unreported and largely unnoticed, may have had some-thing to do with the inability of the fishery to recover. Third, and probably worst, the trawl nets rake the bottom, disrupting eggs, covering nests with silt and destroying the natural nurseries for the young fish, and compromising the food chain. That effect is a death sentence for the fish. With current technology, it does not seem possible that the fishery can recover. As a final result, all the marine life that depends upon those fish – birds, marine mammals – are also in decline.

One would think that the market would limit this destructive harvest. How can these boats bring more and more fish to market and not saturate it? Part of the answer is that there is an increased market for seafood in the developed countries. Part of the answer is that they do not have to make money; because of the romantic associations with Captains Courageous, governments subsidize the fishing industry rather than see the fishermen thrown out of work. (Worldwide, subsidies add up to about $15 billion a year, to keep the $55 billion annual global trade going.)

The economic arrangements for harvesting those fish were troublesome from the beginning. The fishing industry is carried on by thousands of entrepreneurs who own their own boats. It is in each fisher's interest to catch as much fish as possible to sell on the market. He may know that when every fisher does that, there will soon be no fish, but he reasons that his own restraint will not save the fishery, for he cannot count on the others to restrain themselves; he will only make himself poorer, and the fishery will decline at the same rate. Garrett Hardin has called this phenomenon – of independent takers destroying a resource for lack of any way to manage it – "the tragedy of the commons," likening it to the effects of the use of the town grazing commons by many independent shepherds. Since it is to each one's advantage to graze more sheep on the commons, even though that will destroy everyone's livelihood eventually by overgrazing it, each shepherd predictably will graze more sheep on the commons until it is lost to all. Strictly speaking, the oceans are not a "commons" in the historical sense; the historical commons was community governed and very strictly regulated, and any shepherd who tried to graze more sheep than he was traditionally allotted would find himself contemplating dead sheep in the morning. The correct term is an "open access" system. The oceans are open to all; anyone who can buy, or build, a boat is free to send it off into legal fishing waters and catch what he can.

Should the government, or common sense, prod the fishers into some collective arrangement to limit individual take for the public benefit, to reduce the total catch so that the fishery can recover, two large problems await, structural weaknesses for all such arrangements. The first is that unless a large majority goes along with the arrangement, it will not work; the few compliant individuals will suffer the expected individual loss, but the public benefit will not be realized. The fishery will not recover. Then it is foolish to adopt the restraint unless there is some hefty guarantee that the others will cooperate too. The second is the standard free-rider problem; given general compliance, the fishery recovers, but any fisher who cheats and catches more than his quota will reap enormous profit. So there is a powerful incentive to cheat even if the scheme works. (Disarmament treaties suffer from the same kind of instabilities.) Note that the historically individualistic industry shows little inclination toward collective arrangements. To protect the cod, for instance, the best the Groundfish Management Plan of the National Marine Fisheries Service has been able to come up with is voluntary "targets," with individual allotments per boat that the owner promises not to exceed. For the seventh year in a row, the groundfish fleet in New England has exceeded the cod target by a good bit. There is a good-faith effort continuing to end the overfishing, rebuild the depleted groundfish populations, minimize bycatch and protect habitat – but it is very late in the game, and the fish are still in decline.

Government regulation and international covenants attempt to address the overfishing, and the fishing industry claims that some stocks are actually "rebounding," although their numbers are nowhere near their historical norm. But any system of restrictions or quotas suffers from those instabilities. (Even "ITQs," Individually Transferable Quotas to catch certain kinds of fish, the favorite device of market economists because they can be bought and sold on the open market, are difficult to enforce.) Because of the political power of the fishermen, real sanctions are difficult to apply. Limiting the season to fewer and fewer days only rewards the largest and most efficient, that is destructive, boats. Restrictions on permissible gear would work – back to the schooners? – and some progress is being made in some fisheries at designing nets that will (for instance) exclude sea turtles with a grate that shrimp can get through but turtles cannot, or provide escape hatches for juvenile fish. Still, the development of new technology does not mean that it will be used.

What should be done to rebuild the fishery? Should individual fishers do what they want to do, fish to the limits of their own good judgment, with the result that after awhile there will be no fish, but not until after I retire? Or should the people collectively, the government, step in to protect a common resource? What about mandating ocean refuges, no-catch (and no-drag) sanctuaries where fish can be born and grow naturally, until they are adults and swim freely?

⊛ APPENDIX: DECISION PROCEDURES ⊛
FOR ETHICS

Consider the four cases below. They are very different in kind, and require different approaches. Let us take them one at a time:

Case 1. The Impaired Driver
Jack stayed about an hour longer than he had intended to at a very pleasant party with his old college friends. Seems that while Jack was getting his law degree and starting practice, his old buddy Marty made it big on Wall Street. Marty hosted the party in his huge Riverside Drive apartment. All the old college ties were there – great memories, beer, booze, marijuana ... Jack hadn't seen *that* in awhile. Good stuff, too.

Realizing he was late, Jack raced to the parking garage, took the elevator to the third floor, hopped in his SUV, and tore around the turn toward the exit. Smash! There was a small car parked in just the wrong place. He hit it dead center. He backed up, got out, noted that there was extensive damage to the other car – both doors on the driver's side badly dented – but none to his. What should he do?

In fact, he knew very well what to do. There was clearly damage, lots of it, so he should take out his cell phone, call the police, and wait there till they came. When the police saw him propped up against his SUV, they would insist on the inconvenience of a Breathalyzer test. When they got the results of that, they would give him a chauffeured ride to the precinct station and insist further on a urine test. When they got the results of *that*, well, Jack realized he might get to know the folks in the precinct very intimately before seeing the sky again. He might very well – probably would – lose his license to operate a motor vehicle. The fines would be substantial; he might lose his SUV. He might even go to jail. The damage to his reputation, and to his position in his law practice, would probably be irreparable; depending on the state, he might lose his license to practice law. That is a lot to think about. Meanwhile, Jack was the only occupant of the parking garage at that hour.

What to do, indeed. The standard ethicist's injunction, "Do the right thing," may entail a terrible cost, and it is the agent, not the ethicist, who has to absorb it. It is a lot to think about, and one obvious way out is to think about it all the way back to Connecticut, which Jack will probably reach without further mishap. A problem, yes, but this is a *moral* dilemma, a temptation, not an *ethical* dilemma. (It might become an ethical dilemma for Jack if it were not he, but one of his children, involved in the accident.) Throughout the consideration of ethics, in what follows, we will keep this in mind as the kind of dilemma we are *not* talking about.

ADAPT: An approach to moral decision making

People naturally want to do good and avoid evil. For the most part, we limit our attention to morality to the observance of certain inter-personal rules – of courtesy, helpfulness, and respect for privacy, for instance – that serve to make daily life more livable. But sometimes a condition comes to light that interrupts, imposes itself upon, daily life. Consider the following case:

Case 2: The Starving Children
As the wars in the Horn of Africa ground on, enterprising camera crews from the news channels began to filter into Somalia, whose government had collapsed following a coup in 1988 followed by an ill-advised war with Ethiopia. All transportation had been disrupted by the fighting, and there was no way to get food supplies to the civilians. Warlords commandeered all available food for their soldiers and followers. The crews filmed the hunger, the babies with the thinned reddish hair, dull eyes, and distended bellies of starvation; filmed parents, helpless, trying to comfort their dying children; filmed the burial parties consigning their bodies to the earth. Then they sent the film back to Europe and the US, and excerpts started to show up on late-night television.

Laurie, a community activist with four young children of her own, reacted immediately. The pictures of the starving children were continually before her during the day and haunted her dreams at night. She had to act. She rallied her friends, her neighbors, her brother in Atlanta, her cousin in Tacoma, and they started neigh-borhood, then statewide, then national, campaigns to raise money for food for the children. They secured tapes of the television presentations, and showed them in every church and community center. Never mind the politics; those children had to be fed, immediately.

Then she and about one hundred of the activists nationwide found a way to raise much more money than their local churches and women's groups could supply. Many of the world's popular music stars, who had seen the films, were brought together by an enterprising producer to hold a huge fundraiser, called "Africa Aid," for the benefit of the starving children. An enormous amount of money was raised and directed toward famine-ridden Africa. But the warlords got most of it.

So Laurie called her Congressional Representative, to whose last campaign she had contributed generously, and her Senator, a family friend, to try to get some action out of Washington. She and all her friends lobbied Congress to urge the President to send Marines in to protect the Red Cross and the other nongovernmental organisations (NGOs) distributing the food to the children. In 1992, President William J. Clinton was persuaded to do just that, and Marines waded ashore near Mogadishu, the capital, possibly the first invasion ever to be recorded live *looking out to sea from the beach* for US news channels! The Marines' assignment was to protect the distribution of food to the starving children.

Was it a good idea? Not long after the invasion, if that is what it was, the aid workers in Mogadishu noticed that there did not seem to be much famine where they were; the hunger was further in the bush, and would be very difficult to find. Meanwhile, the warlords managed to rally the Somalian people to refuse cooperation with the American invaders, and after one riot, a marine was killed and his naked body dragged in the street, recorded faithfully by the same news channel camera crews and beamed back to the US. That settled that. The troops were withdrawn immediately. Meanwhile, there is no hard evidence that any more food got to starving people than would have if the West had not been there.

Should Laurie have urged this intervention?

The case of the starving children, as we may call the above, and all similar cases, is typical of the kind of moral adaptation that punctuates the normal routine of moral life. The sequence is characteristic:

First, some condition, some situation, or array of facts is brought to light. This condition captures our attention, alerts us to something that stands out from the background noise of our lives as requiring our concern.

Second, that condition is discussed, the information is disseminated through the community, and a community dialog is conducted where public opinion is actually formed. That "community," incidentally, may be as small as a family or as large, as in this case, as the whole world.

Third, the discussion incorporates the moral assumptions that guide our lives, ordinarily without conscious thinking. We do not have to reason out what we ought to do in most situations; most of the moral work is already done.

Fourth, proposals for action are put forward and policies adopted. Decisions are made, implementing the imperatives in a way appropriate to the situation that caught our attention.

And Fifth, the results of the action are tested against the results expected. The test results are fed back into the data from the initial situation: Was the action taken in fact appropriate? Were the imperatives successfully implemented? Or should we go back to the drawing board, and introduce new proposals for action or policy?

Note: The decision process, on review, does not return to the starting point, but only asks after the effectiveness of the policy for action – we have agreed about the ends of the proposed action, and now we seek the most effective means.

From the above, we can put together a normal moral reasoning procedure, easily remembered in the acronym ADAPT:

Attention
Dialog
Assumptions
Proposals
Test.

(Note: Allow me to apologize right now, for this and subsequent acronymic tricks of this sort. They give the appearance of slickness, I know, but they really do help us to remember.) These normal procedures are used whenever changes in our world require new policies in order to continue normal life in accordance with our ordinary commitments.

Now consider the following cases:

(a) You are a physician called in to confer with the family of a terminally ill man in a nursing home. He is conscious, in some discomfort, confused much of the time. He will not get much better, but his heart is strong, and he is not expected to die soon. His children (his wife is dead) are distressed at the length of time it will take him to die. They would like you to inject a fatal dose of morphine to hasten death, on grounds that his estate is being eaten up by the medical and nursing home costs.

(b) You are the production manager of a pharmaceutical company under a lot of competitive pressure. Your boss suggests that you could double productivity if you filled half the penicillin ampules with saline solution instead of penicillin. To be sure, the patients would not get the penicillin prescribed, but most penicillin prescriptions are unnecessary anyway, so probably it would not do anyone any harm.

In practice, Cases A and B would probably not call forth any high-level moral reasoning. They are for you, we may suppose, new cases; but the assumptions that have always worked for you will work here. They do not quite resolve to the easy moral dilemma of the "Impaired Driver" category, but they are not far away. Physicians do not kill their patients; children do not kill their parents to accelerate the inheritance; you do not deliberately adulterate product runs or market trash under a product's label. The answer is no; if asked for reasons, the normal ADAPT-level reasons will do. Try, for instance, "That simply is not done, or is not acceptable." More personally, you might say, "I couldn't sleep nights," or, "I couldn't look at myself in the mirror when I shave tomorrow, if I did anything like that." More spiritually, you might try "My religion forbids me even to consider anything like that," or more ominously, "I don't look good in an orange jump suit." The moral rules that back these up are clear to all: practice medicine only for the benefit of the patient; never tell lies, especially to customers.

Principles and reasoning based on consensus morality are not always in such good shape. Recall the Third Reich, and the fact that in Germany in Hitler's time, it was accepted practice, and in accord with the religious intuitions of the leaders of the country, and definitely in accordance with law, to kill Jews wherever you found them (in an orderly manner, of course). That is why we have to know ethics; to know when the principles and reasoning that we ordinarily use need to be re-examined, criticized, and maybe changed – to know, in short, when ADAPT is not sufficient.

ORDER: From morals to ethics

A problem of moral or of only fundamental ethical concern – like the impaired driver's desire not to confront the cops, the heirs' desire to dispatch their rich father, the boss's desire to make a quick profit, or the starvation of the African children – is not the same as an ethical dilemma. In a *moral* problem, we know what is right, but we may be puzzled about the right way to say "No" or the best means to obtain the best outcome. (Additionally, we may be tempted to preserve our level of comfort by doing nothing at all!) In an *ethical* dilemma, we really do not know what is the right thing to do. Consider the following case:

Case 3: Mother in Decline
Peter and Dora Vlasovic, 51 years and 43 years of age respectively, are at a loss as to what to do about Dora's 67-year-old mother, who lives with them. She is suffering from Alzheimer's disease, and while her periods of confusion are not yet continual, she is becoming too unreliable to be left alone. Both husband and wife work outside the house, and cannot stay with Mother during the day. They started looking into appropriate nursing homes, but Mother, who was a schoolteacher and fiercely independent all her life, has put her foot down: no homes. "Look, you know how valuable my mind and my dignity have been to me," she finally said to them. "I simply cannot endure the thought of ending my days tied in a chair drooling on my lap. See that pillow on my bed? When I can't function any more, my life is over, as far as I'm concerned, and I want you just to put that pillow over my face and sit on it for about twenty minutes. Just call the doctor in the morning and say I died in my sleep. I won't contradict you. No homes."

Meanwhile, the couple has found out that the cost of these homes is well beyond their means, and that Mother will be left on Medicaid after her assets are gone. Their own assets are not large, and they would be totally responsible for the costs if they hired nurses to come to the house to take care of her. They also have teenage children, approaching college, to think about, who will need money for college and probably financial help as young adults after their education is finished.

"How did people used to handle this type of situation? Before there were Nursing Homes?" Dora had once asked her doctor. "Easy," he had replied, "People didn't used to live this long. And when they did, in this state, with no other choice in the matter, people simply left them home alone, tied down or roaming wherever they wanted to roam." That did sound "easy" to Dora, but on balance, worse than the other alternatives. They have the house to think of, too, and leaving Mother alone all day sounds like playing Russian roulette with house and Mother both.

But their first concern is for Mother. The life projected for her does not really seem to be worth living, the more they think about it. "Putting a pillow over her face" is a dreadful thought, of course, but it is what Mother wants, and if they cannot face the pillow, the Hemlock Society advertises many more humane ways to bring life to an end. Should they go the pillow route? Should they explore the "rational suicide" alternatives with Mother? Or should they insist on the home (or put her there anyway after she is no longer organized enough to resist)? Or should they devastate their own financial resources with hired nurses? Are there other alternatives?

In our attempts to reach the good or just solution in this case, what approach do we take? Typically, if we are (personally) in the middle of cases like this, we are strongly tempted to grasp at whatever "solution" appeals to us at the moment: that is, whatever solution accords with our previous prejudices and tendencies. But one of the major objectives of the teaching of ethics is to draw us beyond that subjective stance to one where all rational persons could agree that the right course, or *a* right course, is being pursued. That means that we must reach a course of action that is objectively right, or at least open for public scrutiny.

What would constitute an orderly approach to such problems? First, as participants and decision makers, we should organize our options in the situation – what alternatives are really open to us – and note the probable outcomes of each. What, in this situation, is it possible, and reasonable, for us to do? And what will be the likely results of each of those choices? Which of the outcomes on the list are totally unacceptable? They should be eliminated, and the rest left for further consideration at a later stage. In this step, we are reasoning *teleologically* or *consequentially* (more on these terms below), looking to the means that will produce the most desirable ends.

The Vlasovics, in this case, have the options of

1 Leaving Mother alone – and risking her and the house. That is not acceptable, save for very short periods of time.
2 Bringing in nurses by the day. That will turn out to be very expensive.

3   One of them quitting whatever else they are doing and just taking care of Mother. That will lower the family income, for all purposes, substantially, and no one wants either the burdensome task or the loss of income.

4   Putting that pillow over her face. The thought makes everyone queasy, and they really do not want to go to jail.

5   Putting Mother in a home. She will complain, but she will be safe, and the rest of the family can continue their own lives. This may also be very expensive, until they can establish Mother's eligibility for Medicaid.

Before they act, however, they must review the rights of the various participants, for legally protected rights, in our system, and trump, or override, considerations of right outcome. We must also respect moral (usually legally enforced) **rules** that are held to be valid regardless of the consequences. That is an important point: in this step we are reasoning *deontologically* or *non-consequentially*; that which violates a rule is prohibited by that rule no matter what consequences flow from doing or omitting the act.

Two of the most powerful rights and rules confront us in this situation:

1   First, the *right of the individual to refuse* the well-meaning ministrations, for his or her health and safety, imposed by others without consent. Mother does not want to go into a home, and that should settle that. Medicaid has nothing to do with it.

2   Second, the option preferred by Mother herself, the pillow placed over her face, violates a stringent *rule against voluntary homicide*, "thou shalt do no murder." It is not our purpose at this point to enter the emotional debate about the permissibility of assisted suicide or euthanasia, as requested by a competent patient. At the time that the pillow route would have to be followed, Mother would not be competent to request anything of the sort, and placing pillows over faces does not qualify as physician-assisted euthanasia. The act would be homicide, in fact murder in the first degree, and there are very good reasons why our society forbids it. If Pete and Dora take this option, they will have violated that rule.

Meanwhile, there are other rights to be taken into account. The minor children have an absolute right to their parents' support, for maintenance (food and shelter), affection (yes, that is a right), and provision of education. To what extent will care for Mother have an impact on them?

When we have our options clear and our rights and rules factored in, we should determine our decision, make a disposition of the problem, for the moment. The situation will not wait, after all; an initial decision must be taken immediately. For the moment, Mother is rational, and peaceable enough to be kept at home with her family; also, during her periods of lucidity, she enjoys being with them and they enjoy her. Perhaps a local day-care program can take her during school hours, and the teenagers can switch off afternoons to be with her before Pete and Dora come home from work. Nurses can be hired in occasionally to give everyone a break. The solution cannot last forever; will it work at all? Note that the family *must* act, with very incomplete information. That imperative is typical of such dilemmas. Pete and Dora decide to try it. And then, in a few days, weeks, or months, they must evaluate the effects of the decision. The decision and the action do not, as Macbeth pointed out, trammel up the consequences. The world continues. We need to follow up, to find out what results our decisions have had. The Vlasovics, in this situation, will not be able to avoid the results; Mother is still in the house with them. How much are the teenagers losing from their sacrifice of their afternoons? The answer to that will depend very much on the peculiarities of this family's situation. How is Mother responding to the new program? That depends very much on the peculiarities of Mother. The trouble with ethical dilemmas, as opposed to ethics as a discipline, is that the real solution is empirical, day-to-day, trial and error. Finally, we have to review the situation, reconsider the decision, with an eye toward revision. Nothing, in human affairs, is ever set in stone. We make our decisions, usually, for today, knowing that the decision will probably produce a new situation, with its own new dilemmas, and we will have to take on the whole problem again. The Vlasovics' decision to keep Mother home without round-the-clock nurses, bringing her to day care as often as they can, has saved them money, but after a while it will not work any more: most day-care programs cut off when the disease renders the patient violent or incontinent, and new arrangements will have to be made. But by then, there will be a new situation, with a different set of options, and possibly, a revised set of rights. The children, for instance, will eventually leave home, and confront their parents with a completely different set of demands. The federal government, for another instance, changes its mind every month about what programs to fund for the elderly; these will have to be taken into account in future deliberations.

This decision procedure, like many others in the field of ethics, covers all necessary bases for rational decisions. I prefer it to the others only because it builds in, as others do not, the recognition that nothing is ever decided – not well, anyway – once for all. The temptation to come to resolution, to solve something forever, is enormous. Resist it. Situations change, and the more flexible our decision procedure, the better suited it is to the messy world of human conduct.

Like **ADAPT**, this decision procedure for ethical dilemmas can be remembered easily by its acronym, **ORDER**:

O: options and outcomes
R: rights and rules
D: determination, decision
E: evaluation of effects
R: review, reconsideration

While we are at getting down procedures that are easy to remember, we may take note of three preliminary steps that have to be taken before we can put things in **ORDER**.

First, we have to define the dilemma that we are facing. What conflicts make the situation difficult to deal with?

In the Vlasovics' case, the dilemma is painfully evident: how to ensure Mother's and the family's *welfare* while respecting Mother's *choices* and the most serious *rules* of our society, while allocating the family's not-abundant resources *justly* among the generations that call upon them.

Second, we have to conduct empirical inquiries as appropriate, discover the facts, and get as much information as we can.

What day-care programs are available? What about support groups, for patients and caregivers alike, at the local hospital? Can we get her church involved? How fast is Mother's disease progressing? What should we know about advance directives, living wills, and therapies? Our options, once the decision procedure is engaged, will depend upon what is available.

Third, we have to sort out the stakeholders. We mentioned above that it is important to know whose interests are to be taken into account in making any decision.

Part of the work of sorting out the stakeholders is to make sure that all whose interests are really affected are taken into account. Another part of the work is to see that *non*-stakeholders who seek to attach themselves to a decision – the nosy neighbors, for instance, who do not like the cars of the visiting nurses parked (legally) on the street – are excluded from influencing the decision. Of course, that means that we may not take *their* happiness – the satisfaction they derive from running other people's lives – into account. The rights of the family take precedence over the preferences of their neighbors: rights trump likes and dislikes. This is why mere appeals to the "greatest happiness of the greatest number" are not always sufficient to decide ethical dilemmas. On the same principle, more commonly, we do not allow neighborhoods to exclude persons of an ethnic background different from that of the current residents, even though it would make all the neighbors overwhelmingly happy to be able to do that. The right of the minority family to live where they choose trumps the preferences of the neighbors not to let minorities live there. Of course the neighbors *are* stakeholders to some extent – they certainly have a right to be protected from Mother's wandering, should it come to that. The Anglo-Saxon Common Law, of which we are the inheritors, has spent patient centuries working out the details of the rights that people have *vis-à-vis* the neighbors, and we must be conscious of the whole *corpus* of that tradition.

So our first three determinations, in any ethical decision process, are of the definition, the factual information, and the stakeholders. If it makes it any easier to remember, think of these steps as a "DIS" preface to the "ORDER" decision procedure:

D: Definition of the dilemma
I: Inquiry to obtain all necessary information
S: Sorting out the stakeholders

This leaves us with a procedure whose steps are easy to remember, but leaves the field of ethics in **DISORDER!** Insofar as this DIS-ORDERed formula helps us to remember the essential messiness and anguish of ethical dilemmas, that serves our purposes very well.

Let us revisit Cases A and B in the last section, and add some complications:

Case A, but Dad is unconscious, and expected to remain so. He apparently has no sense or feeling, is unable to think or communicate.

He may be in some pain sometimes, however, and the children, backed up by the court-appointed conservator, request that he be given quite a bit more morphine "to make sure he doesn't suffer at all."

Case B, but your boss suggests only that you speed up the process from penicillin culture to filling the ampules, raising a 2 percent probability that the drug dispensed will not be up to strength. That does not sound good; but there is no evidence that such a change will hurt anyone at all. Meanwhile, the extra income generated will pay off some serious short-term debt and put the company in a better position to carry on its research. The quality control manager, who would prohibit this change on general principles, has just retired, and the company is "searching" for another, so you have a probable three-week window during which you can get the new-standard drug on the market.

In these cases, the need for higher-level reasoning is evident. Terminally ill patients should certainly be kept comfortable; there is nothing to be gained from prolonging this man's life, but a heavy dose of morphine? A balancing act begins, weighing the legitimate, if distasteful, interests of the heirs against the duties associated with the practice of medicine, especially the duty to protect one's patients, especially against this sort of proposal. Ultimately the principle that prevails will be an intermediate one, grounded in the practice of the profession: drugs are there to heal, not to kill, and the patient, probably unable to feel anything and certainly defenseless, may not be subjected to the needs and desires of others.

In Case B, the harm caused by the acceleration of the manufacturing process is not at all certain – even if penicillin was never prescribed unless it was needed, the mix of batches would ensure that no patient actually got perceptibly less than the proper dose. Here an appeal to a middle-level principle is necessary. The manager must ask himself, not, what the consequences of this action are, but, what would happen if everyone did this, and what would be the general consequences of a rule that permitted or required this action? (That formulation of a middle-level principle is found, by the way, in the major works on ethics of Immanuel Kant, John Stuart Mill and John Rawls; see the reference section at the end.) The "Golden Rule," do unto others as you would have them do unto you, is a similar principle. Research is important, and debt-retiring is surely good, but for now they may have to wait for alternative sources of funding.

DEAL: Carrying on without resolution

We may note that we have been presupposing throughout that the parties to the dilemmas were all in agreement on what the problem was and that it must be solved. In the messy real world of human life, these presuppositions do not always hold. Sometimes problems are particularly resistant to solution, because the interests or moral or religious commitments of the stakeholders are resolutely opposed, because the parties simply cannot understand each other, or for some other reason. Consider the following case:

Case 4: The Abortion Clinic
Michael and Maureen O'Connell are college-educated young professionals. Mike is a physician with a practice in Brooklyn and Maureen teaches in the nearby elementary school. They live with their five children (ages 4–13) on the quiet block in Queens where Maureen was brought up, just two blocks from St Luke's Roman Catholic Church, which they all attend. They are staunch Catholics, as is most of the neighborhood, and they uphold all the public teachings of the Church – including the prohibition of the use of contraceptives, the strict rules regarding any sexual relationship outside of marriage, and of course the absolute prohibition of induced abortion.

The neighborhood is mixed residential and commercial, so they are not surprised to find that a storefront three doors from their house is being renovated for use by a new tenant. "Surprise" does not describe their reaction, however, when finally the medical equipment is moved in and the sign is hung in the window: "Pregnancy Termination: Clean, Quiet, and Confidential." They are living virtually next door to an abortion clinic!

The neighbors want the clinic *out*: they all, men, women, and children, picket, obstruct patients and their companions, shout "Abortion is Murder!" sing hymns, pray loudly, threaten individual doctors and nurses, court the press, and plan a lawsuit. The clinic operators, on the other hand, led by two gynecologists, Dr Alan Bennett and Dr Rita Holmes, want the clinic to stay where it is and run successfully. They know that there is a good market for this service, they know that the women, pregnant against their will, will often resort to coat hangers and back-alley butchers to get abortions if safe abortions are not available legally, and they know they have the law on their side. They too spend time explaining their side to the media, and they demand better police protection.

The neighbors bring the lawsuit. It loses. The clinic is entirely within its rights. The police are ordered to protect the clinic and its workers from violence, a job that they detest: many of them are from the Queens neighborhood that produced Mike and Maureen, and attend St Luke's or some church of similar persuasions.

At this point the mayor becomes involved. The common wisdom has it that the elected officials lose three ways in these conflicts. First, they lose the votes of that and all similar neighborhoods, for "allowing the murder of infants a few yards from where our children play." Second, they lose the votes of liberals for not putting a more forceful stop to the demonstrations. Third, they lose the respect of the police department and those interested in law enforcement for diverting resources away from drugs and violent crime. Meanwhile the controversy itself, playing out through the newspapers, presents a very unfavorable view of the present administration. So the mayor wants peace among the parties, peace so quiet that the subject will disappear from the papers, but more importantly, since this is an ongoing issue, peace that will last. How can he, and the city, obtain this peace?

First, can he persuade the neighbors that the business will do them no harm, or the clinic managers to quietly move their clinic elsewhere? We do not usually honor neighborhood objections to a new business in their backyards; as above, not many neighborhood preferences are given enough weight to override the individual's strong interest and *prima facie* right to live where he or she wants and work wherever the zoning laws will permit his or her business establishment. The neighbors should be used to that. But there may be many, and trivial, reasons for locating a business in one place rather than another. Maybe the clinic would not mind moving; his office could help with the moving expenses. Like any good politician, his first thought is to make a **DEAL**.

The mayor chooses Mike and Maureen, as knowledgeable citizens and leaders of the demonstrations, and the physicians, Alan and Rita, as principals in the clinic, to engage in discussions of the issue. There are two reasons for this move. First, they may be able to come to some accommodation that will satisfy both sides permanently (that would have been the purpose of discussion in the last section). But the politician also knows that dialog is good for its own sake: as Winston Churchill put it, "as long as you 'jaw, jaw' you can't 'war, war.'" In the process of talking, the parties become less hostile and less hateful to each other.

No significant accommodation or compromise will work, as it turns out. It does not take the mayor long to learn

1   that Mike and Maureen and all their neighbors strongly believe that the human life of a baby begins at conception, that their belief is informed by medical and scientific knowledge (regarding the implantation of the genetic code, for instance) and firmly and rationally held, and that consequently, and quite logically, they really feel that each and every induced abortion is the murder of an infant. They feel that they are living next door to a Nazi death camp and slave market rolled into one, and that they are bound by religious and moral obligations to speak up and protest the slaughter. They are especially horrified at the prospect of raising their children with this clinic next door, having to tell them what it is about, effectually rubbing their noses not only in state-approved slaughter but in the daily consequences of promiscuous sexual activity!

2   that for their part, Alan and Rita of the physicians' group, the Women's Health Cooperative, that bought the building and set up the clinic, know very well what they are doing and plan to do. They are very much aware of the sexual behavior (if not the sexual ideals) of Mike and Maureen's neighborhood. One half of their first two months' practice were young, unmarried, white, terrified, Roman Catholic girls, mostly from the neighborhood. They feel very strongly not only that they are providing a desired service, but also that they are saving the futures of these girls, permitting them to finish their education, sparing their parents the shame, and the taxpayers the expense, of dealing with the illegitimate offspring, and most likely saving the child from abuse. In the remainder of their practice, mostly older working women of all ethnic backgrounds, they see themselves as permitting adults to carry on their work lives, plan their families and ensure proper provision and education for their children. In both cases, they are an available alternative to the astronomical rates of the offshore clinics, the back-alley incompetents and the terribly dangerous self-induced abortion. Their rates are low; they are not in this for the money, but for the public service, and they belong right where they are.

When pushed to the wall, the mayor notices, the two sides argue very differently, apparently reflecting a difference in the way they see the world. Mike and Maureen cite moral rules and rights – the natural law, the Ten Commandments, the right to life, which hold regardless of situation or consequence. In short, they are reasoning *deontologically* or *non-consequentially*. Alan and Rita, on the other hand, call attention to the pain felt by the women contemplating unwanted pregnancy, the negative effects on employment, education and general life prospects of the woman, from bearing unwanted children, and the welfare costs and other negative outcomes from denying abortions. In short, they are reasoning *teleologically* or *consequentially*. While there are also deontological pro-choice arguments and teleological pro-life arguments, in general Alan and Rita are focused on the problems they are solving, while Mike and Maureen are focused on the nature of the act itself, and there is not likely to be any resolution between the two sides.

So the mayor proposes an experiment in peacemaking. One of the features of the clinic that troubles the neighborhood most is the mingling of the clinic patients and the children as they depart for or return from school. Could the clinic open at 9:30, a bit later than the morning rush, and take a late lunch break at 2:45, as the children return? In return, the demonstrators will not picket weekdays between opening and that break.

That concession – given that each side views the other's work as fundamentally criminal – is strictly speaking *unethical*, for both sides: any concession is incompatible with the moral beliefs that they have set forth and clearly defended.

After a week or so the mayor's office does an assessment of how the experiment is working. The neighborhood seems quieter, and the newspapers have backed off. Good.

So two of his best mediators bring the four principals back together to attempt further progress. Will the clinic accede to even shorter hours in return for complete removal of the pickets? A few more grudging concessions are obtained; since the prospects for further progress are not good, and the situation seems stable as it is, the mediators back away and let the two parties live with the agreements reached so far.

By continuing the dialogue, even more than joining it to begin with – when each party could have claimed a genuine hope of con-verting the other – the two sides have acknowledged each other's legitimacy. While there is no possibility of coming to agree with the other's moral stand, there is no hope of destroying the other. Neither is going away. Distasteful as it is, each must live with the other in peace, even while retaining the conviction that what the other is doing is fundamentally wrong, immoral. This stage of the moral life, a necessity only in pluralistic societies like our own, could be called, possibly, live and let live, or leave people alone!

Change in the neighborhood, or the practice, could upset the unhappy peace that has descended; others must be prepared to step in, should violence break out again, to restart the dialogue. For **DEAL**, the peace process that we have just set forth:

Dialog
Experiment
Assessment
Legitimacy

is, like **ORDER** above, fundamentally an iterative process, continually restarting in slightly different conditions.

Let us conclude the cases we started above:

Case A, with Dad unconscious as before, not expected to wake in this life, but occasionally in some discomfort. But this time the children (two of them, twins) do not agree as to what to do about him. One of the twins wants everything done, including surgery if necessary, to save Daddy's life, and threatens to sue if treatment is "negligently" withheld. The other wants those increasing doses of morphine to "ease the pain" and incidentally to shorten Dad's life, and has brought in a lawyer to argue against "futile" treatment like drugs and surgery. No document signals which of the twins is to have the power to decide.

Case B, modified as above, but the pressures are worse: the company will have to close the plant, ending 10,000 jobs, unless productivity takes a marked turn for the better in the next quarter. It is possible that the weakened antibiotic could cause some harm, at least in some extended sickness, but it is not likely to cause death. On the other hand, it is entirely predictable that if the layoff takes place, dysfunction, sickness, and death – divorce, alcoholism, mental illness, diffuse chronic illnesses, suicide – will claim a solid percentage of those unemployed 10,000. The solution to the manager's dilemma is not immediately clear, and intermediate principles do not really solve the problem (for a thought experiment, try applying the Golden Rule to the case, letting first the workers and then the customers fill the role of "others"). Here the balance must be struck between the obligations to shareholders, workers, local community, and others with a stake in the continuation of the business enterprise, and obligations to customers, reputation, society at large, and others with a stake in the integrity of the procedures of that enterprise. (For instance, the public surely must be notified about the change in standard – but how?) The principles of concern for the welfare of those affected by a decision – primarily the employees, in this case – and of justice, in following the rules applicable to all no matter what the consequences, are logically independent, and there is no safe formula for deciding which shall take priority in a given case.

Given the nature of the situations to which it is applied, **DEAL** does not really yield a conclusion that we can all accept as "ethical." (For another real-life application of this "unethical" reasoning, try the dispute between Israelis and the Palestinian Arabs.) But **DEAL** has much to recommend it, from the ethical point of view. Without further elaboration at this point, we can point out that it accomplishes three tasks, all of which are required by general ethical imperatives.

1   It promotes the maximum social welfare obtainable, by preserving the peace and preventing violence. Whatever may divide the physicians, the anti-abortion activists, and the uninvolved neighbors – and there is much that divides them – they share a common interest in the preservation of life, limb, and property, and the grudging accommodation reached serves to protect those shared interests.

2   It enforces justice, by promoting an even-handed compromise. Both sides find the state of peace with the other, especially with regard to the concessions they had to make to obtain it, really repugnant. But the fact that they both had to make concessions, and that they are required to stick to the deal they made, makes it *fair*, even though the fairness may be much more evident to a dispassionate outsider than it is to the parties.

3   It insists on the dignity, worth, and conscience of every individual, worthy of respect even from those who are utterly convinced he or she is wrong. Neither group has the right to destroy the other, to keep it from the public space or public attention, to relegate it to a slavish state or second-class citizenship. It affirms, therefore, freedom of conscience, and the right and duty of every human being to develop and inform that conscience, to discern, articulate, and defend a moral position on serious matters, especially matters of life and death.

✣ NOTES ✣

1. This summary is borrowed from Ronald F. Duska and Brenda Shay Duska, *Accounting Ethics*, also in the Foundations of Business Ethics series; Oxford: Blackwell Publishing, 2003.

c h a p t e r   t w o

From Ethics to Business Ethics

⊛ AN INTRODUCTION AND FOREWARNING ⊛

The role of this chapter is to give a general background for business ethics. We will not review the terminology and forms of reasoning covered in the last chapter and its appendix, nor will we dig any further into the history of philosophical ethics. The theories we are most likely to refer to are the **utilitarianism** of Jeremy Bentham and John Stuart Mill, the **formalism** of Immanuel Kant, and occasionally the theory of **justice** of John Rawls. Beyond that, we will refer on occasion to the principled duties of beneficence, of justice, and of respect for persons; of the imperative to cultivate virtues appropriate to one's occupations; and of the general relational duties of care and compassion. So that you may be forewarned, the thread of ethical theory that this account of business ethics is most likely to follow is the centrality of human autonomy, choice, freedom, and responsibility, foreshadowed by Immanuel Kant.

Responsibility may mean many things: it may designate an assigned task ("He is *responsible* for cleaning the third floor of the building"), a hierarchy of **authority** ("He is *responsible* to the building janitor"), **accountability** for some event ("He is *responsible* for the cleaning fluid getting into the third-floor smoke alarm"), **culpability** ("and the janitor intends to hold him *responsible* for that"), and **liability** ("and make him pay for the Fire Department's answering a false alarm.") To "assume responsibility" means to acknowledge any or all of those. Responsibility also refers to a trait of character, combining **prudence** (the tendency to think ahead, to foresee any bad outcomes of your actions, and to act to avoid them), **reliability** (the disposition to keep your word and to do what is expected of you), **concern and compassion** for others (the ability, and willingness, to imagine the consequences for others of any of your actions), and the **integrity and courage** to make your actions, with all their consequences, your own (despite any pain or embarrassment it may cause you). A "responsible" person is one who recognizes and assumes responsibility for those areas of activity within his or her power and right.

A "responsibility perspective" on any field of ethics combines a claim of value with a tendency to evaluate the situations, policies, and practices that fall within the field in a certain way. The claim is that it is a good thing for human beings to live lives of responsibility: to recognize the good that it is in their power to do, and to do it; to recognize what harm they may cause, and to act to avoid that harm; and whenever things go awry in their world at least in part because of something that they have done, to acknowledge their part in the situation and act to redeem it without blaming others. The evaluative tendency is to judge according to the degree to which the actors in the cases under consideration take responsibility for their own actions and for situations under their control, according to the tendency of the policies and practices to encourage and demand the development of responsibility as a virtue in all participants in the area covered, and according to the possibilities of creating new areas of responsibility where presently they are lacking. This description of the responsibility perspective may seem puzzlingly general at this point, but it will come up again and again in the areas we will cover in this section, and it should be clear by the end. At least, I regard it as my responsibility to make it clear, and stand to take the blame if it is not.

Given this perspective, we will not always find it necessary to abstain from judgment on the policies, practices, and actions submitted for ethical review in these pages. All ethical perspectives will be considered, all sides of every question fairly presented for evaluation, as required in any text for general use; but the reader will be openly invited to share a preference for institutions and policies that grant the opportunity to exercise responsibility in all dealings in and with business and the professions, and to respect responsible action when it occurs. We hope, through this consideration of the responsibilities of business with regard to the natural environment, to sketch the outlines of an ideal of business practice that would be completely compatible with the moral maturity of all the individuals involved with the economic institutions with which we must deal.

✦ BUSINESS AS A MORAL ENTERPRISE ✦

Why is it so much fun to describe **business ethics** as an oxymoron
(a contradiction in terms), and pretend that all businesspersons are
greedy graspers who will gladly sell their own grandmothers to
improve the bottom line? (Literally, the final line on the quarterly
income statement; figuratively, the net profit or loss in dollar terms
for any person or company.) There is little evidence that those who
make a living in the business world are any better or worse than
those of us who, for instance, teach in college; so why the prejudice?
In this chapter we will try to set out the moral configuration of
business enterprise as a whole, as conceived by philosophers and
economists who have tried to understand it as a whole. We will
try to see why we might be disposed to view business as somehow
fundamentally good or otherwise, and if business turns out to be
a moral enterprise, we will look for the central moral principles on
which its goodness rests.

We will conduct this exploration in several steps. The first series of
steps will trace the roots of the inherited moral opposition to business
enterprise, the nature of work and the growth of the work ethic, the
growth of the city and of commerce, the establishment of the rights
of private property and contract, the discovery of the potential of the
free market, and the emergence of business as a critical arena of moral
growth and accomplishment, a place for the exercise of autonomy,
prudence, and responsibility. The second series will trace the birth of
the modern corporation, the effects of the factory system, the separation
of ownership and control, and the foundations of the moral dilemmas
that confront business now.

The first series brings business from the ancient world to the modern.

Aristotle and the ancient world's class system

If there is a prejudice against the possibility of morality in business
bred in our bones, it may be useful first to find out where that prejudice
came from (and therefore what of it we should retain in our contemporary critiques of business). The Greek philosopher Aristotle (fourth
century BC) was the first to attack the foundations of the marketplace. In the first book of the *Politics*, where he discusses the laws of the
household (*OEconomica*), he distinguishes the worthy occupations
by which a man may support his family from the unworthy ones.

Hunting in all its varieties is worthy; fighting is worthy; farming and animal husbandry are worthy; ruling is worthy; and certain kinds of crafts will qualify. All forms of commerce are unworthy, with retail trade and banking catching the worst opprobrium. Why banking? Because in the practice of usury (collecting interest on loans) it allows money to make more money, "as if cold metal could breed!" (*Politics* I, x, 4; 1258b) Why retail trade? Because it focused a man's mind on money, petty gain, hoarding, and getting more, and all that was thoroughly bad for the character. Crafts, which focused on beauty, were acceptable; farming and herding, which produced necessary food in cooperation with nature, were good; and hunting, with the contest of skill and strength between hunter and prey, was positively ennobling, as was any military endeavor. As a final insult, Aristotle classifies piracy – freebooting – as a form of hunting, and therefore a worthy occupation, as if the merchant, along with all his goods and employees, were just another prey animal to be slaughtered for the hunter's triumph.

Why was Aristotle so intolerant of business folk? It has been said that he was just a man of his time. The landed aristocracy, to which he belonged (or whom he served), had total contempt for the Athenian merchants, whom they regarded as an alien and inferior race given to taking advantage of honest farmers even as they traded the Athenian crops. In fact, Aristotle was not describing the society in which he lived, but one that he preferred. Yet his inherited prejudice, against any occupation that dealt not with natural goods but with the institutions that traded in them, carried the day. The Roman Church adopted the prohibition on usury, and by doing that, significantly slowed the growth of commerce in the Middle Ages.

The monastic movement and the work ethic

In 529 AD, St Benedict founded a Christian monastery at Montecassino. It was not the first celibate colony founded for the purpose of religious retreat and enlightenment (many religious sects had those), but it was one of the first Christian ones, and it made a difference: Benedict's idea was that instead of (only) begging to support a life of prayer and meditation, his monks should work in the fields and at other tasks, to learn humility. (His model was the arresting figure of Jesus, towel wrapped around his waist, washing the feet of his disciples – the task assigned to the lowest of the servants in the Judean household.) As a rule for Benedict's monks, the work assignments made sense. At first, most of them were from the ruling class, and working in the fields was the most humiliating thing they could think of. To leap forward almost a millennium, most of the monasteries that were formed in the first 1,500 years of Christendom taught their novices that for the sake of service to the Lord, it was appropriate to imitate Jesus in the cheerful performance of all useful menial tasks – in short, to work. They did this work as part of their vocation (literally, "calling," the life that they felt the Lord called them to and wanted them to live), and so the work became noble and good. This ethic, so contrary to the aristocratic ethic of Aristotle, that embraced hard work in the world as something ennobling and even holy, played a vital part in the growth of the industrial civilization that followed.

Commerce and contract

When prosperity began to return to Europe, toward the end of the twelfth century, it created among the wealthier nobles and their families a market for the goods of the East – silks and spices, ivory and aromatic woods. A new class of merchants and traders arose, to finance expeditions, by land and water, to the East and to sell the goods when they arrived in Europe. The merchants, agents, and beneficiaries of that prosperity soon formed a new class, a "middle" class between the feudal knights and the serfs who worked the land as tenant farmers.

What did these merchants have, to guarantee that the ship they sent off, Heaven knows where off in the East, would return to them, at least if it survived the ocean's storms, and that they would get the profit from the goods brought back? Very little, actually, except the power of the word – the captain's *promise* that in return for a salary (or more likely a share of the profit) he would not run off with the goods and sell them somewhere else. The agreement made – *quid pro quo*, mutual promising, an agreement to mutual performance of some specific agreement – was a contract. There had been contracts in the ancient world, of course, but through the intervening ages, Europe had relied more on authority, of the Church or feudal lord, or tradition, to command performance. But there was no tradition for the commercial class; they had to make up their own ways of cooperating. So a series of contracts bound together the banker, who put up the funds for the voyage, the merchant who ordered the goods, the captain who set sail with European products in trade, and the distant merchants in storied lands who supplied the riches of the

East for transport. The contract then was a chancy thing at best, with so much time and distance between agreement and performance. But enough of them worked so that the practice, of contract and performance, became an established way to conduct the business of business; by now, it is second nature, and one of the strongest moral obligations we acknowledge, in or out of business.

Social contract and private property

Contract is indeed a powerful concept. We all know about moral obligations – thou shalt do no murder, thou shalt not steal, etc. Moral obligations are non-optional (you do not have any choice about being bound by them), and everlasting – as long as families exist, there will be an obligation to take care of the children and honor the father and mother. But a contract *is* optional. You do not have to agree to a contract. But if you do agree, then you are under a very strong moral obligation to fulfill it – all the stronger because it was of your own free will that you made it. In a world whose major ancient institutions were dying or paralyzed in the throes of change, a world flooded with new possibilities, Europe suddenly discovered a moral principle capable of handling all novel circumstances, one that could engage human reason to decide the patterns of human conduct. Europe emerged into the modern age convinced that this notion of "contract" could underlie all moral obligation and political theory.

Accordingly, when the major political thinkers of our immediate tradition – the political thinkers of the modern age – undertook to challenge the sacred authority of the Church and the divine right of kings, they imported the commercial notion of contract to justify the political authority of the state over the citizen. Thomas Hobbes (1588–1679) was among the first to propose that society (all organized human life) should be seen as the product of the **social contract**, an agreement among freely contracting parties to get them out of a chaotic and violent **state of nature** characterized by Hobbes as "the war of all against all." John Locke (1632–1704) held that people could live in peace with only natural reason to guide them. All of us live under the **Natural Law** (a fixed order of eternal laws, proceeding from God's mind and binding on all humans forever, but accessible to human reason). But the natural law will not protect property or civil rights. The boundaries of a parcel of land are arbitrary from God's perspective, as are the rights of neighbors along a riverbank or claimants of air rights in New York City; to protect property, we need civil government, just to protect the rights given by nature. How may people acquire property in the state of nature? For Hobbes, people seize what they can, but the Sovereign can overrule them if he wants it himself. In Locke there is no such sovereign; people acquire property by using it, by "mixing their labor" with it, and they are free to take from the common stock of unowned land as much as they can use (and no more), as long as they leave "enough and as good" for the next person who comes along. Once it is theirs, it is theirs by entitlement (right); no one may take it from them without their consent.

The wealth of nations

Most of the elements of an ethic of business had come together in the Protestant Reformation. Martin Luther, an ex-monk, preached that *every* person had a vocation from God, to work honestly, to produce excellent products, and to earn a living in the sweat of his brow in the way for which he was best fitted. A practical, middle-class religion, Lutheranism made enormous strides in the cities. Freed from the domain of the prevailing Church, philosophers also tried to capture the new spirit of Renaissance, Reason, and Enlightenment, and one of the best of them echoed perfectly the practical calculations of the merchants. This was Jeremy Bentham (1748–1832), the founder of Utilitarianism.

Writing about half a century after Locke had established property and representative government on a foundation of natural rights, Bentham taught **hedonism** (from ʿedoni, pleasure: the belief that pleasure is the only good and pain the only evil). People are their own best judges on what is pleasurable or not, so all you have to do is ask them what they like and what they do not like and you will know what is right and wrong. By "the common good" we mean no more than the sum of individual goods. To see if a proposed piece of legislation will serve the common good, then, all you need to do is adopt a single unit of pleasure (say, one hour of pleasurable consciousness for one citizen) and apply the felicific calculus (a technique of adding units of pleasure and subtracting units of pain to come up with a happiness bottom line) to get a sum that will tell you not only whether, on balance, the legislation will serve the common good, but also if it will do so better than any alternative.

The moral philosopher and economist Adam Smith (1723–1790) proceeded to apply Bentham's assumptions to the marketplace. Let us assume, said Smith, that Bentham is right; that apart from short and rarely significant bursts of **altruism** (the motivation to help others, with no thought for oneself), people are selfish. Most people, most of the time, want to find pleasure and avoid pain for themselves. In the marketplace, that disposition translates into a determined effort to advance one's own interests – to become wealthier, in terms of money, goods, and enjoyments. The fundamental "capitalist act," on this assumption, is the self-interested voluntary exchange (the willing trade with another for the purpose of advancing one's own interests): two adults, of sound mind and clear purposes, meet in the marketplace, to which each repairs in order to satisfy some felt need. They discover that each has that which will satisfy the other's need – the housewife needs flour, the miller needs cash – and they exchange, at a price such that the exchange furthers the interest of each. The **utility** (the increase in wealth brought about by this exchange) to the participant in the free market of the thing acquired must exceed that of the thing traded, or else why would he or she make the deal? So each party to the voluntary exchange walks away from it richer.

Adding to the value of the exchange is the competition of dealers and buyers; because there are many purveyors of each good, the customer is not forced to pay exorbitant prices for things needed (it is a sad fact of economics that to the starving person, the marginal value of a loaf of bread is very large, and a single merchant could become unjustly rich). Conversely, competition among the customers (typified by an auction) makes sure that the available goods end in the hands of those to whom they are worth the most. So at the end of the market day, not only does everyone go home richer (in real terms) than when they came but also as rich as they could possibly be, since they had available all possible options of goods or services to buy and all possible purchasers of their goods or services for sale.

Sellers and buyers win the competition through high **efficiency** (ratio of quantity and quality of production to the costs of production: "the bang for the buck"), through producing the best-quality goods at the lowest possible price, or through allotting their scarce resources toward the most valuable of the choices presented to them. It is to the advantage of all participants in the market, then, to strive for high efficiency, that is, to keep the cost of goods for sale as low as possible while keeping the quality as high as possible. Adam Smith's most memorable accomplishment was to recognize that the general effect of all this self-interested scrambling would be to make the most possible goods of the best possible quality available at the lowest possible price. Meanwhile, sellers and buyers alike must keep an eye on the market as a whole, adjusting production and purchasing to take advantage of fluctuations in supply and demand. Short supply will make goods more valuable, raising the price, so the producers will make money; and that will bring more suppliers into the market, whose competition will lower the price, to just above the cost of manufacture for the most efficient producers. Increased demand for any reason will have the same effect. Should demand exceed supply, the price will rise until only as many buyers as there are products will be able to afford them. Should supply exceed demand, the price will fall to a point where the goods will be bought. Putting this all together, Smith realized that in a system of free enterprise, you have demonstrably the best possible chance of finding for sale what you want, in good quantity and quality, at a reasonable price. Forget benevolent monarchs ordering things for our good, he suggested; in this system we are led by an "invisible hand" to serve the common good even as we think we are being most selfish.

Smith pointed out that certain virtues (excellences; traits of character that enhance an individual's ability to perform his or her duties, live well, and serve the public good) are presupposed by the operations of the free market. The whole system will not work at all unless the participants are honest in word and deed. That is, they tell the truth, especially about the invisible properties of their products for sale, they pay their debts, and honor their contracts. The capitalism that he describes will not, in fact, work for very long unless the participants are rational (for these purposes, just that they know what their own interests are and are not often subject to emotional outbursts that interfere with acting on them), prudent (foresighted, able to set aside present gratification for long-term profit), industrious (hardworking, not lazy), temperate (moderate in their demands, not greedy), thrifty (strongly disposed to save money; a kind of prudence), and for the most part in possession of some saleable skill that they can use to make a living. Above all they must be responsible: willing to follow up on their commitments and keep their contracts, making sure that their goods are as described and do no harm to anyone, and taking a full and active part to protect the community that underlies their own and their neighbors' business endeavors.

Benjamin Franklin and the bourgeois tradesman

Adam Smith's theory of economic enterprise and the "wealth of nations" came from a combination of the natural law tradition of the seventeenth and eighteenth centuries (exemplified by John Locke) and the empirical tradition represented by Jeremy Bentham. Locke was needed to establish the sanctity of property and contract, and Bentham to establish the priority of self-interest in human relations. Smith translated the conclusions as so many elaborations of the natural law: the law of supply and demand, that links supply, demand, and price; the law that links efficiency with success; and ultimately, the laws that link the freedom of the market with the growth of the wealth of the free-market country.

The point of it all was liberty, or freedom – the natural liberty that every human had from God and nature, and the liberty of exchange in the free market that would increase the wealth of the nation without limits. It is no accident that the currents of liberty, political and economic, came together in the English colonies in the New World. The colonies had been settled first as a business enterprise (the companies that colonized Virginia and Massachusetts Bay expected to make a profit trading the products of the New World), then became a refuge for Protestant burghers of various traditions (English Separatists, French Huguenots), and rapidly came to see themselves as an experiment in freedom. The ferment of freedom came to a head simultaneously in several ways: recall that the year 1776 saw the American Declaration of Independence, and the publication of Bentham's *Theory of Morals and Legislation* and Adam Smith's *The Wealth of Nations*.

The American colonists who agitated most for independence were the wealthy businessmen (like John Hancock) who found British taxation cutting severely into their profits. But the ethic of American business had been laid down 40 years previously, in the widely read issues of *Poor Richard's Almanack* by Benjamin Franklin (1706–1790). Franklin provides a strong restatement of the work ethic, along with assurances that work will provide prosperity. "Keep thy shop, & thy shop will keep thee," he advised. He had no use for laziness: "Employ thy time well, if thou meanest to gain leisure," "Be always asham'd to catch thy self idle," and was sure that honest toil would always yield prosperity. The time invested in apprenticeship was well worth it; "He that hath a Trade, hath an Estate." In such proverbs, aphorisms, and sage advice on a multitude of subjects Franklin addresses the small farmer and businessman who were assumed to make up the population of America, urging prudence, industriousness, honesty, and lapsing repeatedly into simple praise for profitable trade. Aristotle is repaid to the full: Franklin matches his boundless admiration for the small businessman with profound contempt for the foppish "gentlemen" who put on airs around the working folk.

By way of conclusion: The good news part I

So the business system in America certainly started out as a moral enterprise, specifically as the embodiment of that "pursuit of happiness" to which Thomas Jefferson, in the Declaration of Independence, assured us we had a right; the best and only way to promote the general prosperity, one of the purposes (according to the Preamble to the American Constitution) of the founding of this country; and a teacher of virtue, as Benjamin Franklin would have it. The virtue that sums up Franklin's tradesman is responsibility: he owns and is in full charge of his farm or shop, freely exercising rational choice in the decisions for the expenditure of resources (including his own time and effort) in accordance with the dictates of prudence, making commitments appropriate to the flourishing of the business and his family, following up on the commitments, making sure that all work that he does is done right, representing it truthfully and billing only for what was done. With the highest stake in the continuing good order of the community, this tradesman is also the best candidate for holding office in its government, and is the basis for democracy.

Jefferson's letters suggest that he, at least, believed that *only* the small tradesmen and farmers could be relied on to run the country properly. Their property, he believed, gave them a stake in the stability and laws of the country, in contrast to the urban working class that he had encountered in Paris, and most definitely in contrast to the lazy and functionless "nobility" left over from pre-modern civilization. With Franklin, he saw that managing their own property for a profit taught them responsibility and prudence, surely qualities needed to run the state as well.

All of this is good news for a country that needed responsible management in both the economic and the political domains. As Adam Smith had insisted, the very natural self-interested struggle to get a living will teach those virtues that are necessary to ensure not only prosperity and wise administration throughout the land, but mature and adaptable citizens who can be relied on to take responsibility for the government of a state with the same sober industry as they apply to their own business.

✪ BUSINESS AS ARENA OF MORAL ✪ DILEMMAS

Then whence came the images of business as a cruel exploiter of its employees, fat cats fiddling while the public be damned, the purveyor of cheap goods of which the buyer should beware? Business was not perceived as a villain in the United States until the nineteenth century – the age of the limited liability corporation, the industrial revolution, and the civilization of the factory. We now turn to the corporation and the ethical dilemmas that surround its operations.

The nature of the corporation

What is a corporation? A for-profit corporation, the kind with which this chapter is primarily concerned, is a venture financed by **investors** (the people who put their money into the venture, at the outset or later on) for the purpose of making more money, getting a return on investment (ROI) as great or greater than they could get in any other allotment of their money. Once launched in business, a corporation is legally a *fictional person* – as Chief Justice of the Supreme Court John Marshall put it in 1819, "an artificial being, invisible, intangible, and existing only in the contemplation of the law." Intangible or not, it is a real thing that outlives all its members, that can sue and be sued and make contracts like any individual. It is the status as a legal individual of Exxon or Pepsico or General Motors that has us assuming that they can have moral rights and obligations like any one of us.

Any individual or group can carry on business. Why would one form a corporation to do that? The answer lies in a curious point of legal history. Historically, corporations have been chartered by the state, and granted by the state the privilege of limited liability: the members of the corporation (the investors) are financially liable for corporate debts only to the extent of their investments. They can lose the money they put in, but the creditors of the corporation cannot come after their personal funds to satisfy the corporation's debts. From the sketch above of the enterprises that created international trade, you can see why commercial corporations were formed. Each trip to the East put the investors terribly in debt, and if the boat were to be lost, as many were, the creditors could come after the owners' personal funds, houses, and possibly their persons (remember that the merchant of Venice, in Shakespeare's play of that name, nearly lost a pound of flesh nearest the heart!). The East India Company, established in 1600 by Queen Elizabeth I just to undertake the commercial exploitation of Asia, was one of the earliest and largest corporations. The Massachusetts Bay Company, formed to undertake the similar exploitation of the American colonies, was another.

The corporation in the free market

The nations of early modern Europe were **mercantilist**. That is, they assumed that all economic dealings within their borders (or across them) should be monitored for the public good, and that it was part of the prerogative and duty of the state to charter only those corporations that would serve the national interest. Naturally, the officers of the state in charge of deciding who deserved a corporate charter and who did not tended to favor friends and party members, and the entire approval process became cumbersome and corrupt. After Adam Smith, the defenders of free enterprise pointed out that it was also entirely unnecessary. Let people make their own economic arrangements, they argued, and the public good will be served. Furthermore, in the name of liberty, especially liberty of association, there should be no reason why any group of persons should not be able to form a corporation if that is what they wanted to do. So in the nineteenth century the process was streamlined; now all it takes to form a corporation is a form that any lawyer can supply, a fee for the state, and a few signatures. You and I could form one.

Not all corporations are formed for the purpose of making a profit. Charities, hospitals, and universities are also incorporated. For the moment, let us leave the non-profit sector alone and concentrate on the "private sector" corporation, formed for the sole purpose of returning money to its investors – to take advantage of corporate freedom to carry on business and the limitations of investor liability to maximize the chances of personal profits while minimizing personal risks. Corporations enjoy most of the freedoms available to humans (including free speech and participation in political campaigns). Then can they be held morally responsible – requested to honor moral duties of (for instance) helping the poor or supporting the arts, required to control harmful emissions from the factories even beyond the level required by law, urged not to fire those who really need the jobs? Here a real problem arises. To understand the structure of the problem, let us look for a moment at the structure of the corporation.

Ownership and agency

When a corporation is started, it is wholly owned by the investors; its name, all its assets, and all the products of its activity are property, and it is theirs. They can do what they (collectively) like with it and with the return it yields – save it, reinvest it, give it away. Let us suppose a company was started by 10 investors; each would have a one-tenth share in the company (or one-tenth of the stock of the company), and presumably all decisions about what the company should do would be made by a majority vote among those 10. If the local fishermen asked the corporation to install some extra equipment so their toxic waste water would not flow into the creek (equipment not required by law), or the local opera needed money and came to the corporation asking for a corporate contribution, the 10 could take a vote among themselves on whether to install the equipment or contribute to the opera. If they decided to spend the money, no problem – that is their right. It is theirs.

Now, if they want to be about their other business, and so hire a manager to run the corporation in their absence, the manager has none of the rights of ownership. The owners are the principals in this engagement (strictly speaking, the owners collectively *are* the corporation, and the corporation is the principal), the manager is the agent of the corporation, and in this agency relationship the manager has a fiduciary obligation to the corporation to advance its interests. (The principal is the decision maker and initiator of the relationship; the agent is one who acts on behalf of another, not for himself; and a fiduciary relationship [from *fides*, faith or trust] obligates the fiduciary to act for the interests of the beneficiary, the persons or institution for which he or she is the agent.) The agents can do only what they are instructed to do by the owners, and the owners have told the agent to run the business profitably, deduct his or her costs and salary, and send them the profits (the higher the better) as dividends, as a return on their investment. The owners have also, of course, told the agent to run the business in strict compliance with the law, because going afoul of the law can be very expensive; in the worst case, the whole business might be shut down and all the investment lost. So they will spend the money needed for compliance. But if the town asks for control of runoff into the creek beyond the letter of the law, or the opera asks them for money for the next production, they really should do nothing until they have had the opportunity to ask the owners. If the owners are far away, that may be difficult to do. If the agent cannot consult them, they may just have to continue doing what they were told, which is to increase the shareholders' wealth. After all, it is not the agent's money.

The situation gets worse (for the creek and the opera) if the original owners decide not only to sell their shares to other parties, splitting them several ways as they do so, but also to issue more stock, selling it to the public at large, in order to raise capital. (Their small factory has been doing so well that they decide to build two more, and need a lot of money, more than they could borrow from a bank, to start building.) By this time the corporation will have assumed its contemporary form, run not by the shareholders directly but by a Board of Directors, elected by them, whose charge it is to further shareholder interests – in short, to increase their wealth by directing the managers to follow policies that will raise the value of the stock in the market for stock, the Stock Exchange. By the time several new issues of stock have been sold, there will be many thousands, ultimately millions, of shares of company stock outstanding, owned by the public, and the manager is never going to be able to get hold of all the owners. Since, on the stock exchange the shares can be traded (ownership can change) every day, the idea of contacting the shareholders for advice about the pipe or the opera rapidly becomes absurd.

Can the manager assume that the shareholders might *want* to clean up the creek or contribute to the opera? He or she might be wrong, but for most of the corporation's history, they could certainly try. The shareholders, however many and anonymous they were, were at least individual human beings who could be presumed to want the community fishermen and opera patrons to think well of the company, and to possess at least a passing interest in the natural environment and the arts. Throughout most of the twentieth century, corporations could assume at least some responsibility for community support and protection beyond the letter of the law. More recently, even that presumption has been defeated.

Funds, buyouts, and takeovers: The corporate dilemma

In the latest transformation of the corporation, the whole structure of ownership has changed. Since the 1920s we have had mutual funds, investment pools, which give the small investor with neither the time nor the skill to manage his own investments the opportunity to participate in the stock market with an experienced manager to make the investment decisions. Since the 1930s, college endowments, workers' pensions, and many other projects have been provided for by similar funds, money pooled and saved for special purposes, run by fund managers whose job it is to make sure that the fund is properly administered – invested in ways that will make sure that it is there when it is needed and that it will grow, as much as possible. For most of this century, such public funds stayed out of stocks – fund managers bought corporate or municipal bonds (loans to corporations or cities), because they seemed so much safer. Once the fund managers of these large public funds, endowment and pension funds, realized that the stock market was not going to crash again, and that the return on stocks was much higher than that on bonds, they started putting their funds into shares of the corporations publicly traded on the stock exchanges. By now, up to 80 percent of our large corporations may be owned by these funds.

When there are 50 million shares of stock outstanding, the corporation's manager cannot poll the shareholders to find out if they want to give up some of their ROI to donate to the opera or cut back on emissions. But at least in theory, that might be what individual shareholders want to do, and if the cause is very good, the manager may be justified in assuming that they do want to do that. With the funds as the owners, the corporation manager's freedom to make that assumption disappears. The fund managers have no more right than the corporate managers to authorize charity or public-spirited expenses beyond the letter of the law. They were appointed to run their pension fund, or endowment fund, in such a way as to increase its monetary value for the sake of the retirees or the college. They cannot give to charity from the fund's money, and it is difficult to see how they could authorize one of the companies in which the fund is invested to give the money due the fund in dividends away as charity, or spend it unnecessarily on community benefits.

Let us review that structure. Who owns the corporation? The 40,000 teachers in the Florida Public Schools, let us say, pool their pension money and hire an administrator to manage that money for their benefit. The teachers collectively, from whose salary the pension money came, are the principal, the fund manager is the agent, with a fiduciary obligation to the teachers, to increase the amount of money they will have to retire on. The fund buys stock in a major US company. Now the fund owns part of the company, and it becomes an owner/principal of the corporation. The corporate manager is now essentially the agent of the teachers' pension fund and all the other funds. *No one in this picture* has any right to install environmental equipment, contribute to the opera, or undertake any action at all beyond the requirements of law in the name of the corporation. In this bizarre limiting case in the history of private property, no one who knows whose money that is has any power to spend it, while the actual principals – the Florida schoolteachers – have no idea that they are owners of that or any corporation. The money does not belong to anyone who can do anything with it. It is its own. It has developed an engine of its own, and a single direction – to make more money. Cold metal has learned to breed.

We are not led inexorably to the conclusion that business must be unethical – only that business is limited. It is not *supposed* to do creeks and operas. Its *only* job is to make money for investors, and (following Adam Smith) fulfillment of that task must eventually tend to the public good. Milton Friedman, an influential University of Chicago economist, has argued for decades that the only "social responsibility" of business is to make profits. If the society disagrees, the society can make laws restricting the activities of business, and the manager, ever compliant, will make sure that those laws are obeyed. Not all managers agree with Friedman.

This transformation of ownership has led to some sad and confusing developments in US corporations. Starting in the 1980s, a relatively small number of bankers, stock brokers, lawyers, and other financial officers discovered that whole businesses could be bought and sold in a matter of hours. Since the fund managers watched the price of the stock minute by minute, and could buy stock, or sell all the thousands of their shares of a single company's stock, on a moment's notice, all a broker ("raider") had to do was borrow a large amount of money, make a tender offer (an offer of a certain price per share in return for the owner "tendering," giving over, stock in the corporation) on the open market to buy out a controlling share of a company for a price per share a few dollars at most over the going price, and the funds would take him up on the deal immediately. They *had* to: the managers had no choice but to advance the interest of the fund, and a few dollars per share is a huge amount of money when you own hundreds of thousands of shares. So to the extent that US corporations were publicly owned, and actually owned by the big funds, they became very vulnerable to these sudden "unsolicited" sales – the "leveraged buyouts" and "hostile takeovers" of the last decades of the twentieth century.

Next conclusion: The bad news

Generally, being "taken over" in this kind of "raid" did not work out to the advantage of the managers and workers of the "target" company (the company taken over) in the long run, since the only way the raider could pay back his loan was by selling off parts of the company and laying off large numbers of employees. The usual denouement of the affair was that the target company, weakened by loss of its assets and experienced employees, ended up a small part of some other company – and a business enterprise, product of the collective efforts of many people, often over many generations, is no more. Yet doubts about the goodness of the consequences of these mergers cast no shadow on the clear rights of the major actors in these dramas. The corporation is no more than a piece of paper; ownership of it may change at any time; and it is the owners' right to do what they want with it. This chapter of the history of American business is still being written, and one of the enduring problems for business ethics concerns the fate of corporate stakeholders, especially employees, in a time when capital moves with the speed of light across all time zones and all national boundaries. We will return to this problem.

⊛ THE FACTORY AND THE WORKER ⊛

Thomas Malthus, David Ricardo, and the Iron Law of Wages

Adam Smith had predicted prosperity for the nation. Soon enough Thomas Malthus (1766–1834) outlined prosperity's dark side. In his *Essay on Population* Malthus argued that every species increases until it outruns its food supply, at which time starvation brings its numbers down to the carrying capacity of its environment. Humans are no different. The undisciplined sexual behavior of humans inevitably produces more babies than the region can feed. Should Smith's predictions of increasing wealth actually come true, then, the inevitable result would be that more babies would survive infancy, and proceed to adulthood, eating more every year, until they had consumed the available food supply and people started to starve again. The famine will continue until it has brought down the number of potential parents to a point of reproduction low enough to live within the food supply. This must mean that human life is one long cycle of prosperity and famine, and that all people, despite temporary flashes of good living, will generally live a mouthful away from starvation.

How did Malthus' grim demographics influence the conduct of business? Benjamin Franklin knew business enterprise as an affair of small family farms and small shops, in small towns and small cities. It did not stay that way. Adam Smith was the first to sing the praises of division of labor (the fragmentation of each task in production into a series of simple steps, so that even unskilled laborers can perform them) and consequently of the new industrial revolution, then starting.

Consider this: People need shoes. At the time Smith wrote, making shoes was a highly skilled affair. You needed experienced cobblers to fit and make shoes. The cobblers could charge what they liked (constrained by competition with other cobblers). No one could become a cobbler overnight; and in practice, anyone who wanted to become a cobbler first had to persuade an existing cobbler to take him as an apprentice for several years. Employer and craftsman had approximately equal power in any wages negotiation.

Then division of labor was introduced. Now, if you wanted to make shoes, you could feed all the leather in at one end of a very long moving platform along which your workers stood. The first would cut the leather into shoe-size squares. The second, working from a mechanical pattern (a different one for each size and style) would cut the leather into shape – or three workers did that, each making one simple cut. And so forth. By the time the heel is nailed on and the laces inserted, upwards of 60 workers may have had a hand in the making of the shoe, each one performing repetitively a task that it took him or her only half an hour to learn. If one of the workers wants more wages or better working conditions, he or she can be fired on the spot. There are plenty more where he or she came from. That is what Malthus showed us.

David Ricardo (1772–1823), one of the first real economists, was the first to describe the effect of monopoly (legally guaranteed) on the economy; as long as landlords kept cheap grain out of England (the Corn Laws), they could raise the rents for their fields indefinitely, eventually absorbing all the profits of the nation. In his calculations, the new businessmen, the factory owners, would get nothing for their investment. This is because the factory owners had to pay workers enough to get food to live; dead people do not show up to work in the morning. As long as the landlords forced up the price of food, by raising their rents, the capitalist's profits had to go to pay those

subsistence wages. The only limit on the rents was the total profitability of the industrial sector. But then the Corn Laws were repealed,
and the price of food fell precipitously. That moved the profits from the
landlord's pocket to the industrialist's, but the workers were no better
off. If you feed Smith's law of supply and demand – interpreted here
as the law of labor supply and wages – into the projections as given
by Malthus, you conclude that workers will always live on the edge
of starvation. There are more workers than jobs; all workers must
work or they will starve; if any worker wants more than subsistence
wages, there is another outside the factory gate willing to work for
subsistence. This condition only holds true, of course, as long as all
jobs are unskilled, so the worker cannot profit by developing a rare
and necessary saleable skill and charging more money for it.

So the owner rakes in the profits, while workers suffer. He or she
uses the profits to make more money, being a good capitalist; he or
she plows them back into profitable enterprises, building more plants
and using capital equipment to substitute for human skill. That way
they will make sure that all jobs in their factories can be performed
by people without skills. As each worker becomes more productive
(able to produce more of the product per period of time or labor,
because of the aid of the factory's machines), the owner's profit
increases; at the same time, the worker's wages become more firmly
fixed at the subsistence level. (The difference between the value of the
product on the market and the amount given to the worker who made it
is called surplus value, and it all ends up in the employer's hands.)
Increasingly, the society is divided into two classes – the fabulously
rich owners of the factories and the desperately poor workers.

Charles Dickens and Karl Marx: The moral response

The industrial revolution of the late eighteenth and nineteenth
centuries followed much the same path in England and in the United
States. In both places it resulted in a good deal of human misery –
16-hour days of grinding toil, filth, and poverty for the workers, the
blackening of the skies with smoke from the coal-fired machines, and
the noise and grime of the factories. The industrial revolution did
exactly what Adam Smith said it should – increased the wealth of the
nations that experienced it – and exactly what his contemporaries
had feared. The factories could make goods more quickly and much
more cheaply than the village craftsman could, and usually, though
everyone hated to admit it, of better quality in many ways. Parts

were genuinely interchangeable (so the product could be easily repaired by its owner), manufacture was uniform and predictable, and for the making of heavy machinery, factories were capable of feats of strength beyond the capability of any craftsman. The move from shop to factory was irreversible for all but the most marginal goods. Yet in the process, all that Franklin and Jefferson had valued in business was lost – the contact with land and raw materials, the direct service to the customer, the whole nexus of reward for hard work (in the factory, it hardly mattered how hard you worked – you got paid no more), and above all, the opportunity to exercise prudence and responsibility by running a business owned by the craftsman. All that had taught virtue in the farm and shop had been stripped out of the factory. The life of workers was poor in that their work was poorly compensated, but in terms of opportunities to govern their own life and exercise responsibility in their life choices, their life was impoverished indeed.

The human misery caused by the industrial revolution, widely recognized precisely because it was concentrated in the towns and cities where everyone could see it, provoked moral outrage among a wide variety of educated citizens. The Romantic poets praised the farm, nature, and the small shops in the small village, and condemned the ugliness of the factories on simple aesthetic grounds (reasons having to do with art and beauty). Faced with the drab consequences of greater efficiency in production, they created a whole new ethic – some would say a religion – of nature, and of earlier, simpler times, and of the whole escape to country life. The environmental movement really started here.

Charles Dickens (1812–1870), a Victorian novelist, wrote an influential tract called *Hard Times*, with no particular plot but an abundance of outrage. In it he condemned absolutely every aspect of industrial society – the dangerous machinery that took workers' hands and arms, the practice of employing helpless children, the filth of land, sky, and water created by the factory's emissions, the relentless toil and exhaustion, the slave wages, the unimaginative industry-oriented educational system, the factory's unhealthy effect on the character and morals of worker and owner alike, the factory owners for maintaining such conditions, the government for tolerating them, the economists for justifying them, and the Utilitarian philosophers for providing the underlying ethical structure! All this criticism laid the basis for reform, which ultimately came in the form of wages-and-hours laws, the prohibition of child labor, environmental protection laws, and, ultimately, government agencies to enforce those laws and otherwise provide for safe and non-polluting worksites. But all this was in the future.

Meanwhile, reform would not satisfy one critic of the industrial revolution and the factory system. Karl Marx (1818–1883), an economist and political philosopher, was a follower in his youth of the German political philosopher G. W. F. Hegel, who saw the history of the world as a series of ideal ages, or stages. Each stage was called, as it took shape, a **thesis** (statement, or proposition) and each successive idea governed all events during the period of its ascendancy. No thesis lasted forever: as soon as it reached its flowering, it generated its own **antithesis** (a stage whose ruling idea was a direct contradiction to the idea of the thesis). Then, in a third stage, both previous stages were swallowed up in a **synthesis** (an idea which combined the best of both thesis and antithesis in something totally new). Marx found this three-part succession very persuasive, and had been toying with ways to show how it applied to the nineteenth century society in which he lived. Eventually he concluded from his study of economics that Hegel had to be wrong. The phases of history were ruled not by ideas, but by the material conditions of life (food, furniture, housing, and other products and evidences of wealth or poverty), and their evolution one from another came about as the ruling class of each age generated its own revolutionary overthrow.

Marx's theory, especially as it applies to the evolution of capitalism, is enormously complex; for the purposes of this book, it can be summarized simply. According to Marx, the **ruling class** in every age is the group that owns the means of production of the age's product. Through the seventeenth century, the product was almost exclusively agricultural, and the means of production was almost exclusively agricultural land: landowners were the aristocrats and rulers. With the coming of commerce and industry, the means of production became money itself, that is, the capital invested by the merchants in their ventures. It was a short step to turn that capital to investment in the factories of the industrial revolution, and in that step, the old "middle class" merchants and manufacturers became the ruling class.

Life was not good for the workers, Marx observed; and by the laws that had brought the economy to this point, the situation could only get worse. It was in the nature of capital-intensive industry to concentrate within itself more capital. Its greater efficiency would, as Adam Smith and Ricardo had proved, drive all smaller labor-intensive industry (the shops of the craftsmen) out of business, and its enormous income would be put to work as more capital, expanding the domain of the factory and the machine indefinitely (at the expense of the cottage and the human being). Thus would the wealth of society concentrate in fewer and fewer hands, as the owners of the factories expanded their enterprises without limit into mighty industrial empires, dominated by machines and by the greed of their owners.

Meanwhile, Marx went on to argue, all this wealth was being produced by a new class of workers, the unskilled factory workers. Taken from the ranks of the obsolete peasantry, artisans, and craftsmen, this new working class, the "proletariat," expanded in numbers with the gigantic mills, whose "hands" they were. So Marx adopted from Ricardo the vision of ultimate division of Western society under capitalism, into a tiny group of fabulously wealthy capitalists and a huge mass of paupers, mostly factory workers. The minority would keep the majority in strict control by its hired thugs (the state – the army and the police), control rendered easier by thought control (the schools and the churches). According to Marx, the purpose of the ideology taught by the schools and the churches – the value structure of capitalism – was to show both classes that the capitalists had a right to their wealth (through the sham of liberty, free enterprise, and the utilitarian benefits of the free market) and a perfect right to govern everyone else (through the sham of democracy and equal justice). Thus the capitalists could enjoy their wealth in good conscience and the poor would understand their moral obligation to accept the oppression of the ruling class with good cheer.

Marx foresaw, and in his writings attempted to help bring about, the disillusionment of the workers: there will come a point when they will suddenly ask, *why* should we accept oppression all our lives? and the search for answers to this question will show them the history of their situation, expose the falsehood of the ideology and the false consciousness of those who believe it, show them their own strength, and lead them directly to the solution which will usher in the new age of socialism – the revolutionary overthrow of the capitalist regime. Why, after all, should they not undertake such a revolution? People are restrained from violence against oppression only by the prospect of losing something valuable, and the industrialized workers of the world had nothing to lose but their chains.

As feudalism had been swept away, then, by the "iron broom" of the French Revolution, so capitalism would be swept away by the revolt of the masses, the irresistible uprising of the vast majority of the people against the tiny minority of industrial overlords and their terrified minions – the armed forces, the state, and the Church. After the first rebellions, Marx foresaw no lengthy problem of divided loyalties in the industrialized countries of the world. Once the scales had fallen from their eyes, the working-class hirelings of army and police would quickly turn their guns on their masters, and join their natural allies in the proletariat in the task of creating the new world.

After the revolution, Marx predicted, there would be a temporary "dictatorship of the proletariat," during which the last vestiges of capitalism would be eradicated and the authority to run the industrial establishment returned to the workers of each industry. Once the economy had been decentralized, to turn each factory into an industrial commune run by its own workers and each landed estate into an agricultural commune run by its farmers, the state as such would simply wither away. Some central authority would certainly continue to exist, to coordinate and facilitate the exchange of goods within the country (one imagines a giant computer, taking note of where goods are demanded, where goods are available, and where the railroad cars are, to take the goods from one place to the other). But with no ruling class to serve, no oppression to carry out, there will be no need of state to rule *people*; what is left will be confined to the administration of *things*.

Even as he wrote, just in time for the Revolution of 1848, Marx expected the end of capitalism as a system. Not that capitalism was evil in itself; Marx did not presume to make moral judgments on history. Indeed, capitalism was necessary as an economic system, to concentrate the wealth of the country into the industries of the modern age. So capitalism had a respectable past, and would still be necessary, for awhile, in the developing countries, to launch their industries. But that task completed, it had no further role in history, and the longer it stayed around, the more the workers would suffer and the more violent the revolution would be when it came. The sooner the revolution, the better; the future belonged to communism.

Summing up: The bad news continues

Let us review the theoretical conclusions to this point. There is a possible world – Benjamin Franklin, Thomas Jefferson, and Adam Smith thought they lived in it, as a matter of fact – where the practice of business teaches virtue, provides wealth and comfort for individuals, families, towns, and nations, and provides ultimate human fulfillment in the exercise of autonomy and responsibility in the conduct of one's life. Presupposed in this world is a system of *small* businesses – small farms, shops, crafts – competing for repeat customers in a place where everyone knows everyone and word gets around fast if a product or service does not measure up. But the actual world, from the end of the eighteenth century onward to the present moment, has not matched that system. Instead, we seem to have a world of publicly owned corporations (see previous section), which by their nature are unable to be anything but profit-maximizing machines; of heavily capitalized manufacturing, especially in heavy industries (iron and steel, automobiles, mining, building materials) in which entry into the business is limited to those with access to large amounts of money; of mass production, wiping out the skills of craftsmanship and the responsibility of the craftsman for his product; and as a result of all this, *according to the theory*, the creation of a new class of worker, unskilled, dulled by repetitive work, living in abject poverty, and ultimately only an appendage of a machine until he or she dies or is brutally cut off from his or her brutish livelihood. It would be nice if the workers could get their government to pass laws to protect them, or at least get the police and the courts to enforce the laws that are in place now, but these institutions are supported by the rich corporations and really work only for the rich corporations – and the corporations are bound, like it or not, to seek only greater wealth. So reform will not happen. The workers' only hope is to beat their screwdrivers into bayonets and join a violent revolution which will overthrow the government and put in place a benevolent dictatorship of comrades who have their best interest at heart and will make sure to run the society for their benefit, maybe. That is where the theory leaves us.

❀ THE UNEASY COMPROMISE ❀

Why the bad news is wrong

We are not at the point where the theory leaves us, of course. The society triumphantly deduced by Karl Marx has no resemblance to our own. Something got off the track between theory and practice. What?

Ordinarily we distinguish carefully between **empirical laws** (the laws of science, descriptions: generalizations about what, in fact, happens, most or all of the time. For instance, "if it rains, the streets get wet") and **normative laws** (moral rules, prescriptions: general precepts about what to do). Within normative laws we distinguish (after Immanuel Kant) between **hypothetical imperatives** (rules for what to do in order to achieve certain goals. For instance, "eat an apple a day to stay healthy") and **categorical imperatives** (rules that always define appropriate conduct. For instance, "Don't kill anyone, ever.") Note that hypothetical imperatives, like empirical laws, can be shown to be false if the hypothesis fails to hold. If apples make us sick, it is no longer *true* that we should eat an apple a day to stay healthy.

Business theory also has laws, but sometimes it is hard to tell whether they are meant to be empirical or normative, and if normative, what kind. For instance, the "law" according to which the prosperity of the nation will be increased without limit if only "the government" will stay out of the economy, appears to be an empirical law, which means that we could make observations that would tell us whether it is true or false. As a matter of fact, once the industrial revolution happened, the more "government" stayed out of the economy the poorer the workers got, suggesting that the law was not true. But then why would business theorists continue to pretend that it is, except that it was in their personal interest to do so (and they wanted the rest of us to believe it so that their interest would continue to be served)? Or do they mean it to be normative – insisting on the desirability of non-interference even when it obviously fails to maximize happiness? When we argue that because of Smith, and Malthus, and Ricardo, workers' wages must remain at the subsistence level, how do the theorists handle the fact that wages are not, in fact, at subsistence level? Often enough, the theorists argue that the reason Americans are losing out to the Asian nations in manufacturing is just because the wages in the US are "too high," and should be lowered. In short, the Iron Law of Wages was normative, not empirical – never mind the way the world turned out, the theorists seem to be arguing, all those workers *should be* living at subsistence level!

So when pointing out that the laws of economics adduced to govern business in the modern world are really a poor fit with the actuality of business practice, we do not know whether we have disproved the laws empirically, because they turn out not to apply in the early twenty-first century, or whether we are disregarding the normative laws because they seem to us not to be very good laws much of the time. If the Iron Law of Wages decrees subsistence living for much of the nation while the few rich owners feast, who needs the Iron Law of Wages?

The human factor: Legislation and labor unions

What, in fact, happened? Contrary to theory, government did intervene on behalf of the factory worker, limiting the hours that an adult worker could work and abolishing child labor altogether. Minimum wages were set and safety measures required in the workplace. Contrary to theory, labor unions were allowed to form in the nineteenth century, gained strength in the first half of the twentieth, and after World War II became very powerful; the combined power of owners, managers, police, and Pinkerton men was insufficient to stop them. They in their turn negotiated a fine middle-class lifestyle that became part of what we know as the "American Dream"; wages were sufficient to allow the worker's spouse to drop out of the workforce altogether. (With the continuing evolution of globalization, they have not done so well recently.) Communities began to hold their corporate establishments accountable for the damage done to the environment of the town, and the corporations often found ways to contribute to that opera. Why? In the name of the careful definitions we have laid out, how could they?

The short answer is that the most rational corporation is still run by human beings who have to get along with their neighbors in town. Any longer answer would require a book on the subject of corporate obligations in general, of which there are several excellent examples on the market (see bibliography). In brief, by consensus and usually by law, a corporation must satisfy certain duties to all of its constituencies, or stakeholders. Through fulfillment of these duties, the company finds ways to be a moral agent and a responsible citizen in the community despite a business theory that says it should not. To help put the duties to the natural environment, with which we are concerned, on the moral map of generally accepted business ethics, these duties, the result of three decades of debate in search of consensus in the field, may be summarized as 10 imperatives for business in our time. (Other formulations are certainly possible; this list is formulated for simplicity.)

(I)   The corporation satisfies its obligations to its internal constituencies by treating its employees fairly in all respects, respecting their rights to privacy, dignity, and integrity, protecting their health and safety, and adhering to fairness and justice in all decisions having to do with hiring, firing, promoting, and disciplining.

1 *Non-Discrimination.* The corporation shall adhere to fair laws in hiring and promoting, with no discrimination among workers that is not clearly related to the job.
2 *Employee rights.* The corporation shall respect the employee's public and private rights, especially the right to privacy.
3 *Employee welfare.* The corporation shall protect the health and safety of the employees, and maintain a healthy and accident-free workplace.
4 *Employee dignity.* The corporation shall maintain a workplace that protects and nurtures dignity, is free from physical or psychological harassment, and is free from degrading stereotypes.
5 *Employee integrity.* The corporation shall provide channels through which employees may question and criticize company decisions and policy.

(II) The corporation satisfies its duties to its external constituencies – customers, suppliers, local communities, national and international audiences, and the natural world itself – by providing excellent goods and services, by representing itself and its products honestly, by cooperating with civil authorities at all levels and in all places, and by cherishing the natural world as the condition for all human enterprises.

1 *Quality of the product.* The corporation shall do its work well, make safe and functional products, and stand behind them.
2 *Veracity.* The corporation shall be truthful in all of its marketing and advertising, and direct its campaigns to audiences that can understand them.
3 *Citizenship.* At the local and the national levels, the corporation shall carry on all of its transactions in compliance with the law and for the common good, with special sensitivity to local communities that rely on corporate payrolls to survive.
4 *Consistency.* The multinational corporation shall, to the extent possible, carry its ethical procedures abroad and try to follow them there.
5 *Stewardship.* The corporation shall protect and preserve the natural environment, defending the biosphere against its

own actions and the actions of others. The rest of this book will focus on this duty.

It is not surprising to find that there is an ongoing tension between the profit-seeking theory and the real need to be responsive to the community, even at the expense of profits. In fact, the rest of business ethics tracks an uneasy compromise between a single-minded pursuit of profit (the bottom line, the increase in shareholder wealth, whatever we choose to call it) and a conscientious adjustment to the expectations of the surrounding community, present and future, local and global, human and otherwise.

Overview of stewardship: A business ethic for our time

Business in the eighteenth century was a moral enterprise in ways best described by Jefferson and Franklin. Business in the twenty-first century is a moral enterprise in very different ways. In the course of the next chapters we will track the ways in which a fundamentally impersonal person, a corporate enterprise, can assume moral responsibility for the protection of the natural environment, and give some account of the difficulties it will encounter along the way.

It is difficult to overstate the importance of the present effort to protect the natural environment. In the first half of this century, that effort might be understood as an attempt to preserve natural beauty, woods, and songbirds for human enjoyment, and air and water not contaminated with substances that would damage human health. By now the protection of the environment is directed not so much as the preservation of healthy and beautiful surroundings for humans here now, but the protection of the good health of the **biosphere** as a whole, the entire interlocking system of topsoil, plant life, oceans and ocean life, and the composition of the atmosphere itself, including the ozone layer, seen as one interdependent living system. Said another way: for the first half of the century, we were worried about keeping Nature's face clean and her hair brushed; now we are worried that continued deterioration of her lungs may lead to general organ failure and death – our death. For instance, when John Muir pleaded for the preservation of the Western wilderness in the first decade of the twentieth century, he did it in terms of the majesty of nature and our spiritual need for wilderness in our lives; now, seeing the results of the destruction of the forests, we would plead on grounds that the destruction of the topsoil consequent upon clear-cut logging operations will result in mudslides on the steep slopes which will wipe out villages in an hour, the destruction of the salmon industry, the extensive loss of forest-dependent species (of which the spotted owl and the marbled murrelet are only the indicators), and the permanent desert-ification of the mountains, resulting in significant loss of oxygen production in that area. We are worried, in short, about the long-term sustainability of the living processes that make human life possible. In a world where the number of humans is increasing exponentially and the amount of cropland, forest, and ocean is not increasing at all, the general duty to protect the natural environment, and the corporation's part in fulfilling that duty, take on a new urgency. The remainder of the book will explore, from various angles, the corporate interface with the natural environment. The natural environ-ment is as much a theoretical construction as the corporate community, and our first task is to understand the several meanings of "nature" and "the natural environment" as they appear in the ongoing discussions of business and the environment. We now turn to that task.

⊛ CASE 2: HOOKER CHEMICAL & LOVE CANAL ⊛

The key concept for business ethics is responsibility, and the famous case of Love Canal shows just how hard it is to assign responsibility in the case of environmental disaster. As we will discover in the next chapter, Love Canal is not, strictly speaking, an "environmental" case: the fate of the ecosystem, the land itself, is never in the forefront of the controversy. All that is in dispute is the welfare of the people living in the houses, and attending the school, built on the toxic dump – and the assignment of responsibility for whatever injuries they sustained.

The story of Love Canal is well known. When electricity first became widely used, toward the end of the nineteenth century, the technology allowed only for transmission of power by direct current, economical only over short distances. Cities very near power sources promised to become boom towns, so banking on the power of Niagara Falls, entrepreneur William T. Love set out in 1892 to build there a model industrial city. His famous "canal" was to be one of many transportation corridors in the city. Stymied by the slow speed of the work (turned out he was digging through solid heavy clay), a recession at the beginning of the century, and the sudden discovery of a method for transmitting alternating current over long distances, he ended in bankruptcy in 1894. The canal was abandoned. Hooker Chemical bought the site in 1942 for one of their chemicals factories, discovered the abandoned canal, and decided it would be excellent for dumping their waste chemicals, by-products of their manufactures. They had a permit from the city to dispose of waste on their property, so they decanted the wastes into steel drums and put them in the Canal. In the 1940s, the Army contracted with Hooker to supply we-know-not-what chemicals for its wartime operations at home and abroad, and wastes from that work were also stored in the Canal. In 1953, when the Canal was full, Hooker closed the dump, and had a "cap" of solid clay tamped down on top of the collection of drums.

As Niagara Falls expanded, it needed new schools and room for houses; the Hooker property, not in use by that time, seemed to be appropriate for the city's needs, so it persuaded Hooker, under threat of condemnation, to cede the land to the School Board of the city of Niagara Falls for $1. Hooker was very explicit, in the deed of transfer, that the property had a dump on it, that no one living at the time had any idea what might be in the dump, but that it was probably dangerous, especially since, after about half a century of deterioration, it was entirely possible that some of the drums were leaking. They expected no trouble, either for the surface of the earth or the water supply; the bottom, sides, and top of the canal were impermeable clay. No problem putting playgrounds on that property. But if the town should decide to pierce that clay cap, Hooker could not predict what damage might occur, and would take no responsibility for it. Consider the actual language of the instrument of conveyance:

> Prior to the delivery of this instrument of conveyance, the grantee herein has been advised by the grantor that the premises above described have been filled, in whole or in part, to the present grade level thereof with waste products resulting from the manufacturing of chemicals by the grantor at its plant in the City of Niagara Falls, New York, and the grantee assumes all risk and liability incident to the use thereof. It is therefore understood and agreed that, *as a part of the consideration for this conveyance and as a condition thereof,* no claim, suit, action or demand of any nature whatsoever shall ever be made by the grantee, its successors or assigns, against the grantor, its successors or assigns, for injury to a person or persons, including death resulting therefrom, or loss of or damage to property caused by, in connection with or by reason of the presence of said industrial wastes. It is further agreed as a condition hereof that each

subsequent conveyance of the aforesaid lands shall be made
subject to the foregoing provisions and conditions. (emphasis
supplied)

It really could not be clearer. The dump area is dangerous to human
health, and we will not give you this property unless you promise
never to dig it up. Got that?

Lest the attribution of responsibility seem too clear at this point,
consider the conditions under which we might challenge such provisions. If I sell you my extensive wooded property for your use and
development and sale, mentioning on the way out that my pet tigers
roam the woods so watch out for them, do I absolve myself of blame
if they eat your surveyors? I *told* you they were there. If I have in the
past made my property available to the Survivalists for weekend war
games, and I know they have planted mines all over the property
(but I do not know where they are), what kind of clause in the deed
would appropriately transfer responsibility for those mines from me
to you? Note that I have been making money on the deal with the
Survivalists. Should Hooker have absolute responsibility for cleaning
up its mess, no matter what the law and the deed say?

Less than a year later the terms of the deed were forgotten. By the
midpoint of 1958, roads and cellars cut into the old Canal; there were
scattered incidents of children burned by contact with contaminated
soil. Hooker Chemical publicly reissued warnings. No action followed. In 1968 Occidental bought Hooker, acquiring all its assets
and liabilities. It may have come to regret that last in the mid-1970s,
with environmentalism sweeping the nation, when the odd smells
and pets with burnt paws began to register in the neighborhoods of
the Canal. In response to popular complaint, New York State closed
off the dump area in April 1978. In June, Michael Brown of the *Niagara
Gazette* wrote a series chronicling the claims of illness due to exposure
to the chemicals of the Canal. Illnesses alleged (some later disproved)
included reproductive difficulties, chromosome damage, asthma,
seizure disorders, mental instability, and cancer, especially cancer.
That got national attention, and the New York State Commissioner
of Health began evacuating families. Lois Gibbs, a Niagara Falls
housewife with a sick child, emerged as a neighborhood leader; the
residents' action committee eventually seized two Environmental
Protection Agency (EPA) inspectors and held them hostage until, on
the phone to the Carter White House, they received a pledge of help
and money to move to safer places. Ultimately up to 2,500 families

were moved out, compensated for their homes, and relocated at a cost of about $30 million.

Lawsuits were brought against Occidental for the damage caused by everyone except the city of Niagara Falls, disabled from lawsuit by the terms of the deed. The residents sued for $20 million. Occidental was clearly saddled with whatever liabilities Hooker would have had. But the landfill was clearly secure when it was turned over to the city, it argued, so the city should take responsibility for whatever happened; further, it was not clear anything had really happened, since the evidence of real physical illness was inconclusive at best and the mental instability was more likely caused by the media feeding frenzy than by the chemicals. When it became clear that the courts would not see things Occidental's way, they settled that suit. In 1988 Occidental was found liable for all clean-up and resettlement costs, about $250 million. In 1990, New York State brought another lawsuit, on the theory that the Canal was never as secure as Hooker said it was, that although cause could not be shown for any individual injury or illness, substances like Hooker's were known to cause illnesses like the ones in Niagara Falls, and besides, a judgment against Occidental would deter other corporations from polluting the soil and provide money for an Environmental Remediation Fund.

1   Should the state prevail?
2   Should new rules define corporate responsibility, or should the attribution of responsibility be left to the good sense of juries?
3   How do we know when a dumpsite is "toxic," or "dangerous"?
4   Is it wrong to keep companies in limbo, hindered from making future plans, regarding responsibility for past pollution? If so, how should we settle these matters?

From Ethics to Environmental Ethics

✤ INTRODUCTION ✤

The Iroquois Nations in convention issued a simple test for the permissibility of any new technology, change in customs or in hunting patterns: will the choice we make today seem good from the perspective of our descendants seven generations from now? The standpoint they chose was wise: after seven generations, not only will all who made the choice be gone, but all those who heard the elaborate explanations of the choice from their grandparents will also be gone. The choice will have to stand on its own, without any defenders beyond its own wisdom. That may be the best test of "sustainability": that seven generations away, a path chosen still seems to be the correct one. That is the perspective we are looking for in this chapter.

> To deny future generations even part of their natural heritage millions of years old, to destroy it for all time, is just morally wrong...Evolution is not going to replace this heritage in any period that has meaning for the human mind.
>
> Edward O. Wilson

✤ OUR OBLIGATIONS TO THE NATURAL ✤ ENVIRONMENT

Chapter 1 was all about *us*. We are animals that experience pleasure and pain, need and satisfaction; we are social, and need a rule-governed regime that satisfies our sense of justice; and we are free, rational, able to discern duties and take responsibility for our actions. From those three facts about us, we are able to see the general pattern of our intra-species obligations and the source of our conflicts.

Now, can those ethical theories apply to the natural world? A first answer emerged in Chapter 2, as an extension of Chapter 1: granted that we have duties (Chapter 1), granted that our lives in business carry implications of special duties by reason of what we are doing for a living (Chapter 2), one of those special duties turns out to be stewardship of the natural environment. Embedded in the general ethical duty of stewardship are three general concerns – for the law and the community, for the health of this and succeeding generations of human beings, and for non-human nature in some description. Our duty to obey the law and avoid measurable harm to the community follows from our general duty of *citizenship* (whose virtue is *justice*); it is not discretionary. How that duty plays out is described in more detail in Chapter 4. Our responsibility to tailor our activities to guard the health and welfare of other humans is a more general duty of *caring* or *compassion* (whose virtue is *charity*); while compassion is demanded and expected of us, it cannot be reduced to specific duties, nor can we be sued for lack of it. Our duty to non-human nature is *stewardship* proper – there is a world that needs to be cared for, and intelligent human beings are the only ones who can do it. That is us.

No simple ethic will capture our duties to nature in a traditional theory, for the theories were all developed to treat human beings only. "Each one to count as one and none to count as more than one," the first principle of equality and justice, dissolves in confusion if we try to extend it to chimpanzees, woodchucks, mosquitoes, and bacteria. Utilitarianism, the only philosophy that truly supports rights for non-human animals, asks that we seek the greatest happiness of the greatest number in the long run. Happiness of what? The costs and benefits of whaling come out very differently if you count the happiness of the whales into the equation.

It may be that the duties we have to the environment can be turned into partnership with it; nature is ingenious, and so are we, and the limitless capacity of human beings for innovation shows off to very good advantage in a system that rewards marketable innovations. The effort to integrate sound environmental philosophy with sound business strategy is not new. As early as 1988, in his pioneering *Environmental Ethics*, Holmes Rolston III argued that corporations must take into account the integrity of the natural environment, and that it was possible, contrary to the prejudices of many business executives, to incorporate a naturalistic environmental ethic in the workings of the profitable firm.[1] As we shall see in the next chapters (especially Chapter 5 on Green strategies) there are many avenues now available to business that lead to higher profits through more sensitive cooperation with the environment, and many more opening up for the future. The companies that best understand the workings of the natural environment will be the best positioned to take advantage of those opportunities.

The central imperative for partnership with the natural world is to *see it as it is*. This rule sounds simple, but it contains the heart of the problem. *How* do we see nature? When we look at the natural world around us, what do we *see*? This chapter will attempt to put our diverse ways of seeing nature in some kind of order, with an eye to explaining why the parties to the debates so often seem to be talking past each other.

Rachel Carson was not the first to point out that our behavior toward nature would be determined by what we saw when we looked at it; Aldo Leopold has that honor.[2] In 1968, Senegalese ecologist Baba Dioum summed it up: "In the end, we will conserve only what we love; we will love only what we understand; and we will understand only what we are taught."[3] But Carson, summing up the conclusions of *Silent Spring*, her landmark book on the terrible effects of the chemical pesticides of her day, put the problems of our current approach to nature with peculiar elegance:

> The "control of nature" is a phrase conceived in arrogance, born of the Neanderthal age of biology and philosophy, when it was supposed that nature exists for the convenience of man. The concepts and practices of applied entomology for the most part date from that Stone Age of science. It is our alarming misfortune that so primitive a science has armed itself with the most modern and terrible weapons, and that in turning them against the insects it has also turned them against the earth.[4]

The way Carson's adversaries saw nature is simplicity itself – nature is our servant, to be controlled for our desires. But there are other ways of seeing nature. The next section describes that and seven others, in a spectrum from arrogance to humility.

✪ EIGHT PERCEPTIONS OF THE NATURAL ✪ WORLD

At this point it would be desirable to review the major environmental philosophical works and approaches, from Henry David Thoreau to the present, to gain an appreciation of the vast range and individual genius of the masters of the field. Space does not permit this course; the alternative, a bare sketch of that territory, will serve the purposes we set for this volume. We will describe a descending (or ascending, depending on your perspective) series of possible orientations to the natural environment, to employ in the chapters that follow to throw light on environmental critiques of business enterprise. The following "positions," or orientations, on the natural environment are cobbled together from a very rich and varied literature, and there is an arbitrariness in any such spectrum that must set the scholar's teeth on edge. But for our very practical purposes, the classification may help us get a handle on an otherwise overwhelming body of thought. For convenience, the items on the spectrum are ranked from least appreciative of the natural world to most appreciative; the first four positions are anthropocentric (that is, only human beings can be valued or valuers), the last four positions center value on something outside humanity. At the end of the chapter we will sketch some directions for profit-oriented enterprise in a market economy, although the larger part of this discussion will take place in Chapter 5. (The reader will note some changes of tone in the positions that follow, as we attempt to adopt the point of view being described to give it a fair hearing.)

The first, and most widespread, of the orientations to the natural environment is the **resource** orientation: The woods are just trees, the trees are just wood, and there is no reason for us not to cut the wood for our purposes. Two subgroups are part of this orientation:

Unlimited exploitation

On this principle, humans take what they want, and see no limits in their appropriation from the natural world of absolutely anything that might be of use, materially or symbolically. This approach to nature is currently unfashionable, but is still the rule for environmental behavior over most of the world; it has persisted since the origin of agriculture, when recognition of the possibility of mastery, dominion, over the natural world replaced "animism," the pagan recognition of utter dependence on nature. This perception seems to arise naturally in any successful society; more poignantly, it is the only orientation possible anywhere in the world where people live at the edge of starvation, and that includes, to our everlasting shame, much of the world right now. People who need firewood for their evening fire will not heed "Please do not disturb the forest" signs, nor will the hungry respect endangered species. There is nothing we can do to change such perceptions without feeding the people, for survival comes first. The survival imperative is not the only source of terrible environmental damage; in Russia and Eastern Europe during the ascendancy of the Soviet Union, heavy industry polluted land, water, and air without limit. In that case, an overpowering ideology created the perception of a need to industrialize areas that had been governed only by peasant cooperatives or remote lords, with no history of responsible self-government. A mindless agenda of industrial production led to a managerial orientation of damn-the-waste-stream, full speed ahead, and left Eastern Europe with a very badly treated landscape. Throughout the history of business in the US, for that matter, most of the emphasis has been on the increase of *profit* or *shareholder wealth*, with environmental damage treated as an "externality" of no concern to the manager. In a highly competitive international business environment, corporations might argue still today that there is just no room in their survival plan for caring for the trees or land they need for the business. Theists of varying persuasions tend to extract a human right to treat nature this way, as no more than raw materials and a convenient dump, from the Bible, the book of Genesis, Chapter 1, where Adam is given by God a right of *dominion* over all non-human nature.

Wise use

The name of this orientation, the original conservation movement, was chosen by its first exponent, Gifford Pinchot, President Theodore Roosevelt's chief of forestry.[5] Resources are there to be used, on this orientation, and the natural environment is to be seen as nothing but resources for our use, but they must not be wasted. We must provide not only for our own generation but for our children, too. Like any prudent householder, we must conserve natural resources for future use, and make the most efficient use of those we have. So Pinchot had forests set aside, to be managed in order to supply wood for construction materials and other products into the indefinite future. While the woods were standing waiting to be cut, they should be managed for other purposes – watershed protection and recreational uses, for instance. Thus the multipurpose National Forests were born. Pinchot argued for nothing more or less than enlightened self-interest, where "interest" was defined purely economically. If we are enlightened about keeping pollution under control, for instance, we should be able to have clean air and water without damaging our lifestyle. There had been a predecessor movement, on which Pinchot drew, beginning in the 1870s: as industrialization and settlement advanced west, wealthy families of whom enjoyed the chase saw their hunting grounds begin to disappear, so purchased and preserved large tracts of woods for hunting, to be held by their clubs or associations. When Roosevelt and Pinchot first started talking about setting land aside, then, to keep for the future, a significant number of the people who mattered, including Roosevelt's family, already approved of the concept.

The second orientation, one that the US only discovered in the past century and struggles with still, is a **protection** orientation, one that seeks to conserve wildness wherever it is found. Again, there are two branches:

Conservation

Mark Sagoff is a powerful spokesman for an orientation of aesthetic or spiritual conservation (as opposed to Pinchot's economic conservation). Nature is perceived as threatened and as valuable, requiring our protection. We should be willing to modify our extravagant lifestyles in order to save scarce valuable resources. First of all, the hunting of endangered large animals for commercial purposes should be stopped (elephants for their ivory, tigers for their pelts, whales and dolphins for cat food). The preservation of these beautiful animals is much more important than the indulgence of tastes for exotic rugs and carvings. Second, there should be parks, where future generations can enjoy unspoiled nature; parks should be the appropriate monuments of the US, corresponding to the great castles and cathedrals of Europe, available to the American people and the world in perpetuity for rest, recreation, education, and spiritual inspiration. Further, there should be quiet but firm pressure on all consumers to buy less polluting cars, to install energy-saving windows, turn out lights and turn off computers, recycle all materials that can be recycled, and so forth. Our most valuable resources should be available not only for private profit, but for public use. The natural world has limits, which we are approaching, and we must work to eliminate the wasteful practices that damage it. We must remember that we are responsible for keeping the world beautiful and healthy for our grandchildren, and support organizations that engage in responsible educational activities to teach young people the value of nature and the ways of preserving it. Theists of this persuasion also derive their authorization from the book of Genesis, but from Chapter 2, where God puts humans in the Garden "to tend and to keep it," imposing upon us a duty of *stewardship*.

Preservation

This approach, traced to John Muir, attributes to natural tracts a life and value of their own, and requires us to preserve them for that value. Proponents insist that the conservation orientation, economic or otherwise, will never succeed in protecting the natural world. As soon as it is suggested that wilderness should be "accessible to the public," we have created a dilemma between wilderness preservation and public access, and preservation is unlikely to win. Already, only a century or so after their founding, our National Parks are being "loved to death" by a public all too eager to "appreciate nature" and all too unwilling to leave their preferred lifestyle behind. Asphalt roads, enormous parking lots with electrical fixtures and plumbing to accommodate the recreational vehicles assembling in flotillas every summer, trash cans, rest rooms, and concession stands for food and souvenirs are required. Handicapped ramps and places where wheelchairs may be brought to carved out "scenic points," carefully fenced, to enjoy the view are required. The wilderness that spanned the country when our forefathers arrived is not being preserved by such "parks." Future generations will be best served by inheriting intact ecosystems, large expanses of forest that will remain untouched forever, available to people who want to walk in, pack their food in (and pack their trash out), and just enjoy the woods as they always have been and (as long as we do not cut them) always will be. They are not just for recreation; these ecosystems are our future universities on the workings of the natural world, and our storehouses for generations of pharmaceuticals, foods, and other materials not yet discovered. We cannot afford to lose them. No roads are necessary, nor any special care; the forest can tend itself just as it always has (including surviving forest fires). When we have conducted polls on the subject, a substantial number of people have answered that they are in favor of the preservation of Wilderness Areas not for any projected use of theirs but *just to know that they are there*, forever, for their grandchildren's grandchildren and on to the seventh generation. The preservation of untouched nature has what can only be called a moral value, a satisfaction built into the stewardship itself.

The third orientation is a **rights** orientation, growing out of the increasing American habit of settling whatever conflicts we have by going to court and arguing them out as entitlements. Here, we are talking about moral rights as well as legal rights. What, beyond human beings, might be "morally considerable," or "entitled" to respect? There are two answers.

Attribution of rights to animals

The "animal rights" orientation has several branches and is difficult to summarize; let us attempt. The most familiar, associated with Peter Singer, stems from utilitarianism: as (the higher) animals can suffer, *they should not, as a matter of right, be subjected to painful or confining circumstances* for human purposes. It is not sufficient to hold the simple "humane treatment" orientation, that we conduct ourselves as virtuous human beings when we are kind to our animals, which appreciate our kindness but have no right to it. Animal rights advocates point out that southern slaveholders were urged to be kind to their slaves, too, but kindness is just not the same thing as protection of one's rights under law. If we take animal welfare seriously at all, we must go beyond the patchwork "cruelty to animals" statutes to a robust concept of animal rights. They do not urge that non-human creatures be given the full panoply of civil rights, from non-discrimination to the franchise; animals have essentially the rights of children, not to participate in the political community, but to be protected from harm by its members. Tom Regan, on the other hand, holds that all creatures who can be "subjects of a life," subjects of an existence that can go better or worse for them, deserve to have their interests in *living a better life* respected. Whatever their theoretical stance, animal rights advocates agree on certain practical conclusions. First, save in circumstances where it would be equally acceptable to use babies as subjects, animals should not be used in scientific research. Second, animals raised for food should live in freedom, in natural settings, drug-free, and eating food that would be theirs in nature, prior to slaughter. Third, pets and working animals (racehorses, hunting or racing dogs, participants in animal acts) should be treated well, and cared for or humanely put down when they are no longer useful in their work. Fourth, many advocates for animal rights (but not all) would argue that animals with special mental capacities (whales, dolphins, and the great apes, primarily) that remind us eerily of ourselves – the most intelligent animals – deserve special rights of preservation and care; not only should we care about those temporarily in our power (dolphins in Sea World, for instance, or chimps in traveling shows), but to the greatest possible extent, we should protect the habitat of these beasts so that they can live together in freedom according to their own laws. Many of the animal rights persuasion, but by no means all, think that we should all be vegetarians; some believe that we should not eat, or use in any way, any animal products at all.

Attribution of rights to ecosystems

"Should Trees Have Standing?" Christopher Stone once asked, in response to a case where the trees were threatened but it was difficult to find a threatened human. In *Sierra* v. *Morton*, the case in question and a classic of environmental law, the Sierra Club sued to prevent Disney Enterprises from developing an amusement park and ski area on Mineral King, a particularly beautiful stretch of California mountains. They argued that the mountain itself and the wild area that depended on it had a right not to be destroyed, and they claimed only to represent it. The judges threw out the case, and required the Sierra Club to come back into court with some human beings who would be hurt by the development (which it did, and won). But the claim retains its interest. The fundamental living unit of the natural environment is not the individual organism, but the ecosystem, the entire system of biological relationships that makes it possible for the organisms in it to live and thrive. Therefore, if we wish to preserve environmental values, we should be concerned to preserve whole ecosystems (forests, deserts, and wetlands, for example). We have learned, as per the argument above under "Animal Rights," that protection of anything, human or otherwise, entails assigning legal rights to that thing, and the right to sue, itself or through a proxy, for its own entitlements. To this end, ecosystems should be permitted to sue for protection in their own names, through the advocacy of environmental associations.

The fourth orientation is **holistic**, starting with the notion that nature as a whole is a complete and privileged system or organism, and that we as humans are bound by obligations of contract or participation to defer to its interests.

Community holism

This category contains a variety of perspectives, having in common the land ethic of Aldo Leopold, which "changes the role of *Homo sapiens* from conqueror of the land-community to plain member and citizen of it."[6] Egalitarian relationships with plants and animals may take the form of mutual accommodation over centuries – between, for instance, shepherds and their flocks, farmers and their oxen, all of us and our dogs. The fundamental insight of this orientation is that we and the natural world evolved together, and support each other by mutual forbearance and cooperation, acknowledging each other's right to exist and to flourish. It is not surprising that this mutual recognition can turn into love and affection; the Pygmies of Central Africa insist that the forest gives them affection as well as providing them with food. Edward Wilson and Stephen Kellert have pioneered studies in "biophilia," the dependence phenomenon of human health and wholeness with association with the natural world.[7] Community holism begins with an appreciation of the land, which entails *seeing* it as the organic whole that it is. It is not a blank slate on which we can write at will, but a living, breathing community with its own laws and understandings, which we must learn. The unseeing, the ignorant, regard the land as simply ground to be worked (or trampled), and regard holism as so much fanciful anthropomorphism, but they are wrong. There is important knowledge to be gained from nature, if we will but be patient, look, and learn to interpret what we see.

Deep ecology

This view, the final move in what is called radical environmentalism, initiated by some very original thinkers (Arne Naess, Bill Devall, and George Sessions, among others), is difficult to pin down. Its simplest interpretation is that the living organisms of the world are so many organs in the single organism of the biosphere, and that we must therefore live subject to the organic laws of that system. (In some streams of radical environmentalism, but by no means all, this biosphere is designated "Gaia," the earth goddess.) We are the brain in this organism. We have the ability to discern the workings of the whole, to see what we must do to preserve its health and beauty, and to behave accordingly. Our moral development is found in increasing identification with all living things.[8] In theory, should severe injury occur to the earth (say, from contact with an asteroid), we would have the responsibility to repair the damage, if the earth could not do it itself. Above all, we have a duty, if we can call it that, to discover the laws of the biosphere as they apply to us and abide by them, not interfering with the other members of the biosphere or attempting to modify or thwart any of its purposes. The most dramatic suggestion from some of this literature is that humans in the great body of nature have completely betrayed their trust; no longer the stewards and protectors of the biosphere, humans are *at this time* acting as a cancer (and have been for the last 10,000 years), expanding their number, their cells, beyond the carrying capacity of the body, filling up the habitats and working spaces of other species, destroying other organs apparently at random, and poisoning the processes of the whole body with the toxins given off in the process of metabolism. Accordingly, its most dramatic requirement is that the population of humans on earth be very significantly reduced. It would seem to follow that the only way that humans should live is by foraging, leaving no footprint at all on the earth, as they did before the period of fatal expansion began. It should be noted that no current thinker recommends that path, and the entire move to make "nature untouched" the centerpiece of environmental ethics tends to be dismissed as fruitless romanticism by mainstream environmental philosophers.[9]

Rights and duties

Of all these orientations, the "rights" perspectives are the first to make major claims on our attention, and are already affecting our legal system. Why does it make sense to attribute rights to animals? In the philosophical literature, most discussions of this question turn on some "feature" of animals that is supposed to link them with us, or more likely, separate them from us. Syllogisms abound, of the sort, "All creatures that can suffer (like humans) are worthy of moral consideration;

the higher animals can suffer; therefore the higher animals are worthy of moral consideration." (Jeremy Bentham reasoned so, putting the matter much more eloquently.) Or more likely, "Only creatures that can reason are worthy of moral consideration; nonhuman animals cannot reason; therefore nonhuman animals are not worthy of moral consideration." (Those syllogisms are not strictly in form, but they are valid.) Such reasoning is easy to tear apart. There turns out to be no simple way to separate the "higher animals" (those with nervous systems like ours) from the "lower animals," and if we have pledged ourselves to cause no suffering, where do we stop? Scallops cannot get arthritis, but can they feel pain when they are scooped out of their shells? If, on the other hand, we restrict moral consideration to creatures that can reason, we exclude infants, the demented elderly, the emotionally disturbed (for the most part), and a wide range of developmentally disabled humans. The rights claimed for animals are precisely those extended to such humans – to be taken care of, fed and sheltered if they are in our power, and treated respectfully. Incidentally, the history of the philosophical treatment of this question is not encouraging; there simply is no "set of characteristics" that distinguish the human from the nonhuman. Are animals valuable? There are other examples of simple difference in perspective on the subject of the natural environment, but none so clear and so potentially divisive. Let us look at that potentiality.

Animal rights advocates are not just intellectually convinced that whatever it is that makes humans worthwhile also makes animals worthwhile. Many of them genuinely love and respect the animals they defend, so they are genuinely passionate in their defense of their perspective. They tend to regard those who disagree with them as "speciesists," on the analogy of racists, willfully blind to the natural worth of animals, blinding themselves for the sake of continuing the exploitation, to serve their own convenience and pleasure. *Animal rights advocates perceive a being that has value, moral considerability equal to our own, where others do not.* In this respect, their advocacy is much like the anti-abortion faction of the American public now, who see a being of equal value in the unborn human where others do not, and they have been compared to abolitionists on the slavery question. As in both those similar campaigns, the potential for violence is not far from the surface, and several animal rights factions (including the Animal Liberation Front, ALF, and PETA, People for the Ethical Treatment of Animals) have engaged in criminal trespass and other violations of law to "liberate" animals from laboratories and farms.

We find much the same potential for the defense of ecosystems. Violence is not as likely in defense of trees, which lack soft fur and appealing brown eyes, but in the redwood forests of the West Coast, where confrontation has been the rule for too many years, tree-sitters and Earth First! saboteurs have courted criminal proceedings as a regular tactic.

The rights orientation asks primarily for protective laws, and where animals are concerned, they have got laws on the books. On the simple hypothesis that animals have a right to be cared for humanely, all animals used in laboratory experiments are now subject to strict regulations regarding veterinary care, cage space, food, and "cruelty" – any infliction of pain beyond the needs of the research being done, any signs of filth or neglect, any evidence (from tapes of the experiments, for instance) of callousness or enjoyment of the animal's suffering. Prohibitions on cruelty to animals dating back to the middle of the nineteenth century forbid the public abuse of domestic animals (whipping, for instance), and serious neglect of animals in our care (starvation, filthy quarters, general poor health). No statute forbids us to kill any animal in our care, as long as it is done humanely, but laboratory and domestic animals at least have laws to hold their owners to account for treatment. (Campaigns on behalf of farm animals have not enjoyed the same success.) Neither in the case of animals nor in the case of ecosystems do we have any law in place that attributes rights to the natural object to sue in its own behalf – neither animals nor ecosystems have legal standing – but laws restricting human activity that may harm natural objects, solely on the justification of harm to humans, are very much with us.

Let us note, and keep in mind, the conceptual gulf between perspectives 3 and 4, conservation and preservation. Conservation has us protect the environment only for human use, but along dimensions that include many human values beyond the purely economic – recreational, health, spiritual. This ambivalence lands it in a perpetual dilemma between preserving the environment and ensuring public appreciation, with all the parking lots, rest stops, recreational vehicle (RV) hookups, and Internet cafés entailed by that responsibility. Preservation assigns value, not to the ecosystem being preserved in itself (that is the goal of the ecosystem rights move, perspective 6), but to the value *we* place on having that ecosystem preserved, as it is, for our grandchildren's grandchildren, and to the seventh generation. Yet both these orientations form part of our approach to the environment, and both are valid.

⊛ ENVIRONMENTAL CRISES: A SHORT ⊛ CATALOG OF BAD NEWS

Facing the problems

If these perspectives are possible approaches to the subject matter, what is the subject? What are the basic environmental challenges that must be dealt with in our generation? This is no place to rehearse the problems in any detail, especially since (as all good ecology texts point out) we cannot begin to understand environmental problems without a strong basis in the actual workings of the healthy environment, the interconnected cycles of the elements. But we have to have some notion of the major problems in the field, if only to find out what corporations will be expected to deal with in the near and middle future. A short list of environmental problems, according to the consensus of the field, might follow any of a number of organizing principles. *This is only a sample of the most pressing environmental problems.* For convenience (and ease of remembering), we will adopt the startling image suggested by the deep ecologists, in perspective 8 above: human-caused environmental damage may be likened to the working of cancer in the human body, a lethal cancer, which unchecked, leaves the body that it invades a nonliving *corpse*. What does cancer do to the body (and humans to the earth)?

Sometimes cancer simply changes the metabolism of the whole body. Similarly, the first and most far-reaching environmental offense, and the one most in the headlines, is **climate change**, the gradual warming of the world through the effects of human activity. We know how it takes place. Some of the heat received from the sun is not absorbed in the earth but is reflected back into space. Our canopy of atmosphere, especially the gas CO_2, carbon dioxide, product of the respiration of all living beings, catches some of that reflection and sends it back down to earth as warmth. That is why life is possible; on planets without atmosphere, the sun may shine down brilliantly, but none of that heat will be retained. Because of what has been called the "problem" of the greenhouse effect, we and all life are alive. The problem arises, of course, when we get too much of a good thing. When carbon dioxide builds up in the atmosphere, due primarily to the burning of fossil fuel, the whole earth warms up. In fact, atmospheric concentrations of carbon dioxide have increased and are still increasing; people released 6.44 billion tons of carbon into the atmosphere in 2002, a 1 percent increase over the year before, bringing atmospheric carbon dioxide to 372.9 parts per million by volume in 2002. (It was about 320 parts per million in 1960.) And global temperatures, famously, have increased: the average global temperature was about 13.8°C in 1880, when they started keeping records, and was about 14.5°C in 2002.[10] The polar icecaps seem to be shrinking,[11] the sea level is rising (threatening many small island nations),[12] and we seem to be on our way to the earth of two and a half million years ago, when the oceans nearly swamped the earth. Who should take responsibility for the increase in global warming?

The second offense, and the way we recognize most cancers, is **overpopulation**, the simple crime of proliferation, overgrowth, a mass of a certain kind of cells, more than there should be for the sake of the body. If it does nothing else, this mass of one kind of cells displaces other organs, blood vessels, or in the case of the environment, habitats of other species. There is too much of it for the health of the whole.

The population figures are well known. It took until the modern period for the human race to achieve its first billion on earth; we reached 2 billion in the 1930s, 3 billion in 1960, 4 billion in 1976, 5 billion in 1989, and 6 billion in 1999. That is a very rapid increase, achieved primarily by lowering the human death rate (for we are not having that many more children). At this rate, we expect the seventh billion by 2012 and the eighth by 2025. But the rate has moderated, due to a further lowering of the fertility rate, and the United Nations now estimates that there will be only 8.9 billion people on earth in 2050, not 9.3 as previously thought. That is a very large "only"! Nor are they very happy people: according to the *World Development Report 2000/2001*, 1.2 billion of the world's present 6 billion people live on less than $1 per day, and 2.8 billion people live on less than $2 per day.[13] Actually, the population figure has to be modified to take into account that some of those masses of cells are a lot more dangerous (malignant?) than others. Because the impact a human makes on the earth is not a simple function, one human one impact: the affluent humans, who consume many more units of a given resource than the poor ones, have a much larger impact. Further, where technology aids the consumption, that technology adds its own environmental degradation and pollution per unit of resource consumed. (Example: An American uses three times the amount of wood used by a typical Indian, simply in consumption of chairs, tables, houses, and paper pulp. But even per unit of wood used, the American consumes more than the Indian, for cutting down a tree with a simple axe produces no pollution or destruction of the soil, while felling the tree with a chainsaw causes several types of pollution, and dragging it out of the forest with a bulldozer does enormous amounts of damage to the soil.) So we can draw up a simple equation to summarize the environmental impact of population:

P(Population) × A(affluence, consumption) × T(technology)
= I (Impact)

The implications of the equation are disquieting: even though the major increases in population are happening in the less developed world, it is the developed world, especially the United States, that is causing the greatest environmental impact.

If overpopulation is the second offense, the third is **resource depletion**, stemming from our monopolization of the resources of the body or the earth. The reason we lose weight when we have cancer is that the tumor commands the body's resources for itself, even spurring the growth of new arteries to direct blood to itself at the expense of the other organs. Similarly humans, instead of adjusting their choices out of consideration of the needs of the other life on earth, crowd into whatever ecosystem seems appropriate to their needs, and proliferate without regard to allocation of scarce resources. One way of expressing the human impact on the biosphere is by calculating the fraction of the net primary production of the earth that humans appropriate. Net primary production is the energy left in the biosphere after subtracting the respiration of primary producers (photosynthe- sizing plants) from the total amount of energy (mostly solar energy) fixed biologically. Net primary production is, in effect, the total food resource on earth. Humans, only one among the millions of animal species on the earth, are already using 40 percent of it – more, on some calculations.[14] That is a lot. Since 1950, the use of lumber has tripled, the use of paper has increased sixfold, the fish catch has increased nearly fivefold, grain consumption has tripled, and the burning of fossil fuel, a non-renewable resource laid down as part of earth's capital millennia ago, has quadrupled.[15] We know that this consumption is impossible to sustain, even if only humans needed the product; but we are taking from every other life form as well.

The next major category of problems is **pollution**: of air, water, and the earth itself. When a tumor grows, it gives off waste products, toxins that may destroy the ability of the liver to function. When people expand, they give off more waste products too. Air pollution includes the "greenhouse effect" that causes *global warming*. Another cross-border complaint comes from the impact, in Canada, from America's Midwest power plants. You know the problem: the tall stacks of the power plants route the smoke up above its surroundings, and successfully remove the pollutants from the homes and businesses of the citizens of the local towns, who control its permissions to operate (and pollute). The smoke contains nitrogen oxides (NO_2, NO_3, generally summarized as "NO_X") and sulfuric oxides (SO_X) that are picked up by the rain and transformed into liquid acids (nitric acid, HNO_3, and sulfuric acid, H_2SO_4) that change the chemical composition of the waters wherever the rain falls. *Acid rain*, or acid deposition, is charged in the United States with killing fish (and everything else) in the lakes of the Adirondack Mountains in New York, and killing the trees of the highest mountains in the Eastern mountain ranges – the Green Mountains of Vermont and the Smoky Mountains in North Carolina, in particular. It is becoming a huge problem in China (where the rain occasionally approaches the acidity of vinegar), South America, and parts of Africa. Air pollution also comes in the form of little specks, *particulate matter*, that invade the lungs. The burning of diesel fuel, especially in badly tuned engines, creates a constant stream of such particles. We do not know what other harm it does in its incomplete burning, but we know that it is a major trigger for asthma, especially in children. At least the emissions from smokestacks and fixed engines is locatable, *point source emissions* that we can find, should we want to control them; more troublesome are the *non-point source emissions*, from moving targets like cars and trucks, rain runoff from the lands around the watercourses, and the oil spread through the waters from motorized recreational watercraft.

The atmosphere is not the only recipient of the waste products of our enterprises. The waters – creek, rivers, and oceans – have been our industrial sinks and sewers for about two centuries. Among the worst of the water polluters are *pathogens*, germs, microbial life that cause diseases in humans if humans drink the water. Strictly speaking, the problem is only one of public health, if the rest of the ecosystem is not harmed by the microbes, but it is a serious problem: according to a 1995 World Bank study, contaminated drinking water causes about 80 percent of the diseases in developing countries and kills about 10 million people annually. That is 27,000 deaths a day, more than half of them children under the age of five.[16] Pathogens at least die and disappear in the ordinary course of events. Persistent chemicals like *polychlorinated biphenyls* (PCBs) do not die, at least not in the real time of human use. These chemicals were discovered and manufactured all through the mid-twentieth century, valued as insulators and lubricators for machinery precisely because they reacted with nothing, never changed, and never broke down – once they were anyplace, they were there, for all practical purposes, to stay. Predictably, tons of them ended up in the waterways, most notoriously in the Hudson River in New York, near the old and leaky General Electric plant that made them. PCBs exhibit the problem peculiar to many persistent organic pollutants (POPs): they are not soluble in water, but are soluble in fat, so when fish ingest them with food, they accumulate in the fish's body fat. When the birds eat the fish, they accumulate in the bird, more PCBs with every fish meal, and there they stay. If we eat the fish, the same thing happens to us; PCBs gather in the fat and in all body fluids that contain fat – for instance, the breast milk of nursing mothers. There is evidence that they eventually wreak havoc on the hormonal system of the body; and we do not know how to get rid of them.

The land, too, accumulates pollution. Most visible on the horizon are the "landfills," the enormous dumps in which we put our solid waste. Solid waste is simply any unwanted or discarded material that is not a liquid or a gas. The United States generates about 10 billion metric tons (11 billion US tons) every single year – about 44 tons per person. With only 4.6 percent of the world's population, the United States manages to produce a third of its solid waste. Before consumers start feeling guilty about that, it should be pointed out that almost 99 percent of that waste comes from mining, oil and natural gas production, agriculture, and other industrial activities. Mining waste is the worst offender.[17] Attempts to reduce the reducible portion of this enormous pile of waste (and that part includes none of the mining waste) center on alternatives like compacting it and burning it as fuel for the waste treatment process; recycling might be more effective. Possibly more serious than just the sheer volume of waste is the toxicity of some of it. Toxic, or "hazardous," waste is defined as any waste that is corrosive (tends to eat the tanks you keep it in), reactive, explosive, easily inflammable, or contains one or more of 39 defined toxins – carcinogens, mutagens, and the like. The list contains a good many pesticides, solvents, and paint strippers, but does not extend to the exotic wastes generated by special industries – the radioactive wastes from nuclear power plants, for instance, and the slag from mining operations. These, also, have to be dealt with by systems that may not be fully prepared for them.

After the poisoning of air, water, and earth, the next most serious problem is **species extinction**, the rapid loss of the biodiversity of the world. As cancer quietly displaces and destroys parts of the body that it consumes, so the human race seems to be displacing too many animals and plants that have been on the earth for more millennia than we have been. Most species loss is attributed to habitat destruction. About 50 percent of all species on earth, for instance, are endemic to the tropical rainforests (that is, they are found nowhere else). According to the World Resources Institute, 7–8 percent of tropical forest species will become extinct each decade at the present rate of forest loss and disruption. That is about 100 species per day. Since 1950, almost a third of all tropical forests existing then have been cut down, and the land changed for other uses; we have very little idea of how many species we have already lost in that wastage.

The sixth and last complaint in this sample of environmental abuse is **energy waste**, the systematic abuse of energy worldwide. Outside of the small contributions of geothermal and nuclear energy, we have only one source of energy, the sun. The sun not only gives us warmth and light, it is virtually the only source we have for the energy to run the world. For most of the developing countries of the world, all cooking and heating is done with wood – the energy of the sun transformed by photosynthesis into long organic molecules and stored in trees and bushes. Wood is potentially renewable, where population pressure is not great; unfortunately, the poorest areas of the world have serious problems with population. At the other end of the economic spectrum, the United States, with only 4.6 percent of the world's population, uses 24 percent of the world's commercial energy, primarily from fossil fuels – the energy of the sun transformed by photosynthesis into forests, as above, then compressed within the changing earth into pure carbon (coal) or condensed hydrocarbons (oil and gas), burned for heat, light, electricity, and transportation. (India, with 17 percent of the world's population, uses only about 3 percent of the world's commercial energy.) None of our energy use is very efficient. Eighty-four percent of all commercial (fossil fuel and nuclear) energy is wasted. Forty-one percent of the energy is necessarily lost; by the second law of thermodynamics, no transformation of energy from one form to another can be completely efficient. But 43 percent is wasted unnecessarily, "mostly by using fuel-wasting motor vehicles, furnaces and other devices, and by living and working in leaky, poorly insulated, poorly designed buildings."[18] According to energy expert Amory Lovins, energy waste in the United States alone comes to over $300 billion per year – an average of $570,000 per minute, and about three times the amount needed to get through the first phase of rebuilding Iraq (by earlier estimates). But the wastage is not confined to the developed world: the open fires on which the poorer residents of the developing world do their cooking lose much more heat than they retain. Any worthwhile environmental policy aimed at reducing this waste will have to address every facet of the human use of energy, and the problem promises to be monstrously complex.

The list above only scratches the surface of environmental problems that have to be addressed. It is a short list, and easy to remember: just think cancer, and **CORPSE**, for the problems identified. (Climate change, overpopulation, resource depletion, pollution, species extinction, and energy waste.) The metaphors are compelling, but a metaphor is not an argument. Let us develop, very briefly, the environmentalist point of view, the orientation of the one who will argue, vote, support organizations, march, and maybe even lie down in front of a bulldozer to defend the natural environment against activities of government or business.

The case for environmentalism

Environmentalism is not just a political position, "cause," or "special interest." By definition, it cannot be a special interest, like the sugar lobby or the hotel workers' union. Along with other contemporary causes adopted simply because they are good causes – feeding the poor of the world (Oxfam) or the protection of human rights (Amnesty International), for instance – environmentalism conceptually excludes the link between advocacy and economic advantage typical of the special interest group. (The homeowner who wants the woods bordering his property protected in order to preserve his property value is *ipso facto* not an environmentalist, at least not when he advocates for "protection" for those woods.) There is no reason why environmental measures cannot also create economic advantages – the thesis of this book, after all, is that there is an enormous range of actions that benefit both the environment and the bottom line of business, sooner or later (see Chapter 5). But for present purposes we are exploring the non-economic side of an increasingly popular movement, with coherent purposes and undeniable influence on the global scene.

Nor is environmentalism just a political position, adopted from a vision of the public good. It is that, but for its participants it can be considerably more: it can be a life-absorbing care and dedication, like a family, and it can be, or fill the place of, a religion, deserving devotion and service even when external indicators suggest the cause is hopeless. Given the emotional power of the commitment, it is worth an attempt to understand just where the movement is coming from.

How does the environmentalist see the present situation? Like this: We are in a car, hurtling down the mountain toward the cliffs from which the car will plunge into the bottomless ocean. We are all passengers in the rear seat, while the front seat holds the corporations and the governments, chatting amiably. It is hard to see who is driving, but the likely end of the trip is very clear. Please, sirs, could we stop? Or at least, slow way down? *Now*, please?

Somewhat surprisingly, this perspective is not shared by the folks in front. They seem to think that the car is going *up* the mountain, in a course of human progress charted by their great mapmaker Adam Smith, who believed that cutting down forests, clearing fields and damming rivers all made nations wealthier. They do not. They destroy the working capital of the nation and mortgage its future. But the folks in the front either do not know this, or they do not care. They are doing very well on this route – which they see as creating value and the environmentalist sees as planned plunder – and they see no need to stop the car. They think the complaining passengers are just a bit nutty, corporation-haters, tree-huggers, political ideologues, or worse.

To be sure, most of the passengers in the rear are not complaining. The vast majority of them are so concerned with day-to-day survival that they have no time to complain about anything, and a solid number of those who remain are convinced (probably by paid agents of the folks in front) that their livelihoods depend on opposing the nuts that are complaining. But the complainers see with crystal clarity the decline of the conditions for human existence and indeed all life on the planet, and they are not to be deterred; they have the numbers on their side. They see the situation for humans and the planet as somewhere between very serious and desperate, they see their role as saving a world from a small group of insensitive and selfish schemers, malefactors of great wealth, and they are willing to put into their work the energy appropriate to such a battle. People who are convinced of the rightness of their cause are unlikely to flinch from dying in battle. It might be worth remembering that.

The problem is not that the environmentalist has a "political position" that he or she refuses to "compromise." True, the genius of democratic governments is an understanding of compromise. But compromise is unavailable, given the nature of environmental problems.

Consider resource depletion, say, the logging of an old-growth forest. If the environmentalist reluctantly agrees to let the timber folks take 50 percent of the forests, on condition that they leave the rest, there goes 50 percent of the forest. But loggers do not just need jobs this year. They need jobs every year. Two years from now, when the 50 percent they took is all gone, they are going to come back for the rest. And the year after, when that is gone, they will ask for another "compromise." Old-growth redwood forests, at least, do not regrow, even if (as is not always the case) they are replanted, not for 1,000 years. Nor do toxic wastes, like PCBs or pesticides, go away; they are bioaccumulative; they persist and get worse, in the body of the human and in the body of the earth. "Compromise" compromises the future of the earth and the human race with it; the environmentalist cannot compromise.

What do the environmentalists want? They want the salvation of the world. The car is hurtling toward its destruction, and they want to stop it. If they cannot do that, they at least want to slow it down, in hopes that the time purchased by slowing it may provide the opportunity for the drivers, or at least a larger number of the passengers, to realize that they are on the wrong road. All the clanking machinery of government – the Environmental Protection Agency (EPA), the state and local Departments of Environmental Protection and Conservation Departments, the Clean Air Act, the Clean Water Act, Superfund (CERCLA and SARA), and the recycling requirements on federal, state, and local levels – are stopgap measures. As William McDonough points out somewhere, when you are trying to go from Washington to Baltimore, and you find yourself on the way to Atlanta, slowing from 90 miles an hour to 45 miles an hour will not really solve your problem; you need to turn around and go the right direction. But if the driver continues to refuse to look at a road map or ask directions, at least slowing down will mean that when you do finally turn around, you will not have so far to go. And if you lose the battle, and they never do turn the car around, at least your grandchildren will live slightly longer and happier lives than they would have if that earlier speed had been maintained.

What can be expected of the environmentalists and the numerous organizations that they support? They cannot be expected to go away, or come round to the driver's view that the earth's carrying capacity will somehow expand to allow a population of 9 billion (foreseen for the middle of this century) to live at the standard of the suburban North. They can be expected to work for future environmental protection legislation; Chapter 4 will explore business strategies in the face of this likelihood. They can be expected to constitute a disconcerting global presence, influencing international dealings to an extent not predicted by their US influence; Chapter 6 will suggest areas of vulnerability abroad that companies should be aware of. They can be expected to work through Civil Society Organizations (CSOs; also known as private voluntary organizations or nongovernmental organizations, NGOs) like Greenpeace, which have attained an outsized world influence through coordinated and dramatic environmental campaigns. Chapter 7 will examine the new role of the CSOs and consider what methods may be found to work fruitfully with them, or around them.

The problem right now is to achieve some sort of engagement in the dialog with the people in the front seat. There are two approaches to dialog. One is confrontative (shoot out the tires): we will talk about this in Chapter 7. The preferred other approach is cooperative. For that we need to refocus the perspective as an opportunity to get something good done. In the next chapter, we look at more orderly methods of confrontation. In Chapter 5, we will revisit the possibility that the perspectives of the corporate manager and the environmentalist are not so far apart that they cannot work together. For the near and middle future, hope lies in the increasing realization that the natural environment must be preserved as a condition for the continuation of any successful enterprise, business included.

⊛ CASE 3: GREAT APES AS BUSHMEAT ⊛

"In a clearing in the jungle of the Congo river basin," Laura Spinney writes, "local hunters hold an illegal market twice a month with workers from a nearby logging concession to trade bushmeat for ammunition, clothes and medicine. Among the carcasses that change hands are chimpanzees, gorillas and bonobos (pygmy chimpanzees), all of which are protected species."[19] That is not the only market. All over the tropical forests of West and Central Africa, Latin America, and Asia, increasing numbers of commercial hunters are slaughtering the primates, especially the great apes, for food and also for export. Conservationist Jane Goodall, the world's foremost expert on the chimpanzee, has stated that unless this hunting is stopped, "in 50 years there will be no viable populations of great apes left in the wild."[20]

It is not easy to tell people in poverty not to hunt monkeys and apes. They are traditional food in Central Africa, and to the hunters,

"They're just animals."[21] A hunter will get $60 for an adult gorilla, and a full-grown chimpanzee would bring almost as much. (Since gorillas bring a better price than chimpanzee, chimpanzee meat is often sold as gorilla.) Concerned observers in the area often have reservations about the practice, but end by defending the hunting. As David Brown of the British government's delegation to the Convention on International Trade in Endangered Species of Wild Fauna and Flora (CITES) put it, bushmeat is "a major component of the economies of much of equatorial Africa. It is a primary source of animal protein and the main export commodity for the inhabitants."[22] He therefore thinks that the "industry" should be "managed, not stigmatised and criminalised."

Hunting is now a greater threat than habitat loss to ape populations already strained to the breaking point. According to Spinney, "The World Wide Fund for Nature estimates that there are no more than 200,000 chimps, 111,000 western lowland gorillas, 10,000 eastern lowland gorillas and 620 mountain gorillas left in the wild." With respect to bonobos, their "numbers are thought to have halved in the past 20 years..."[23] Why has the hunting of primates increased so dramatically, especially in Africa? In all probability, the hunting is triggered by the African population explosion of the last 20 years, which has increased the density of human population all through the forest and countryside, and left a hungry population in the burgeoning cities. The pygmies, for instance, in Congo and Cameroon, used to eat anything that moved in the forest with no fear of impacting the species: there was one pygmy for 10 square kilometers, and with their poisoned arrows, at that density, they could do no real harm. They would probably do no harm at ten times that density.[24] But now there are many more people than that, not only pygmies but loggers (to pay off their debts and develop their nations, West African governments often contract with foreign companies to log the remaining rainforests), commercial poachers, prospectors, and other mine and lumber workers who live off the land while they work in the forests. In one logging camp alone, in one year, according to a report released by the Wildlife Conservation Society (WCS), more than 1,100 animals were killed, totaling 29 metric tons.[25] The WCS estimates that the annual harvest of bushmeat in equatorial Africa exceeds one million metric tons.

In 1998, a coalition of 34 conservation organizations and ape specialists called the "Ape Alliance" estimated that in the Congo, up to 600 lowland gorillas are killed each year for their meat. While the initial exchanges of that meat take place in the bush, the bulk of the meat is sold in the cities. The railway station at Yaounde, the capital of Cameroon, houses a bushmeat market that does not close; one ton of smoked bushmeat, largely chimpanzees and gorilla, is unloaded there on a daily basis.[26] It is no secret. "It's a 500-foot stretch of sidewalk only a few blocks from the presidential offices and the $200-a-night Hilton Hotel..." Behind the antelope stalls are "piles from which long arm bones protrude, obviously those of chimpanzees and gorillas. At the fetish stalls, you can buy chimpanzee hands, gorilla skulls, round slices of elephant trunk or the bright red tails of endangered gray parrots."[27] (If you boil the finger of a gorilla, the people believe, and add the water to the baby's bath, the baby will be strong like a gorilla.)[28] Thousands of chimpanzees are killed each year. Chimpanzees reproduce at the rate of one baby every four years, gorillas usually more slowly than that. The apes do not have the reproductive capacity to bounce back from this kind of assault.[29]

There can be no doubt of the West's reaction to the facts as we have discovered them. A World Wide Web query on the subject of "bushmeat" yielded "about" (the search engine's word) 26,100 entries in 0.20 seconds, and a random search showed all of them linked to an organization determined to stop the slaughter and protect the apes. In April 1999, the same month that the WCS report came out, 28 organizations and agencies, led by the Jane Goodall Institute, came out with a major statement on the protection of the apes. The consensus statement enumerated the measures that would have to be taken immediately if the apes were to survive, calling on educators, governments, and corporations in general, and above all, the logging, mining, and other extractive industries to take immediate action to protect the apes.[30]

Yet clearly the developing world does not agree. The sense of revulsion that attends the contemplation of the market in ape hands and fingers, shared by so many in the nations of Europe and North America, is obviously not shared by the hunters, the loggers, or even by the African and Asian governments nominally in charge of the hunting grounds. How come we feel it? Why are we so sure that the bushmeat harvest is fundamentally wrong?

Who are the great apes? First of all, as we all know, they are our relatives. Furthest from us in the family are the "lesser apes," the gibbons (*Hylobates*) of Southeast Asia, who show amazing dexterity and acrobatic skill, but who are distinguished from monkeys only by their tendency to walk upright. The "great apes," our closest relatives, are the orangutan, the gorilla, and the chimpanzee. They are fascinating species, well worth intense study. For our purposes, all we need to know about their physical makeup is that they are genetically very similar to us; the chimpanzee shares 98.5 percent of our DNA. (Does that make the consumer of bushmeat 98.5 percent a cannibal? Karl Ammann, a defender of the apes, would contend that indeed it does.)[31]

The extensive similarities between the species obviously raise serious moral questions about the great bushmeat hunt. Recognition does not stop with DNA. Chimpanzees use tools. They extract termites from their mounds with straws and sticks, and they crack nuts with hammers. They pick out "anvils," depressed knotholes of harder wood where a nut can be positioned securely, find "hammers," pieces of hard wood or stones for the tougher cases, bring their piles of nuts to the anvils, and start hammering.[32] The behavior is in no way instinctive. It is learned, taught to each new generation by the last. Further, it is cultural; in different areas, different groups of chimpanzees have learned different ways of cracking nuts, and use different tools to catch termites.[33] The gorillas, for another example, live in foraging tribes much like our own hunting-gathering forebears, where dominant males protect and lead the troop and gentle females painstakingly rear their widely spaced infants. The chimpanzees hunt in groups, as the gorillas forage in family tribes. They communicate complex messages, we know not how. Language, as we know it, is impossible for them because of the placement of the structures of their throat; they cannot guide air over a voice box as can we. But they can learn Language: chimps have been taught American Sign Language, lexigrams, and token languages. They can communicate with us when we are willing to use these languages, not at any high intellectual level, but at least at the level of a young child.[34]

Even more significantly, they share our worst faults. Jane Goodall, in her lifelong study of the chimpanzees, documented incidents of psychotic behavior and out-and-out purposeless murder, even (since the target of the attacks was an entire group) genocide. Whatever humans do, for better or worse, chimpanzees also do. So far from challenging the conclusion above, the psychotic and genocidal behavior reinforces it: the great apes are alarmingly human. Their lives are much like ours in the foraging period. Their families are much like ours. They sin. They have rituals of forgiveness for individual sin and are totally unconscious of group sin. They are just like us. When we look into the eyes of the ape, we look at our own not-so-distant past.

Is it that fact primarily that grounds our conviction that we must somehow protect the apes from slaughter? Where, ethically speaking, are the apes? There are different, and occasionally incompatible, ethical grounds advanced for our determination that they must be protected. Let us look at a few of them.

Apes in the wild: Keystone species and the preservation of endangered ecosystems

In the objections to the uses of apes for meat, one of the first points always noted is that apes, as species, are "protected." What is the rationale for "protecting" species? First, let us be clear that it is not the "species," in the sense of a certain pattern of DNA that is being protected – we could freeze a few tissue samples and preserve the species forever, in that sense. Nor is it, except in desperation, the individuals that we want to save. The entire ecosystem itself is always the object of conservation activity, the forest, in this case, in which the species operates. We may think of every species as a unique tract, a text from nature, a storehouse of information, infinitely valuable; and each species is a chapter in the book of its own ecosystem. The species and the ecosystem evolved together and must be preserved together.

The great apes in the wild play an important role in the forest, as *keystone* species of the ecosystem, the animal near the top of the food chain without whose presence the balance of all the other species could not be kept. (Recall the destructive overpopulation of whitetail deer that resulted from the removal of the bear and cougar from the woods of the northeast US.) The African forest cannot be saved unless we can save it with all its chimpanzees and gorillas flourishing. The keystone role must be distinguished from the apes' second role as symbol of the ecosystem, or *flagship* species, the large and attractive species featured in campaigns to save the forests. Just because they are like us, the apes attract sympathy and support. Our question is, should they, or rather, since we know they should, why?

Apes in the laboratory: Utilitarian benefits and troubling claims of right

The chimpanzee shares 98.5 percent of our genetic endowment. Then why does the chimpanzee not get asthma, rheumatoid arthritis, acne – or AIDS, even when the virus is clearly present in the bloodstream?

How can the apes harbor a similar virus harmlessly? What can we learn about human diseases, now and in the future, from experimentation with these animals? And after the uses of chimpanzees' bodies for medical research, what else may we learn from that overwhelmingly similar genome? Since the great apes can learn language, and seem to experience all emotions that we know, they may provide an irreplaceable subject for the study of language acquisition and human psychology. This possibility alone is worth the effort to keep the apes off the menu.

What do experimental animals deserve from us? All animals deserve *humane* (as opposed to human) treatment: they may not be beaten, tortured (as part of the research or for the amusement of the staff), abused, neglected, caged without fresh air or exercise, starved, or left to die of infection in uncleaned cages. Clearly such treatment is wrong, and wrong for reasons that have nothing to do with the special qualities of the apes; if research is to be done ethically, what sorts of restrictions should apply to the use of animals in the laboratory? Should regulations be suspended if the purpose of the research could be better achieved if they were?

But humane treatment is not the only issue with the apes. With chimpanzees in particular, their very similarity to us raises questions about the way we do our research. In the major studies of chimpanzee research, especially Roger Fouts' semi-autobiographical account of his life with the chimpanzees,[35] questions of right and humane treatment tumble over each other. He abhors the "prison-like" setting of most experimental labs, roundly condemns the scientists who do research for their own professional purposes, and ends up suggesting that no matter how useful it is, we ought to abandon animal research altogether.[36]

Why? One story is worth a hundred arguments. Consider this one:

> Twenty years ago I met a chimpanzee named Bruno. He was one of a group of chimps being taught American Sign Language to determine if apes could communicate with humans. Last year I went to see him again. The experiment is long past, and Bruno was moved in 1982 to a medical laboratory, *but he is still using the signs . . .*[37]

He had learned how to talk in the community in which he found himself. Then, the experiment over, his ability to talk was of no further use to the members of that community, so they had shipped him off to someplace where he could be used as an oversized lab rat to test vaccines or new drugs. But he still wants to talk, to communicate. He is not content with the secure and well-fed life. He is like humans, and he wants to reach out to humans as they once reached out to him. What right have we to impose such isolation?

Apes in court: Should they have the rights of persons?

Bruno seems human. Shall we extend to him, and to his species, the rights of humans? John Blatchford, a British zoologist, suggested as much in 1997.[38] David Pearson, of the Great Ape Project (a systematic international campaign for rights for the great apes, founded in 1993) took up Blatchford's suggestion in January 1998, calling attention to a "paradigm shift over the past 20 years or so in our understanding of the complex emotional and mental lives of the great apes – a complexity that demands we confer the basic rights of life, individual liberty and freedom from torture on all great apes."[39] By 1999, the Great Ape Project joined the New Zealand campaign for full "human rights" to apes; the campaign failed, but not by much.

The campaign continues, calling for a United Nations Declaration of the Rights of Great Apes. This declaration would include all the above rights as well as the right not to be "imprisoned" without due process. Due process? The language necessarily causes nervousness, not only among the zookeepers, but also among those who carry on research designed to protect the welfare of apes. Must they obtain informed consent in the future?

Primatologist Frans de Waal of the Yerkes Regional Primate Research Center in Atlanta argues that according rights to the apes puts us on a "slippery slope" toward the absurd. "[I]f you argue for rights on the basis of continuity between us and the great apes, then you have to argue continuity between apes and monkeys," and so on down to the laboratory rats.[40] Philosopher Peter Singer, author of *Animal Liberation*, is less worried about rats obtaining legal rights, and wonders if the slippery slope cannot be tilted the other way: "[I]f you deny chimps certain rights, then logically you have to deny intellectually disabled children too."[41] Do we?

Ecotourism and respect

Suppose we decide that apes are, indeed, sufficiently like ourselves to deserve human rights. What follows? Should we treat them the way we treat human beings with limited mental capacities – lock them in homes or institutions, with staff to make sure they dress in the morning, use the bathroom properly, and eat healthful food until they die? God forbid. The central right for any creature with rights is to live according to its own laws with its own community, and that surely cannot happen if we dragoon the apes into human society. (Whether or not they would survive such "care" is another question, one that need not be answered.) That central right alone entails that the apes be left in the wild and left alone, their habitat protected from infringement and their communities respected as we would respect any human community. In short, the implications of full rights for apes are the same as the conclusions of the conservationists. We must work to preserve the forests where the apes live, we must end all poaching of "bushmeat" immediately, and we must structure our encounters with all the apes to reflect the respect owed persons with rights, living according to their own customs and laws. Can we do this?

The major problem with this solution is, as above, economic. Can we help the apes support themselves economically? The best way to set up an industry to sustain the apes is through enabling "ecotourism," entertaining tourists who want to visit the apes in the wild. Tourists have been traveling to Africa and Asia to see the animals for several centuries, after all. In ecotourism, they do not come to shoot, but to enjoy and to learn. When ecotourism is established and running well, the tourist dollars support the local economy. For this reason it is in everyone's interest to make sure that the animals are not harmed or frightened, so that the tourists will enjoy themselves and will come back bringing more dollars. Ecotourism will allow apes to stay in their wild habitats and preserve the ecosystem. If the populations of apes flourish, there seems to be no reason not to allow selective recruitment of individuals from these populations for research and even, possibly, for exhibit.

Some concluding observations and questions

1   As far as we can observe, chimpanzees recruited into traveling shows thoroughly enjoy the experience. Apes regularly associating with humans have no objections to them, and seem to enjoy the attention and company. They do not even mind being dressed up in tutus. May such practices continue?

2   As above, it would be tremendously useful to be able to continue research with chimpanzees. But how can we do this? If we must treat them as humans, they cannot give consent, so we

cannot use them. We can treat them as animals, very humanely, no doubt, but they will still be forced to live in cages and suffer blood draws and strange diets and possibly odd surgeries. Is this justifiable?

3   When an infant (now known to the world as Baby Fae) was born with hypoplastic left heart syndrome some years ago, a baboon (Goobers) was killed so that her heart could be transplanted to the infant. It did not work, and no one has tried it since. But what if we could make it work? Would it be justifiable to kill an ape to get its heart for a child?

4   Are we under any duty to enhance the lives of the apes? If they find themselves in an environment that is not totally to their liking, what is the extent of our duty to go beyond protection to ensuring the flourishing of the community?

5   Should we discover, as Goodall did, a chimpanzee community systematically killing off the neighboring community, do we have an obligation (a) to intervene, in order to stop the slaughter, (b) not to intervene, in order to let chimpanzees live and die by their own laws? Note: We have problems answering this question where human beings are in question.

⊛ NOTES ⊛

1. Holmes Rolston III, *Environmental Ethics: Duties to and Values in the Natural World*, Philadelphia: Temple University Press, 1988. See especially Chapter 8.
2. The references are to Aldo Leopold, *A Sand County Almanac and Sketches Here and There*, Special Commemorative Edition, New York: Oxford University Press, 1949, 1987, and Rachel Carson, *Silent Spring*, commemorative edition with an Introduction by Vice President Al Gore, Boston: Houghton Mifflin Company, 1962, 1994, but especially the book that she was working on when she died, *Help Your Child to Wonder*.
3. Cited in Elliot Norse, "Marine Environmental Ethics," from *Values at Sea: Ethics for the Marine Environment*, ed. Dorinda G. Dallmeyer, University of Georgia Press, 2003. Cited in *The Environmental Ethics & Policy Book*, ed. Donald VanDeVeer and Christine Pierce, 3rd edn., Belmont, CA: Wadsworth, 2003, p. 240.
4. Rachel Carson, *Silent Spring*, op. cit., p. 297.
5. The name is problematic, because recently (in the last years of the twentieth century) an anti-environmental movement of the same name has emerged, fueled by the philosophy of Milton Friedman and the subsidies

of the less-enlightened extractive industries. There is no relation between Gifford Pinchot's philosophy and the new organization.

6. Aldo Leopold, op. cit., p. 204.
7. Edward O. Wilson, *Biophilia*, Cambridge: Harvard University Press, 1984.
8. Guidance in this section especially, and throughout the chapter, was provided by John Nolt of the University of Tennessee at Knoxville.
9. See Holmes Rolston III, op. cit., p. 290.
10. Molly O. Sheehan, "Carbon Emissions and Temperature Climb," Worldwatch Institute in cooperation with the United Nations Environment Programme, *Vital Signs 2003*, pp. 40–41.
11. See *The New York Times*, August 19, 2000, p. A1, cited Lester R. Brown, *Eco-Economy*, op. cit., p. 27.
12. David Taylor, "Small Islands Threatened by Sea Level Rise," ibid., pp. 84–85.
13. Akin L. Mabogunje, "Poverty and Environmental Degradation: Challenges Within the Global Economy," in Robert Griffiths, ed., *Developing World 03/04*, p. 167.
14. Peter Vitousek, Paul R. Ehrlich, Anne H. Ehrlich, and Pamela Matson, "Human Appropriation of the Products of Photosynthesis," *BioScience*, 36 (1986).
15. See G. Tyler Miller, *Living in Environment*, 9th edn., Belmont, CA: Wadsworth Publishers, 1996, p. 8.
16. Ibid., p. 533.
17. Ibid., p. 579.
18. Ibid., p. 397.
19. Laura Spinney, "Monkey Business," *New Scientist*, May 2, 1998, p. 18.
20. Ibid.
21. Donald G. McNeil Jr., "The Great Ape Massacre," *The New York Times Magazine*, May 9, 1999, pp. 54–57.
22. Fred Pearce, "Eating Our Relatives," *New Scientist*, April 29, 2000.
23. Spinney, op. cit.
24. Ibid.
25. "Bushmeat: Logging's deadly 2nd harvest," ("Wildlife Harvest in Logged Tropical Forests") news item without byline, *Science*, April 23, 1999.
26. Ibid.
27. McNeil, op. cit., p. 56.
28. Eugene Linden and Michael Nichols, "A Curious Kinship: Apes and Humans," *National Geographic*, March 1992, pp. 1–45.
29. Ibid.
30. Jane Goodall Institute, Press Release of April 1999.
31. Joseph B. Verrengia, "Bushmeat Hunters Push Primates to Extinction," Associated Press, July 23, 2000.
32. Linden and Nichols, op. cit., p. 22.
33. Ibid., p. 24.

34. Ibid., pp. 32–33.
35. Roger Fouts, with Stephen Tukel Mills, *Next of Kin: What Chimpanzees Have Taught Me About Who We Are*, New York: William Morrow & Company, 1997.
36. He pointedly ignores the efforts of other research centers, especially the Yerkes Regional Primate Research Center in Atlanta, to improve the treatment of apes in captivity. See Deborah Blum's review of the book, *The New York Times Book Review*, October 12, 1997, pp. 11–12. Interestingly, Fouts' career tracks those of Fossey, Galdikas, and Goodall, from research scientist to activist on behalf of the apes.
37. Eugene Linden and Michael Nichols, "A Curious Kinship: Apes and Humans," *National Geographic*, March 1992, p. 10. Emphasis added.
38. John Blatchford, "Apes and gorillas are people too," *New Scientist*, November 29, 1997, p. 56.
39. David Pearson, "Justice for Apes," *New Scientist*, January 3, 1998, Letters, p. 46.
40. Rachel Nowak, "Almost Human," *New Scientist*, February 13, 1999, p. 20.
41. Loc. cit.

chapter four
The Law and the Natural Environment

What lies at the heart of environmental law in the United States? Let us look at some of the elements with which we will be dealing in this chapter, in an account of the experience of Allen Hershkowitz, senior scientist for the Natural Resources Defense Council (NRDC), in the House Commerce Committee's mark-up session for the National Recycling Act Bill on June 6, 1992. Lobbyists for industry tend to crowd these sessions (Coca-Cola had 40 lobbyists assigned to the bill, to ensure that it did not mandate bottle deposits or recycled container content), and in the end environmentalists were able to squeeze only three people into the room. Most of the industry representatives had not waited in the numbered line, but had been "walked in" to the committee room through back doors by legislators with whom they had very friendly relations. (That is how Hershkowitz got in, too, cashing in on an old friendship.)

As the day went on, the reason for the heavy industry presence became clear: many retrograde industry-sponsored amendments were to be jimmied into the bill. The plastics industry managed to get their waste incineration defined as recycling; there was a provision couched in language that made it seem as if the well-being of the nation depended on allowing the federal government to override local zoning ordinances forbidding the siting of incinerators; and the paper industry had succeeded in getting amendments into the bill that allowed virgin timber byproducts to be labeled as waste recycling. At day's end, but before the legislation was voted on, the enviros felt compelled to kill the bill they'd worked flat out on for so long. Threatening to release them to the national media, they issued to committee members and their staff press releases that attacked the legislators for drafting what had now essentially become an antirecycling bill, one that would, if passed, set the progress already made in recycling back twenty years.

In response to the press releases and the fear of committee members that they would be pilloried by their constituents for being antirecycling, the bill was never even reported out of mark-up and never voted on. By two-o'clock in the afternoon, it was dead. The industry lobbyists were ecstatic. No directives about recycling municipal waste would become federal law. And none has been issued since then with the exception of Presidential Order 12873, signed by President Clinton in 1993 – despite a pitched battle mounted in Congress by the paper industry trying to prevent it – requiring all federal agencies, including the Department of Defense, to buy recycled paper.[1]

We will assume, in this chapter, a basic knowledge of how American law works – public law as distinct from private law, civil law as distinct from criminal law, case law (the common law interpreted by judges) as distinct from statutory law – and we presuppose some appreciation of the elaborately layered and dovetailing (or conflicting) accretions of case law, statutes, the executive orders, and the enormous body of regulatory law with which all businesses must deal. There are many wonderful (and readable) works dedicated to the explication of environmental law, some of which appear in the bibliography for this chapter, and there is no reason to try to duplicate them. We will attempt, in this chapter, only to supply a survey of the growth and directions of environmental law, along with some philosophical concerns that accompany it, and the fields of concern for future legislation. Part of ethics is compliance with existing law; that assumption is built into any democratic system. Part of the history of environmental law is slow, uneven, but continual evolution along lines suggested by ethics. If the directions of environmental law are reasonably clear, prudent managers can save their companies significant costs by discerning the reasonable direction of public ordering of business activity for the sake of the preservation of the environment.

In the US everyone is given, in school, a basic understanding of how the law works; where *How a Bill Becomes a Law* is probably read, that elementary instruction on civics and the American legal system. But if *How a Bill Becomes a Law* is relied on to understand

Hershkowitz's experience in the House Commerce Committee, you will note that the text left out a few crucial steps in the lawmaking process, steps that significantly modify the lawmaking and law-enforcing process bequeathed to Americans by the Founding Fathers. In the extract above, note first that the bill arrives in committee pretty much as its drafters expected, capturing a significant amount of the national interest in recycling. But access to lawmakers is highly selective, strongly favoring those whose campaign contributions have endeared themselves to committee members. Those who have (in essence) purchased access and a favorable hearing proceed to amend the bill until its initial purpose is completely lost, in fact, reversed. This is not provided for in the Constitution. But the response of the "enviros" is equally instructive. They counter not with superior votes, which they have, or had at the time, but had no way to mobilize, nor with money, which they do not have, but with publicity or the threat of publicity, promising to bring the activities of the legislators to an unfavorable light and undermine their support at home. Note that our legislative system is supposed to operate on votes, on the will of the people – but it is controlled by two currencies, money and publicity, that are nowhere explicit in the Constitution. (It could surely be argued that Alexander Hamilton foresaw, and approved, the role of money, and that Thomas Jefferson foresaw, and approved, the role of the newspapers, but neither could have foreseen the national and global position the two would occupy at the outset of the twenty-first century.)

The second aspect of the story to note, the aspect that will occupy most of this chapter, is the tone, mood, bent, predisposition, and unwavering commitment of the two "parties" to the dispute (not to be confused, except occasionally, with the Republican and Democratic parties). This is war. It seems that there is a tendency in the United States to promote recycling; the industries affected are dead set against it; they dedicate mind-boggling resources to find ways to destroy it (40 Coca-Cola lawyers must cost as much as several surface-to-air missiles); and are "ecstatic" when it is clear that no recycling initiative will pass through Congress in this term. Presumably, the enviros would have been ecstatic if it had passed in its original form, their pleasure heightened by the wailing and gnashing of teeth from the industry side.

What is this war about? How has the legal system become part of it? Or is it that, given the traditions of Anglo-American law, the legal system is essentially adversarial in nature, and all proceedings of environmentalists and industry have simply taken on that coloration? We will argue in other chapters that there are many ways in which industry and "enviros" can work together outside the adversarial framework; in this chapter we will consider the role that an essentially adversarial system can play in governing the uses of the natural environment.

✤ IN THE BEGINNING ✤

Law is based on the notion of "desert," justice. Justice is done, said Aristotle, when one is done by as one has done, or suffers in return for one's action. Law originates in the fact that humans sometimes do things that damage the condition of their neighbors, in mind, body, or estate, and that something deep within us insists that the victim should be made whole at the expense of the offender. Ultimately, all our legal provisions for the protection of individuals, in the criminal and the civil law, originate in that sense. There is a larger sense of justice, which requires all government to pass good and useful law, regulating the lives of its citizens in such manner as to protect their safety, health, welfare, and morals. (This is the requirement that we summarize as the "police power" of the state.) In providing predictability and order in the lives of the citizens, government makes possible all private enterprise and family stability.

In law, a "windfall" is a significant benefit, usually the sharp increase in the value of property, which has come to the party enjoying it for no reason other than sheer good luck – he or she happened to be holding the stock when the oil well was discovered, he or she happened to have the inventory when a disastrous fire led to a worldwide shortage and sent the price skyrocketing. A "wipeout" is a similar loss – through no one's fault, value simply disappears.[2] Windfalls and wipeouts are very difficult to deal with in regimes governed by notions of desert and distributive balance. If enormous benefit comes from hard and ingenious work, fine, the one who did the work gets to keep it with no injustice arising from the situation; if the loss comes from the criminal acts or civil negligence of certain parties, then those who have been hurt deserve to be made whole by those responsible for the loss. (For instance, in the catastrophe surrounding the downfall of Enron Inc., the employees who lost their pensions due to the negligence and thievery of the executives deserve to have that money repaid by those who cashed out their shares for millions.) But what if the benefit, or loss, is just there, caused by no one at all?

Nature is like that. We know nature as an enormous windfall. No one earned the fish, game, or edible plants, or underlying them the fertility of the soil, the purity of the water, let alone the breathable air – they just came that way. They could not possibly have been manufactured by humans, earned by any work (since without them we can do no work at all), or purchased. But if there is no way to "acquire" nature, how can any part of the natural environment be anyone's *property*?

The notion of "private property" in nature is late. The foragers mentioned in the Introduction had no property in land, any more than the other animals in the area. The first "rights" seem to have evolved from the "defended territory," a concept of land use that we share with many of the higher animals.[3] Many species need territories or spaces (with reasonably defined centers, even while the edges might be contested) in order to hunt, forage, or reproduce success-fully; it is possible that the notion of territoriality is the link between the natural life on the land lived by all earth dwellers and the enduring notion of property claimed by humans.[4] Rights to use land certainly preceded ownership as we understand it – hunting rights for semi-nomadic aborigines, or gardening rights for slash-and-burn farmers, who like the nomads, had no permanent residence. Historically, property rights seem to have grown out of sedentariness, and were well established by the earliest empires. We have inherited these rights, and that is why they are there. But what makes them right? Why is it right for us to have ownership in something we did not make or earn?

⊛ GROUNDING THE OWNERSHIP OF LAND ⊛

Why would such a theoretical question trouble the practical discipline of business ethics? Because when environmental matters come under the purview of law, either in private or public action in the courts, or through legislation and the actions of regulatory agencies created by statute, suddenly the force of the right to private property, at least property in land, becomes a hotly contested subject. Virtually every environmental regulation you can think of limits the right of some owner to use his or her private property as he or she would prefer (or as would be most profitable to himself or herself and to his or her shareholders), and litigation over the extent to which this limitation is legally acceptable inevitably turns on the theoretical question of the true extent of the right of private property. Take, for example, the beach house that David Lucas wanted to build on the Isle of

Palms in South Carolina. The local authorities pointed out that his beach house would violate the Beachfront Management Act, which was passed specifically to prevent property owners from making further inroads on the local ecosystems, then badly threatened, and on the basis of that law forbade him to do it. He claimed a Constitutional right to build on his own property, based on the Fifth Amendment's prohibition of "taking" property without compensation. Eventually the case reached the US Supreme Court, which considered the fundamental question: Should traditional individual property rights take precedence over traditional local powers to protect the community from harm?

The line between "protecting" and "taking" is theoretically clear. If the state is restricting the owner's use of the land *in order to prevent the owner from doing a harm to his neighbors*, then the regulation is part of the normal police power of the state, and the owner deserves no recompense – the law forbids you to do harm, and we are not going to pay you to obey the law. That goes even if the state renders all economic uses of your property impossible (the case that made that point was a lawsuit brought by a moonshiner who complained that the revenuers were making it impossible for him to earn a living with his expensive still). But if the state is restricting that use *in order to provide a public good*, say by opening it up as a park, then that is a "taking" under the Fifth Amendment, a condemnation, and the state must compensate the owner for the property. But finding that line in practice can be very difficult indeed. One test for the location of that line can be the "natural" use or state of that property: if the owner proposes to use a property for a purpose that is "natural" to it, then that use cannot be construed to be a "harm" or "nuisance"; but if he intends to do something "against its nature," then it can be.[5] This distinction is notoriously difficult to apply, and is therefore open to political interpretation. Justice Antonin Scalia's conclusion is given below:

> It seems unlikely that common-law principles would have prevented the erection of any habitable or productive improvements on petitioner's land... The question, however, is one of state law to be dealt with on remand. We emphasize that to win its case South Carolina must do more than proffer the legislature's declaration that the uses Lucas desires are inconsistent with the public interest, or the conclusory assertion that they violate a common-law maxim... As we have said, a "State, by *ipse*

dixit, may not transform private property into public property without compensation..."[6] Instead, as it would be required to do it if sought to restrain Lucas in a common-law action for public nuisance, South Carolina must identify background principles of nuisance and property law that prohibit the uses he now intends in the circumstances in which the property is presently found. Only on this showing can the State fairly claim that, in proscribing all such beneficial uses, the Beachfront Management Act is taking nothing.[7]

Another court might have reached the opposite conclusion with equal logic.

The question of the nature and extent of the right of private property, along with its limitations, has a rich history that we cannot pursue in this space.[8] To simplify just a bit, we may say that theories of property rights fall into three groups. The first group argues from rights, and holds that private property should be held as a matter of right, presumptively against all state purposes, to be alienated only at the free decision of the owner. The second group, following Aristotle,[9] argues from utilitarianism that the lands and other durable resources of the earth will be better cared for in private hands than in public, and that therefore it is good policy for the state or other power to protect private property. (Given the time needed for investments in land to pay off, state protection cannot be a short-term matter if the policy is to achieve its objective; the protections for private property, while allowing exceptions for public purposes, should be settled and durable.) The third group argues that neither of the above theoretical bases is ultimately valid, and that property in land has no moral foundation at all. When homeowner and Department of Conservation square off in court, we see these abstract theories of property take very immediate (and often ugly) form.

⊛ ENVIRONMENTAL REGULATION: ⊛
A BRIEF SURVEY

Background: Wilderness and pollution

In the last chapter we traced the conflicting and complementary orientations to the natural environment that have played a part in the environmental history of the United States. One of the major trends in that history has been the slow recognition that wild lands should, on occasion, be preserved. Even during the wilderness-conquering nineteenth century, the Federal government moved to preserve certain forest reservations: Arkansas Hot Springs in 1832, Yosemite Valley in 1864, and Yellowstone National Park in 1872. Gifford Pinchot, Chief of the US Forest Service under Theodore Roosevelt, preached the "wise use," that is, the intelligent conservation, of resources, and helped to found the Yale School of Forestry to teach it. The Preservationist move, led by John Muir, formed itself in the first decade of the twentieth century in the (ultimately futile) battle to save the Hetch Hetchy Valley from a dam that would provide water to San Francisco. By the early 1950s there were more than 300 conservation groups in the United States, and when the government proposed another dam for Echo Park at the Colorado–Utah border, the preservationists won. The environmentalists made further progress in the 1960s, which saw the passage of the Wilderness Act of 1964, the Land and Water Conservation Act of 1965, the National Historic Preservation Act of 1966, and the National Wild and Scenic Rivers System in 1968. In the 1970s, the US moved beyond specifying certain lands as forever wild, and public, to preservation of resources wherever they might be, on public or private land. The Endangered Species Act of 1973, the strongest protection for biodiversity in the world, forbids any activity or construction that will endanger any plant or animal with extinction; the Clean Water Act of 1970, strengthened in 1977, protects wetlands on private as well as public land.

Attempts to mitigate pollution of air, water, or earth have a meager history until after the middle of the twentieth century. After World War II, the US had the only industrial plant left standing, and industry rapidly expanded – especially into the new fields of organic chemistry, with the manufacture of plastics, synthetic fibers, and pesticides. The increasing intensity of this industrial activity in the US in the 1950s, in the almost complete absence of any consciousness of environmental sophistication, led to massive poisonings of birds and wildlife from the use of pesticides, and massive accumulations of chemicals eventually recognized as toxic in waterways and landfills all over the country. Biologist Rachel Carson's groundbreaking book, *Silent Spring*, in 1962 brought the attention of the nation to the damage that was being done; but more importantly, it brought to our attention the uncertainty of all scientific pronouncements (DDT had been declared harmless; children even ate handfuls of the stuff in public demonstrations of its perfect safety).

In the clamor that followed *Silent Spring*, the major lineaments of the environmental decades took shape. In 1963, the environmental activist group Scenic Hudson was formed, and it saved Storm King Mountain on the Hudson River from hollowing out as a pumped-storage area for a hydroelectric plant. Incidentally, the 1972 decision sparing Storm King, in *Scenic Hudson Preservation Conference* v. *Federal Power Commission*,[10] was the first judicial proceeding in which an environmental group was granted standing to sue. In 1967 the Environmental Defense Fund (now known as Environmental Defense) was founded to oppose the use of DDT in agriculture in New York State; by the twenty-first century, it had become one of the largest and most respected of the environmental organizations.

By 1970, the nation was ready for a clear commitment to the legal preservation of the natural environment, in the US and abroad. In 1970, following the first Earth Day (a student-led, privately initiated and privately run national celebration of the Earth, calling attention to the lengthy agenda of environmental protections needed), Congress created the Environmental Protection Agency (EPA) and passed the Clean Air Act. Environment was high on the list of priorities for the 1972 campaign, and the political momentum continued: the Clean Water Act of 1972, the Resource Conservation and Recovery Act (RCRA) in 1976, and the Comprehensive Emergency Response, Compensation and Liability Act (CERCLA) in 1980. It was CERCLA that authorized the first "Superfund," of $1.6 billion, for the purpose of cleaning up toxic dumps (paid for by the industries that create them). In 1986, that amount was raised to $8.5 billion. Since the 1970s, some of the enthusiasm has gone out of the legislature, but until 2003, when President George W. Bush authorized suspension of the Clean Air Act in order to allow utilities in violation of the law to continue operating, a strong national consensus was in effect: there would be no going back to the pre-Earth Day regime of environmental exploitation and neglect. Now, we shall have to see if that consensus endures.

The problem with regulation: The case of the lake

It could be argued that we ask the law to do too many things at once. Suppose, for instance, that we want to make sure that the water in the lake is pure enough to drink. Suppose further that there is a commercial establishment upstream from the lake that allows certain water from its operations to run off into the stream that feeds the

lake. We want to stop the company from doing that if it is polluting
the lake. How shall we proceed? First, we have to find out if the
company is prohibited from allowing its runoff to enter the lake, no
matter how small or harmless it is. If it is, then it is in violation of
a *law*: a federal or state *statute* or municipal *ordinance*, and it can be
told to cease and desist or pay the penalties set by law. That is the
easy part. But what if there is no law expressly forbidding such
runoff? In that case we are thrown back on the common-Law notion
of *nuisance*, describing the acts of one party (in this case the company)
that damage the lives of its neighbors (in this case the people who
drink the water from the lake.) Or do they? If the company has been
releasing water into the stream for 20 years, and no one has gotten
sick yet from the water, is that proof enough that the runoff is
harmless? Well, no. After all, people have drunk the water and
gotten sick lots of times; what we do not have is a connection
between the two. If some new form of intestinal distress suddenly
emerges, is that because of the water, or from something else?

We can test the water. Suppose we get trace amounts of benzene.
Is that from the plant up the stream, or from a small landfill on the
southern edge of the lake? Is there enough benzene to do any harm?
If there is not enough to hurt humans, is there enough to hurt the
salamanders, and if so, is that a reason to try to do something about
it? Stuck in the middle of this kind of problem, we can do no better
than sketch its boundaries:

1   *Scientific uncertainty is a fact of life.*   Strange are the ways of
    statistics. People get sick, and die, sometimes of strange and
    horrible diseases, often completely at random. There may be
    98 cases of a certain rare and fatal leukemia in the country
    every year, scattered at random among the 50 states. If four of
    those 98 cases show up on the lake one summer, does that mean
    there has to be some common cause? Nope. Could just be the
    result of random assortment. If cases kept showing up at the
    lake, summer after summer, eight and ten of them each year,
    we might wonder if *something* up there had something to do with
    it, but even then, in the eyes of the universe, that occurrence
    might still be absolutely random. At what point of widespread
    illness in the community might we want to blame the water?
    Can we ever be absolutely certain that the water caused it?

2   *We do not want to delay too long.*   Things happen while we are
    fiddling around, doing yet one more study, to find out if it is

really the water to blame. People get sick and die. Salamanders die, and sometimes whole species go extinct. If the benzene is accumulating – in the wetlands, in the salamanders, in the predators that eat the salamanders, in us – the problem may very well spin out of control while we do our studies. If there is a danger, we have to act now. Of course, we do not know if there is a danger.

3   *We do not want to overreact.*   If we march in a body to the factory and demand that it shut down its effluent, over its insistence that the outflow is harmless, it may discover that the costs of internalizing that flow are too high, and it might decide to close down, and there go most of the town's jobs with it. If we demand that the landfill be closed, its contents removed and taken elsewhere, we will hand the town a very large tax bill. In both cases, we put all future corporate residents on notice that the atmosphere of the town can turn from friendly to hostile overnight, and might discourage some of them from coming to the town at all. Overreaction has very nasty costs all around.

How do we settle problems like this? In the US, there is really only one forum for solving problems, at least solving them without violence, and that is the law. If we are to do anything about the lake that concerns us, we are going to have to pass a law at some level – federal, state, or local – and enforce it. If we do that, and the company disagrees with the findings that led to the law, the company can sue to have the law overturned on grounds that it is arbitrary and capricious and therefore unconstitutional. If it is successful in getting rid of the law, a local citizen can still sue the company to stop the effluent, even after the company has won its case – for the fact that a law is ill-drawn (a finding in constitutional law) has nothing to do with an injury that has been suffered by one of the plant's neighbors on account of the plant's negligence (a civil action under the common law). The system is not simple to navigate, and every single one of these actions is very costly. From the perspective of the owner of the plant, the safest rule to follow might be the general rule of environmental caution – nothing but nothing goes from this plant into the local stream.

Why do we need environmental law at all? Recall Chapter 2, and the structure of the modern corporation. The managers are instructed by the board of directors to maximize the return on investment (ROI) for the company; the board of directors are instructed by the shareholders who elected them to make sure the managers do just that and nothing more; and the shareholders, more likely than not, are the fund managers for large pension funds, who have been instructed by those who speak for the participants that they are to invest only in companies that promise the highest possible ROI. Nobody has any choice about that; we are looking at an unbroken string of fiduciary responsibilities. So to ask companies to renounce that goal, and accept less than the highest possible ROI for the sake of preserving the environment, is to ask the impossible – strictly speaking, to ask the unethical. But if each company blazes full speed ahead in total disregard of the environment, the result will likely be the end of the industry, and the company. The situation throughout becomes a replay of the case of the New England Fisheries that con-cludes Chapter 1 – the tragedy of the commons. If each logging company takes just as many trees as it can cut, it will drive the price down, requiring even more trees to be cut to make any profit, and in company with all its competitors, will destroy the forest. The shep-herds will destroy the grazing common, the fishermen will destroy the fishery, and all the polluting industries together will destroy the air, water, and land. If we ask companies voluntarily to withhold sheep from the common, or pollutants from the air, or nets from the water, they will respond, quite correctly, that their shareholders do not and cannot authorize compromising profits for environmental (or any other) reason. If some "voluntary" limitation regime (quotas somehow assigned) is agreed upon, or mandated by an anti-regulatory government, the temptation to cheat will be irresistible: first of all, probably no one will pay any attention to the quota anyway, so if I restrict my taking, I hurt myself without helping the resource; second, if everyone adheres to the agreement except me, we all get the benefit of the restored resource and I can "voluntarily" except myself from the rule (since my small contribution will not make any difference anyway), and rake in an enormous profit. That, of course, is the problem known as "free rider": where there is general compli-ance, it is very much to the material advantage of one of the players to defect from the cooperative scheme and catch as much fish, all sizes, as he or she wants. So we have to have laws, laws that will make it possible to hunt the cheaters down and put them in jail – or at least levy sufficient fines that they will not be tempted to do that again.

To review just the last few paragraphs: All Americans agree that if industrial activity of any kind is doing serious damage to our drinking water, so we might get sick, whatever they are doing should stop, and we are willing to use the collective force of the state, the law, to make sure that it does. What we do not agree on is: whether a tiny percent of benzene will make us sick (and it is very difficult to find that out, no matter how many experimental mice we kill), whether, in the face of that uncertainty we should err on the side of caution (stop the effluence) or on the side of clear economic common sense (let it continue), whether the benzene will sicken any other form of life in the lake, and if so, whether that effect is worth doing anything at all about – in short, what weight should be assigned to it. Since we cannot decide any of these matters by the seat of the pants in the individual instance, we have law, a collective-decision power that settles dubious issues in advance on the strength of the best available knowledge and the democratic process. Then, should a decision be made that will affect many persons, whose voluntary compliance would have to be complete in the absence of law, the history of free riders and voluntary regimes generally suggest that we pass enforceable law to protect that decision.

The limits of law: The case of the Australian silver gem fish

The story is all too typical. The Australian fishery started slowly; Australia is far away from everything, and Australians preferred red meat, so there was not much of a market up through the 1960s. In the 1970s, foreign markets became more accessible, and the population of Australia increased and varied its tastes. With the increasing market for fish, fishers developed much more sophisticated deepwater gear, and by the mid-1970s started to catch previously unknown deepwater fish like the orange roughy (*Hoplostethis atlanticus*) and the silver gem fish (*Rexea solandri*). They are delicious; catches increased by leaps and bounds, peaking in the mid-1980s after which they started to decline. By this time, fishery scientists had figured out that these deepwater breeds (1) cannot survive being hauled out and tossed back, so efforts to limit catch by size were fruitless, (2) live about 100–150 years, (3) do not even start to breed until about the age of 25, and therefore (4) cannot take any pressure at all on their numbers. Against the inevitable protests of the fishers, the Australian government slapped limits on the catch of both fish in 1988; the "total allowable catch" (TAC) of the gem fish was reduced to zero in 1993 as the species continued to decline. It may be too late for the gem fish, especially since the waters are still fished, and the gem fish cannot survive being caught, even if released. The numbers of the orange roughy also continue to decline, and stricter limits are being contemplated.

For both fish, it may be too late. The law, good law, required an informed legislature to vote for it and enable its enforcement. For the legislature to act, it had to have information. The scientists acquired information. But the scientists could not get the information for some time after the fishing had started – these investigations take time. As soon as the scientists figured out what was going on, they told the legislature and the legislature acted responsibly. Life just does not wait for the proper procedures to be followed. The profit was immediate, the fishing was extensive, and the stocks of both these deepwater fish may be damaged beyond repair.[11] The law is too slow.

The limits of regulation: Politics as usual

When law is well passed, and well oriented toward the public good – an accomplishment in itself, as the previous cases illustrate – it is still wide open to interpretation by the administration in power. This is a good thing; no one can foresee every contingency, and some flexibility in the administration of law by the EPA and the current executive branch is to be expected and applauded. But this flexibility returns the conduct of government to the adversarial pattern shown in the opening case: where the preservation of the natural environment is concerned, there are two parties in the US government, not necessarily connected in any way to Republicans or Democrats. One party wants privately owned profit-oriented business to flourish freely with absolutely minimal restraints based only on absolute public necessity; the other party wants to preserve environmental values as an American birthright for generations to come (including public health and unpolluted natural systems), with profit-oriented business asked to prove at every step that it is not degrading those values. (In Chapter 5 we talk about the ways that the two orientations may collaborate for mutual gain; this chapter is about the face-off between them in the politics of the ordinary.)

What shall we call these parties? The opening case in this chapter refers to them as "the enviros" (environmental activists) and the "lobbyists" for industry. But the sides are much deeper and wider than that. In the nineteenth century, we could have called them "conservatives" and "liberals"; classical conservatives were in favor of keeping the commons in grazing and woodlots, preserving the ancestral forests and ancestral customs of stewardship, while the "liberals" were all for free enterprise, free trade, and the endless expansion of the economy. Even in the first third of the twentieth century, "conservatives" were generally the privileged protectors of the wild places, while "liberals," or "progressives," by now with strong ties to the urban labor movement, spent very little time worrying about the environmental impact of the expansion (or recovery) of the industrial sector. To judge from recent literature, the terminology has changed places: Rena Steinzor, whose account of current environmental controversies I will generally track in what follows, calls the industry side "conservatives" and the environmental protection side "progressives," which is historically weird.[12] Rather than fly in the face of either history or current usage, I will name the sides by the normative thrust of their activities: those who would protect the environment I will call "conservationists," those who would release business enterprise from such protections I will call "industrializers."

It is no secret that in the US in 2000, whatever one might think of the election, the industrializers gained a friendly administration. The best way to characterize the change is by a series of "tilts," changes in emphasis rather than direction, which have become part of the environmental regime at this point. Most obviously, new administrations appoint different people; industrializers pick personnel for the EPA and the Department of the Interior who are known to be friendly to industrialization by instinct as well as by party affiliation and history. But there are other predictable differences. Some examples:

1 *Elitism.* Industrializers tend to argue that environmental quality is a luxury good, to be purchased by those who have the money and the inclination, and not given away for free by universal protections like anti-pollution legislation. The notion of a "public good," that should be purchased by everyone for everyone, does not often enter their calculations.

2 *Monetizing.* Industrializers argue that the only way to compare goods is to put a monetary value on them, so that they can take their place in the calculations of greatest advantage. Even the quality of human life is to be quantified in "QALYs," quality-adjusted life years, so that we can make clear decisions on proposals that impact different groups differently. (This system of quantification has been accused of being as elitist as the first

example, since the life of the young Harvard MBA investment banker is clearly of higher quality than that of the immigrant who cleans his building at night.)

3   *The cost–benefit analysis.*   Industrializers tend to solve social dilemmas by a "cost–benefit analysis," a balancing of the costs and benefits to be expected from the adoption of the various options available in the situation. The method is certainly not irrational; it is no more than applied utilitarianism (see Chapter 1). But in cases, and they are many, of scientific uncertainty (see above) the insistence that the best available cost–benefit analysis must solve the problem leaves the conservationists very uneasy. This is because it seems to them that protective action, in public health or in preserving the environment, is *always* justified in the face of uncertainty (according to a rule known as the *Precautionary Principle*), while to the industrializers, if the general calculation, assuming that the uncertainties fall evenly on both sides, leaves a "preponderance of evidence" on the side of non-protection, then protection is unnecessary. Conservationists worry that choices made to adopt new technologies in the face of uncertainty could produce irreversible damage before the true costs are known.

4   *Trading systems.*   The industrializers prefer to use "credit" systems to reduce pollution. Sources of pollution (power plants, for example) receive "credits" or "allowances," essentially licenses to create a certain amount of pollution over a certain period (for example, a ton of NO_x in a year). If your plant is cleaner than that, you can sell some of your allowances to a dirtier plant that needs them, thereby providing both of you with a financial incentive to become and stay clean. Conservationists think the whole arrangement is crazy. Why not just say, no pollution, and tax or fine any pollution that remains, the more pollution the more tax? That gives everyone a financial incentive to get and to stay clean, without apparently creating entitlements and property rights in permissions to pollute.[13] Under the previous administration, the EPA had abandoned credits plans; in 2001, they started them up again. The systems could, conceivably, work, but much more work (on the norm, or "cap," for instance) is needed to make them realistic.

5   *The disappearance of the poor.*   Conservationists tend to keep an eye on the overall effects of any pollution-abatement regime, to

make sure that no population is being unfairly targeted; industrializers, placing all pollution credits on the open market, tend not to notice when wealthy neighborhoods insist that their utilities clean up their acts, making lots of credits available for sale, which are then snapped up by old and very dirty plants in the poorest neighborhoods, generally the homes of people of color, since in those neighborhoods there is no pressure to cut pollution. The result, from the conservationist standpoint, amounts to environmental injustice, but since the free market creates it, there seems to be little that can be done about it.

6   *The relaxation of enforcement.*   A starving watchdog has difficulty concentrating on the job. By systematically cutting back on the workforce and other resources available for the enforcement of environmental laws, the industrializers accomplish several objectives at once: they save money in the government, making those funds available for other purposes; they make it very difficult for public agencies to prosecute offenses, offenses likely committed by persons sympathetic to the industrializers; and they require that pollution reduction (a goal that everyone approves) take place through free-market mechanisms. We can expect that if an administration friendly to conservationists assumes power, those funds will be restored and all three momenta will be reversed.

7   *Partnership with industry.*   Sadly, one of the most noticeable characteristics of an industrializer administration is a loss of interest in preventing conflict of interest. For instance, the General Accounting Office (GAO), the government's watchdog, concluded in 2001 that the Science Advisory Board "routinely neglected to obtain information from candidates for peer review panels that would enable screening for conflicts of interest and bias."[14] Two of the panelists who participated in a decision not to upgrade butadiene to a "known" human carcinogen, for instance, owned stock in companies that made the chemical.

Those six developments are typical, emblematic, of the kinds of changes that happen when political changes occur in a democracy. Note that no one seems even to be suggesting that the basic legal framework of environmental protection – Clean Air, Clean Water, CERCLA – be removed or even seriously reformed. Steinzor mentions in passing that if real efforts were made to repeal our structure of environmental protection, a powerful political backlash could be expected; knowing this, industrializer administrations work primarily through executive orders and other means that do not need to be shared with the electorate at this time.

The major problem that attends the domination of the process by either group is the loss of the contribution of the other. There is an irresistible human tendency to exclude and marginalize those who disagree while enjoying power. In conservationist administrations, the expertise that industry may contribute to the protection of the environment is systematically ignored. In the present industrializer administration, the danger is that the forces above will combine to permit what is called "capture" – the absorption of the functions of the public agencies (as assigned by the law) by industry associations. Should that happen, the perspective of the conservationist party may be marginalized to organize itself around the fringes of the polity – the "backlash" that Rena Steinzor mentions. The resulting division, between a visibly triumphant industrializer party and a stealthy conservationist party striking through the Internet, could seriously compromise the public perception of open and democratic government.

Transparency suffers when the environmental protection process falls into the hands of uncontested power groups, which is why democracies work better with lots of contest. The search for perfect "objectivity," that god-like detachment that makes it possible to evaluate all scientific information without regard to political or economic consequences of decisions based on that information, is surely fruitless. All we can hope is that with adequate information about the process, the contending sides will be able to present their cases and pass the decision on to the people.

The direction of regulation

In the next chapter we take up the areas of environmental protection (or at least, non-damage) that businesses should adopt simply in their own short- and middle-term interest, with some forays into long-term interest. The tone of the chapter will be that Green business is always good business. But it is not always so, is it? At least in the short term, if in a highly competitive industry, one firm decides to adopt expensive pollution-control technology, the others not doing so, it puts itself at a distinct competitive disadvantage. Environmental regulation exists because of free riders, whether they be in the majority (in which case the heroic firm which insists on adopting the technology dies gracefully in short order) or in the very small minority (in which case the majority labor under the burden of the agreement while that minority make out like bandits). When we pass a law, we level the playing field and make it possible for all companies to do the right thing without losing competitive advantage. We also change the playing field. When the rules of the game change, the team that can most quickly develop new strategies to avoid the new obstacles and take advantage of the new opportunities created will win the league; the company that can produce the new low-emission automobile or clean power plant will drive the competition out of the market. Business strategy in the face of environmental law, then, should be one of instant compliance (since the quicker the new limits are in place, the sooner the company will be able to assess the actual economic changes in its operations), and full-court-press innovation to take advantage of the opportunities created.

There is a cliché among those who watched the Japanese automotive firms take over the American market in the 1970s: that when Clean Air legislation went into effect, the Japanese firms gathered all their best engineers, presented them with the new lower emissions requirements, and told them to design cars that could meet them; American firms, on the contrary, gathered all their best lawyers and sent them to Washington to get the new regulations repealed. Some of the regulations may still be repealed, but no matter: the companies that were in there with the regulations-compliant product will have grabbed off a nice chunk of the market share, and think of all the money it will have saved on lawyers.

Where may we expect regulation? All over the global commons, we may expect. On the national level, we may expect legislation on air (emissions control of the NO_x and SO_x, particulates, lead, mercury, and all other metals), water (effluent control, especially where the waste products are immediately toxic, but also whenever, however harmless, they are massive and obvious), land (disposal of solid wastes), and especially on toxic wastes, paint, nuclear spent rods etc. Right now we have no national consensus on such matters, and we are unlikely to get good law absent such consensus.

There will then, we can safely predict, be three major determinants of environmental law in the remainder of this century:

1   *Political education and organization.*   In the last great push for environmental reform, in the 1970s, the majority of the American electorate understood, studied, and reacted to presentations on the threatened state of the environment. The famously short

attention span withdrew soon afterwards, and in the feel-good administrations that followed, long-term threats were hidden from view. That alertness would have to be rekindled for any further sweeping environmental regulation to find political support.

2   *Availability of resources.*   We have the technology now to make fresh water out of salty water, and to replace our terribly inefficient energy consumption patterns, for instance, with much more efficient ones. But strong laws, well enforced, will be required to transform the automobile (worse yet, Sport-Utility Vehicle [SUV]!) culture to a more sustainable way of life. It is unlikely that we will have the political will to force such changes until it becomes clear that the resources simply will not be there to use, at any price (petroleum is expected to run out at mid-century, for example).

3   *The increasing power of international society.*   Right now the US is in a position to veto, at least for application within its borders, any provisions for environmental conservation put out by any international body or any international ad hoc Congress – witness its treatment of the Kyoto protocol. But this position will not last indefinitely: as other nations become more powerful economically and politically, and as the US dependence on foreign trade increases, the US will find itself required to go along with international protocols or face unendurable trade sanctions. The speed with which this rebalancing of world power will take place is one of the unknowns of the century; but the direction of law is toward global scope.

Law, by definition, is the ordering (not simply the prescribing or proscribing) of human conduct by rules; law can create conditions where it is to our advantage to act in a way that benefits the public interest. If we want to order individual activity in order to conserve energy and lower harmful emissions, for instance, we will have to change the incentives surrounding the purchase of vehicles. The simple legal move to make "light trucks" (once farm vehicles, now SUVs) comply with the same fuel efficiency standards applicable to all cars would save us a million barrels of oil per day.[15] As far as the natural environment is concerned, it is the market that is most in need of ordering. Voluntary compliance with environmentally sustainable practices, in the absence of law, cannot be expected of any publicly traded company; the careers of too many fund managers (not to mention too many corporate officers) depend significantly on the next quarter's earnings. Only when law levels the playing field can companies compete vigorously within the market system and simultaneously avoid environmentally damaging practices. It is to be hoped that innovative companies will recognize the competitive advantage that good environmental regulation will give them, and will join the conservationists in their attempts to get such law on the books and enforced.

✸ CASE 4: PACIFIC LUMBER AND THE LAW ✸

World War II found the redwood forests of the Pacific Northwest largely in private hands, save for a few parks and National Forests, primarily in northern California. After the war, the huge building boom made it profitable for the private owners to clear-cut their parcels, especially of the old-growth trees. At the time, no one noticed. When the environmental movement began, two decades after the rush, only one company, Pacific Lumber, still had most of its groves standing. Its company policy, for most of the twentieth century, had been to cut only sustainably, to make sure that it had wood into the indefinite future. That policy required replanting; in numerical terms, it required that it survey its forests every year, and make sure that it had more board-feet of timber standing at the end of each year than it had at the beginning. From the perspective of the seventh generation, that is a good policy, but it is surely not the most efficient use of resources from the point of view of present profitability, and Pacific Lumber was publicly owned (as it always had been). When "hostile takeovers" became considerably easier to bring off, in the 1980s, a financier from Houston, Charles Hurwitz of MAXXAM, made a bid for Pacific Lumber with borrowed money, gained control of it, and started clear-cutting the most beautiful groves remaining in private hands. Protests began immediately.

The Pacific Lumber case well exemplifies the history of adversarial dealings between corporations and the environmental movement. In the redwood groves, spontaneously compared by many who have seen them to the most glorious cathedrals of Europe, the case has an accessible and beautiful heart (unlike, say, the snail darter); it has a suitably shameless corporate voice in Charles Hurwitz (who not only engineered the hostile takeover, one of dozens in his career, but also plundered the company's pension fund to pay off the debts incurred in the takeover, and canceled most of the benefits that had become traditional in the company); and it has a history of environmental activism which includes not only appeals to Nature and Beauty but also persuasive economic models of alternative uses of those groves by the people of the region.

For six months of the year, it rains every day in the Pacific rainforest. The currents of the Pacific Ocean, providing warmth and abundant moisture to coastal northwest United States during millions of years of evolution, ultimately brought forth the ancient evergreen forests, or "old-growth forests," at the heart of the controversy. The forests probably appeared in their present form about 6,000 years ago; at present, they have stands of trees up to 1,000 years old, trees that are 300-feet tall with 10-foot diameters, at least twice as massive as those found in tropical rainforests. Each tree, to put this in perspective, contains enough lumber to build two houses. These forests once extended unbroken from the Alaskan panhandle (Sitka spruce) south through Washington and Oregon (Douglas fir, western hemlock), to northern California (several varieties of redwoods, ponderosa pine). Despite the poor volcanic, basaltic soil, these forests contain the largest examples of the 25 species of conifers found there. The dead trees (snags) may stand for up to 200 years, as it takes 200–500 years for them to decay; nevertheless, the forest floor and streams are littered with decomposing trees that provide nutrients for the living ones, and habitat for thousands of animal species (1,500 invertebrate species were counted on a single tree). One of the species, the northern spotted owl, has become, at least for legal and political purposes, the focus of the controversy. Its endangerment, brought about by loss of habitat, is the major tool the public now has to protect the forests. We will leave the northern spotted owl, and the general question of biodiversity, to one side, since our focus is the trees and the logging company. But it should be noted that our system has a certain Alice in Wonderland quality to it: we want to save the groves, but there is no way that a grove of trees can be declared a species, let alone an endangered one, so we have to find a species that is endangered by loss of habitat, and then we can protect the habitat, the trees, by application of the Endangered Species Act of 1973, for the sake of the endangered owl. Should we try to get Alice back through the Looking Glass, and simply assign rights to the ecosystem itself? (see Chapter 3).

The redwood trees of the Pacific Northwest come in two species, *Sequoiadendrum giganteum* and *Sequoia sempervirens*. What is left of *giganteum*, the largest of trees, is almost completely within the boundaries of state and national parks. At issue for this case is *sempervirens*, the coastal redwood, to the best of our knowledge the tallest trees that have ever lived.[16]

Once established, this forest has proved almost immune from change by natural forces. Most ecosystems are characterized by change and succession: their species change with time, from pioneer species, through more stable species, to the most stable, climax species, only to change again when some violent event upsets their balance (the eruption of Mount St Helena is a good example). No such event has disrupted the redwood forest for millennia; the forest has remained, grown, and reproduced itself, resulting in some individuals as old as or older than Christendom. To quote an admirer, Sallie Tisdale, "There is little on this earth so close to immortal."[17] Unfortunately for those who hope for their survival, these trees are the most commercially valuable in the United States.

This harvest is strictly limited by nature. Once those old-growth trees are logged, there will be no more: the trees are gone forever. The second growth does not have the characteristics of the old growth in its resistance to insects, disease, fire, and decay (we may suppose that the twentieth century remainder of a 2000-year-old forest is composed of the best survivors of all attacks: the less resistant succumbed centuries ago), nor, of course, is it as massive. The old growth is then an irreplaceable asset, more valuable every year into the indefinite future, demanding careful husbanding and conservative forestry practices. Wise management would require very sparing cuts of the old growth, along with encouragement of plantations of new trees to satisfy demands for no more than ordinary lumber.

It is worth pointing out that the failure to manage such lumber harvest wisely has effects beyond the loss of the wood. Besides the imprudent depletion of a valuable resource, rapid harvesting has serious environmental effects on the region and perhaps on the world. The fish and wildlife of the area may suffer severely from the same destruction of habitat that disrupts the owl. Once the trees go, the erosion of the denuded hillsides in the ceaseless rain carries topsoil into the streams. If there happens to be a small town at the bottom of the hill, the town, too, will get buried in mud.[18] Once the topsoil is gone from the hills, where it formed only a thin layer, the land is useless for growing trees even if a lumber company conscientiously replants; once layered into the streams, the topsoil smothers salmon fry that must hatch in the clean pebbles of the bottom of a stream.

One very serious environmental effect of overharvesting, presently unmeasurable, is the contribution to global warming. The old growth is a huge storehouse of carbon, and carbon dioxide is the most important of the "greenhouse gases" credited with causing the projected global warming. While alive, the trees absorb huge amounts of that gas from the atmosphere in the photosynthetic process. Nature's recycling laws of course require that the same amount of the gas be returned to the atmosphere, as it is through the trees' respiration and eventual decay, but that happens, as noted above, over a period of hundreds of years. When the trees are felled the photosynthetic carbon dioxide absorption stops, and compounding that effect, when the "debris" is burned, the stored carbon is abruptly added to the atmosphere as more carbon dioxide.

Rarely do we see a direct face-off of the conservative business approach (oriented to the long-term maximization of value from assets, the careful accounting of interests of all stakeholders, the long-term competitive positioning of the company itself, and the continuity of its arrangements with suppliers, customers, and employees) and the radical grab-the-profits-and-run approach made famous in the decade of the 1980s.

Pacific Lumber was founded in 1869. In the 1930s, the company adopted a policy of perpetual sustained yield: mature trees were marked for selective cutting, felled, snaked out by the "cat" tractor, and milled. With more light in the forest, the younger trees matured faster; where bare spots were left, the company reseeded. In theory, such practices should "keep the company supplied with redwood logs from its own lands in perpetuity."[19] The sustained yield policy is economically sound and kind to shareholders. Pacific Lumber's financial statements for the years through 1984 show small cyclical adjustments to demand, but steady earnings on its outstanding shares.[20] The company took just as good care of its workers, supplying housing, all municipal services, college scholarships, and guaranteed employment for the workers' children, and a securely overfunded pension plan.

In 1986, Charles Hurwitz, CEO of MAXXAM, seized control of Pacific Lumber (with $900 million in Drexel Burnham junk bonds), immediately terminated the pension plan, and accelerated the traditionally measured timber harvest. He used $55 million of the pension funds to pay down part of his buyout debt.[21] An insurance company controlled by Hurwitz, Executive Life, bought more than one-third of the junk bonds, and issued the "annuities" required by federal law to replace pension funds when their managers deplete them. Executive Life collapsed when the junk bond market did, leaving the workers without pensions beyond what the truncated company was able to supply on a temporary basis.[22] Repayment of the same debt required that Hurwitz get money off the land as fast as possible; forestry practices changed, to harvest groves that the old Pacific Lumber had been saving for the end of the century, to clear-cut where selective cutting had been the rule, to speed up the pace of logging, and to abandon the costly projects of replanting that had insured the future harvest.

The selective cutting and replanting, besides providing for future harvests, had held the soil in place after logging, and prevented erosion of the steep slopes in the relentless rainfall of the region; under new management, the soil began to wash into the streams. As stated above, that erosion is bad for the slopes (which cannot then grow more trees), bad for the banks of the stream, which overflow with regular spring floods, and fatal for the salmon, which cannot breed when soil from erosion covers the gravel at the bottom of the streams.[23] These practices continued without limit until 1991, when US District Judge William Dwyer declared a moratorium on the cutting of the old-growth habitat critical for the spotted owl.

Did Hurwitz do anything wrong in clear-cutting the old groves? It could be argued that protecting the environment was *not* part of Hurwitz's job. Environmental issues are beyond the competence of business to decide. Everything Hurwitz did was within the law. After all, if the American people, through their elected officials, wish to keep more of certain kinds of products (like trees) in the ground and away from the market, let them pass a law to that effect, and law-abiding businesspersons will adhere to the law. But in a publicly held, profit-oriented corporation, it should not be management's obligation, or option, to look after the long-term fate of the trees. Pacific Lumber was in business to make money for the stockholders, not to act as unpaid trustee for the North Coast forest.

As for the laws to protect the trees, it should be added that a good businessperson would regret, as a citizen, the loss to the economy that such a restriction would represent, and would feel obliged to bring to the attention of the citizens the potential cost in jobs, tax revenues, and so forth. In this effort, the company presidents, contemplating profits and prices per share, would be joined by the loggers, contemplating their jobs. As a matter of fact, the major initiatives to limit the effects of the Endangered Species Act (ESA), and to free more acreage of old-growth timber for cutting have come from the workers and the small businessmen of the affected regions, with the major timber companies, Pacific Lumber included, taking a back seat. The loggers believe that they have very few options. Most of them were raised in the region, either in the Pacific Lumber family or in similar areas with similar expectations. They do not see themselves as having the skills to move elsewhere; for them, only a job of cutting down trees (or milling them, or serving those who do) stands between them and permanent unemployment. "Jobs or woodpeckers?" their signs demand; their bumper stickers insist that they "Love Spotted Owls: Fried, Boiled, Barbecued...," or that "Loggers, too, are an Endangered Species." With such strong political alliance, it might be pointed out, the companies have little motivation to retrain them for other employment.

We have here a direct and serious confrontation of environmental values and short-term economic imperatives – the imperatives that rest on the rights of private property and the responsibilities to shareholders. Adam Smith held that business enterprise of all kind is limited by supply and demand, and would have held out hope for the trees in the very saturation of the market. There is a demand for only so much redwood lumber, he would argue; ultimately it will cost Pacific Lumber more to mill the logs it cuts than they will sell for, and then they will have to scale back logging until demand returns. But if the market includes players who are operating by different rules – the Japanese, say, who pursue long-term instead of short-term economic interests – that reasoning fails to apply. Because the lumber companies have by now disposed of their mills, as costly and unpredictable, they sell raw logs overseas, enjoy sales completely unlimited by domestic demand, and leave their workers to be taken care of by the government.[24] The closing of the mills, not the restrictions on the logging, seems to be the real cause of unemployment in the area.

Aristotle and Adam Smith both argued, in very different ways, that property (specifically, land and all resources for production) was better off, more likely to be taken care of, in private hands than public. This assumption, that the private owner is the best caretaker, underlies the importance we attach to the right of private property. Is the assumption now, at least in these cases, false? The redwoods of Pacific Lumber are clearly not safe in Charles Hurwitz's hands. Outside of the option of taking the property as eminent domain, which requires that market price be paid for the groves by the taxpayer, do we have any legal right, or structure, to take the land away from him to protect it? Should we?

Even timber executives agree that in a competitive climate, government regulation will be necessary to limit environmentally destructive practices. Then by what means, and to what end, shall the government regulate? What is the public interest at this point?

The heart of the problem, from an environmentalist point of view, is the old-growth forest. From the loggers' point of view it is jobs. The owl, the financier, and the alphabet soup of regulatory agencies are bit players in an agonizing twentieth-century drama of loss and conflict. We need not search for villains; once we all thought that the forests were unlimited. The timber industry's managers, who watched the old growth disappearing before their eyes, and did not know that it could not be restored – that once gone, it would be gone forever – were no more ignorant than their regulators, their customers, or their fellow citizens. The environmental movement is not the sole property of Eastern Elitists, as the loggers suspect, nor is the timber industry a series of tintypes of Charles Hurwitz, as the environmentalists are convinced. Protecting the forests will require the abolition of a way of life, one that has been honored and valuable in our immediate past. For the moment, the very agenda of protection raises a series of questions that will not go away; we conclude with the questions.

1   What are the business imperatives of a company that logs redwoods? Is it sufficient to replace 2000-year-old groves with young stuff that can be harvested in 40 to 80 years?[25] Sufficient for what? What, exactly, are we prepared to do to compensate and redirect the people orphaned by preservation? Or, on the other hand, are we prepared to spare ourselves that difficult decision by allowing the forests to be destroyed?

2   Are there environmentally friendly ways to carry on logging operations? Once the trees are gone, the industry will die, and the workers will be unemployed, but then it will be their problem, not ours. How much are we willing to lose in order to avoid the pain of making a decision? Our history would suggest, quite a bit.

3   Are there new directions that the environmental movement should be taking? Should it abandon the "endangered species" approach and reorient itself to ecosystem integrity?[26] Or will that move succeed only in disorientation, discouraging followers

by forcing an admission that previous efforts were wrongly conceived, and plunging them into indefinable terms and inchoate goals? The ESA has at least the virtue of clarity.

The ironies abound, not the least of which is the agencies within agencies fighting each other. But the most disturbing aspect of our political response to these dilemmas is the hypocrisy, of the United States urging Brazil and other Third World countries to halt the cutting of their tropical rainforests in the interest of preventing the worsening of global warming, while we cut ours at a rate of about twice theirs. To quote an official with the Oregon Natural Resources Council, "It's interesting that we're telling Third World countries, 'don't cut your forests' [while]...we're wiping out our fish runs, we're wiping out our biotic diversity, we're sending species to extinction...we're not a Third World country. We're not so poor that we have to destroy our ancient forests. And we're not so rich that we can afford to."[27]

Consider the following questions:

1 Where valuable natural tracts are concerned, should there be special legal protections to buffer the tracts from the market in corporate control?
2 If it could be shown (and it very possibly could be) that it would be cheaper in the long run to pension off every logger with $45,000 per year, just to bring the industry to an end, should we recommend such an unprecedented entitlement?
3 We have always protected private property in land (while denying it in air and on the ocean) on the grounds that the land would be best cared for under the control of one who hoped to make a long-term living from it. Now we have entrepreneurs who are not interested (at all) in the long term. Should we re-examine the entire concept of private property in land?

⊛ NOTES ⊛

1. Lis Harris, *Tilting at Mills: Green Dreams, Dirty Dealings, and the Corporate Squeeze*, Boston: Houghton Mifflin Company, 2003.
2. See Donald G. Hagman and Dean J. Misczynski, *Windfalls for Wipeouts: Land Value Capture and Compensation*, Washington, DC: American Planning Association, 1978.

3. See Robert Ardrey, *The Territorial Imperative: A Personal Inquiry into the Animal Origins of Property and Nations*, New York: Athenaeum, 1966.

4. A suggestion I owe to Thomas More Hoban and Richard Oliver Brooks, *Green Justice: The Environment and the Courts*, Boulder, CO: Westview, 2nd edn., 1996, p. 34.

5. See, for these distinctions, *Just* v. *Marinette County*, S.Ct.WI 1972, 201 N.W.2d 761, cited and discussed in Hoban and Brooks, op. cit., pp. 21–35.

6. *Webb's Fabulous Pharmacies, Inc.* v. *Beckwith*, 449 US 155, 164 (1980).

7. *Lucas* v. *South Carolina Coastal Council*, No. 91-453 (US June 29, 1992) 22 *Environmental Law Reporter* 21104.

8. But see Lawrence C. Becker, *Property Rights: Philosophic Foundations*, Boston: Routledge & Kegan Paul, 1977; Bruce A. Ackerman, *Private Property and the Constitution*, New Haven: Yale University Press, 1978; among more recent works, see Stephen Munzer, *A Theory of Property*, Cambridge: Cambridge University Press, 1990; Margaret Jane Radin, *Reinterpreting Property*, Chicago: University of Chicago Press, 1994. Richard Epstein, *Takings: Private Property and the Power of Eminent Domain*, Cambridge: Harvard University Press, 1985, and parts of Garrett Hardin and John Baden, eds., *Managing the Commons*, San Francisco: Freeman, 1977, will be discussed in the text.

9. Aristotle, *Politics*, II, v.

10. 407 US 926 (1972).

11. I am indebted to my reader, Michele Hoffman of DePaul University in Chicago, for bringing the story of the silver gem fish to my attention. See also the FAO Fisheries Department Circular #920 FIRM/C920; www.fao.org/docrep/003/w4248e/w4248e28.htm.

12. Rena I. Steinzor, "Toward Better Bubbles and Future Lives: A Progressive Response to the Conservative Agenda for Reforming Environmental Law," *Environmental Law Reporter (ELR)* 32: 11421–11438 (December 2002).

13. To be sure, Title IV of the 1990 Clean Air Act Amendments states explicitly that allowances to emit sulfur dioxide do not constitute a "property right" vested in the entity that receives them initially or purchases them on the open market. 42 USC #7651b(f), ELR Stat. CAA #403(f). Cited Steinzor, ibid., p. 11424. But buying and selling things for awhile sure makes them feel like property, and if the "entitlement" ever gets established in law, the credits regime may become very expensive to bring to an end.

14. US GAO, EPA's Science Advisory Board Panels, Improved Policies and Procedures Needed to Ensure Independence and Balance (2001) (GAO-01–536), cited Steinzor, ibid., p. 11432.

15. "Warming Up," editorial, *The New York Times*, January 25, 2004.

16. Catherine Caulfield, "The Ancient Forest," *The New Yorker*, May 14, 1990, p. 46.
17. Sallie Tisdale, "The Pacific Northwest," *The New Yorker*, August 26, 1991, p. 54.
18. Eric Brazil, "Pacific Lumber to Pay Millions in Landslide Suit," *The San Francisco Chronicle*, March 9, 2001, A12.
19. Hugh Wilkerson and John Van der zee, *Life in the Peace Zone: An American Company Town*, New York: The Macmillan Company, 1971. pp. 112–113.
20. In the third quarter of 1984, for instance, Pacific Lumber reported that its net earnings rose 50 percent over the previous year ($11,337,000, or 47 cents per share, compared to $7,547,000, or 31 cents per share, for the third quarter the previous year.) See: Pacific Lumber annual reports, years 1981 through 1984.
21. Gisela Botte and Dan Cray, "Is Your Pension Safe?" *Time*, June 3, 1991, p. 43.
22. Ibid., also James Castro et al., "A Sizzler Finally Fizzles: In America's largest life insurance company collapse, California officials seize control of shaky giant Executive Life," *Time*, April 22, 1991. "Nightline" (ABC) did a program on the dire straits of workers who have lost their pensions in the collapse of insurance companies in general, with special attention to Pacific Lumber, on June 18, 1991. The program featured interviews with aging retired workers, bewildered and frightened, demonstrating in the streets, demanding the return of their pension fund.
23. Grant Sims, "Can We Save the Northwest's Salmon?" *National Wildlife*, October–November 1994, pp. 42–48.
24. See G. Tyler Miller, *Living in the Environment*, 9th edn., Belmont, CA: Wadsworth Publishers, 1996, pp. 296–298.
25. Shepard, Jack, *The Forest Killers*, New York: Weybright and Tally, 1975, p. 33.
26. Kathie Durbin, "From Owls to Eternity," *E: The Environmental Magazine*, 3(2), pp. 30–37 (March/April 1992).
27. Caulfield, op. cit., p. 67.

c h a p t e r   f i v e

Green Strategies and New Opportunities

To stay competitive, a company must keep costs down, quality up, and innovate, innovate, innovate. This chapter is about strategies that a company can adopt to become and remain competitive – strategies that centrally involve the natural environment. The key notion for all these strategies is *sustainability*: the ability to continue a profitable practice indefinitely without having an environmental limit suddenly appear to end it.

1   We will start with the cost of basic services; to the extent that they are provided by nature, how much would it cost to replace them? Could a business, any business, survive at all if the services were not provided? Think of it as the ultimate supply chain problem: What strategies should be adopted to make sure that the company does not suddenly have to replace or do without some crucial natural service?

2   The second section we might call "Seven Easy Pieces," steps that any firm can and should take to increase profitability and environmental stewardship simultaneously. Most of these come under the heading of "eco-efficiency" in the literature; they are simple applications of the imperative for efficiency along the environmental interfaces.

3   The third will outline "Seven Harder Pieces," outside-the-box long-term strategies that will reinforce both environmental integrity and corporate profitability for the long run. These strategies call for the development of new structures, physical

and organizational, and the recognition of new efficiencies and new metrics for business success.

The importance of the enterprise cannot be exaggerated. The environmental problems are very serious, and must be addressed very seriously, in the context of the working economy. "To put eco-systems in economic terms," suggests Lester Brown in *Eco-Economy*, "a natural system, such as a fishery, functions like an endowment. The interest income from an endowment will continue in perpetuity as long as the endowment is maintained. If the endowment is drawn down, income declines. If the endowment is eventually depleted, the interest income disappears. So it is with natural systems. If the sustainable yield of a fishery is exceeded, fish stocks begin to shrink. Eventually stocks are depleted and the fishery collapses. The cash flow from this endowment disappears as well."[1] We already have, in our legal system, the notion of *fiduciary duty*; it makes sense to ask what obligations fall upon managers, as trustees of that endowment, to maintain it; to ask as well, what consequences will follow, should that capital be dissipated.

THE ECONOMIC WORTH OF NATURE: THE VALUE OF NATURE'S SERVICES

If we are to choose economic strategies for the natural environment, we should begin by recognizing the economic value of what is already there. The first acknowledgement is that in the end, there is no capital but nature's. Solar capital – the energy, in all its forms, from the sun – and earth capital, living and nonliving, provide us with all we have to work with. These are the life-support systems on which we depend; we have no other source of wealth or access to life. How big is this endowment? How much is it worth to us? The value of nature's services has been variously estimated (depending on what you are counting) to be as low as $16 trillion or almost as high as the world gross national product (GNP) of $18 trillion (1997); counting a more complete array of services, the value came to $54 trillion.[2] In 1997, Robert Costanza estimated (on average) $33 trillion in all, and that estimate is generally accepted. But there can be no certainty. As Janet Abramowitz points out, nature simply has different values to people in different times and places, and as with any market valuation, different surveys will yield different values for the same goods.[3] With nature we are in worse shape than with other services for finding "market value," because we have no accepted way to express that value in our currency. While we struggle for the translation, we still have to act as if we knew how to do it, for we are under a strong obligation to do what is in any case in our best interests – to conserve that endowment, if possible to enhance it, and above all to avoid any action that would diminish the capital and endanger its future.

The effort is not helped by the fact that our economic counters are not only not adapted to express the value of nature's systems, they are perversely set to count destruction as gain and preservation as loss. The forest intact and standing, for instance, presently enters economic calculation only as unrealized ("underperforming") assets, even as it performs extensive services for human life and economy. Uncut and otherwise unexploited for "economic" value, it provides habitat for pollinators, birds and animals; by sheltering biodiversity, it serves as a reservoir of potential lifesaving pharmaceuticals; its roots and canopy control floods, buffer wind, and preserve the soil from erosion, thereby preserving the fertility of the soil and saving the fish-bearing streams from silting. It preserves, simultaneously, the productivity of soil, stream, and the vast web of life of an intact ecosystem (ask the Army Corps of Engineers what it costs to restore *that*, after the forests are gone – if it can be done at all); its leaves absorb and filter pollutants from nearby industrial areas; and through its photosynthetic activity, it manufactures oxygen for us to breathe and locks up carbon, preventing further warming of the globe. How much would we be willing to pay for all this – or just, for instance, for the oxygen alone, if we could not get it from the forest? The amount rises into the billions very quickly. But how does that forest look on the balance sheet? Like a tax burden. When we start to destroy it, decreasing the real net worth of the forest's services to us, the destruction does not show up on the negative side; on the contrary, everything suddenly looks economically positive. The salaries of the woodcutters, the profits of the companies who supplied the chainsaws and bulldozers, the profits of the lumber company selling logs for housing, furniture, pulp, or just for storage at the bottom of Japanese lakes, the profits of the construction industry, the furniture retailers, the paper companies, all figure in the gross domestic product (GDP). The forest does not. Further, when the paper company kills all the fish in the river with its wastes, no value at all is attached to the uncaught fish and the ecosystem that supported them. But when the federal government mandates a cleanup, all the wages and machines that go into the cleanup are part of the GDP, as are the landfill expenses for the unrecycled furniture scraps and the carting expenses for the mountains of paper we use. Yet those efforts result in no useful product whatsoever, except a partial restoration of what was there before, the economic value of which, we recall, was reckoned as nothing. Since the value was nothing, the cost of the depletion – the loss of the forest's services – is counted as nothing. Janet Abramowitz's favorite example: "the damage from a massive oil spill is not subtracted from a nation's GDP, but the amounts spent on cleanup and health impacts are counted as additions to the national economy."[4] It is time to learn better accounting.

The attempt to account for "natural capital," and calculate the value of nature's services, rests on the recognition that intact habitat worldwide (forests, coastal wetlands, prairie) is often more valuable to us than the products (like timber) or productive uses (fields, fish farms) into which it could be converted. Wild habitat may, like the forest, pay its own bills.[5] Examples abound. Famously, New York City, by investing in upstate real estate to surround its water supply, saves itself the $6 billion filtration plant that would be necessary otherwise to ensure the integrity of its water supply, which is one of the best in the country. (Or up to $7 billion; all writers use this example, and estimates vary.)

But the services listed above are worth much more than that. Medicines from natural wild products are worth about $40 billion a year worldwide; 25 percent of prescription medicines contain substances from wild plants. "Biodiversity prospecting," searching the rainforest for new pharmaceutically useful substances and species, has been advanced as one commercial reason to protect the tropical rainforests. (It would be nice to share that bounty with the indigenous peoples, but that is another problem.) Harvested wild goods, products that would disappear if the wild areas were converted to lumber or farmland, play enormous roles in local economies and households over much of the developing world. Mangroves and other coastal wetlands are crucial nurseries for commercial fisheries, worth much more than the suburban developments or shrimp farms contemplated for their locations. Eighty percent of the world's cultivated crops depend on wild and semi-wild pollinators, not only the carefully hived honeybees but all their wild relatives – not to mention the bats. Consider, in this context, the chemical pesticides we poured on our crops to increase productivity in the 1950s and beyond: they tended to hurt the more sensitive pollinators, specialized for the crops they serviced, more than the tougher and more adaptable targeted insect pests. They also decimated the predators that ate the pests, including many birds, whose evolutionary mechanisms for adapting to environmental threats like pesticides are much slower than the insects. (The farmers might consider leaving the insect control to nature. Bat colonies in Texas can eat 250 tons of insects each night. Many types of birds eat the leaf-eating insects that destroy the crops.[6]) Consider the frogs of Bangladesh: seeking new Western markets, Bangladesh exported untold quantities of frogs' legs in the 1970s and 1980s. Agricultural pests exploded; pesticide imports went up 25 percent. "By 1989, Bangladesh was spending three times as much each year on pesticides – $30 million – as it was earning from exporting frogs' legs."[7] When they stopped the trade, frogs rebounded, and the pesticide bill dropped.

Anecdotes do not make a method. "Replacement costs," like calculating the cost of preserving land in the New York City watershed versus building a filtration plant, make for dramatic comparisons, but do not give us a method. "Avoidance costs" estimate how much it would cost us if those services had to be purchased. But the value of natural pest control, as stated above, pollination, flood control, soil fertilization, and water filtration are very difficult to count, since actual expenditures are avoided completely, not even hypothetically measurable, if the natural ecological services are intact and working properly. Photosynthesis would be impossible to replace. So we simply have to estimate what we would do if suddenly the service failed. Could this kind of contingency be gamed on computers? The only other measure we have is from the realtors: How much could farmers get for their farmland if they sold it for development as a suburban subdivision? But that, of course, is part of the problem, not part of the solution.

Possibly the greatest service nature provides is its resilience. Our world is full of shocks, storms, emergent diseases, volcanoes, and uncontrollable fires. Nature, rich with the possibilities of biodiversity, generally responds quickly and innovatively, to colonize the devastated area, bring back life, and stabilize the soil. The regeneration of the original will take time, but it will happen. The insect blights that most trouble us – the gypsy moths, tent caterpillars, even locusts – generally only have a year or two to wreak their devastation in any given locality. After that some novel microorganism infects the attackers, or birds from the next state find them. Those two years are not time enough to hurt mature trees, and the ecosystem will recover. The most important demonstration of resilience is in episodes of epidemic disease. When one species is struck by a blight of any kind, members of the same genus are available to help reconstitute the damaged population, spread genetic protections (often one allied species will have the gene that confers immunity to the disease), and confer desirable characteristics. Farmers know this: that is why the wild landraces of cultivated crops are maintained wherever possible.

What is all this worth? How do we measure the worth of the resilience of a genus? Between 1949 and 1970, China lost 90 percent of its varieties of wheat in the interests of "more efficient" mono-cultures. Indonesia lost 1,500 local rice varieties in the last 20 years. The United States at the beginning of the twentieth century grew nine times the varieties of fruits and vegetables that are now available on the market. This standardization is typical of contemporary agri-culture, but alarmingly wasteful of biodiversity, one of our greatest natural assets – if one species fails, there have always been several to take its place. We are putting too many eggs in one basket.

The awareness of natural capital, its value and its fragility, is a necessary precondition for designing environmentally friendly busi-ness policy (or business friendly environmental policy). At this point, we should be able to sketch out some steps that may be respectful of nature while not hurting the objectives of business.

⊛ CORPORATE DISCERNMENT ⊛ (OF GREEN IMPERATIVES): SEVEN EASY STEPS

It looks, pardon the metaphor, like a military problem. The land-scape across which we advance our troops has changed its character over the last several decades, and continues to change now. Let us sum up: In the 1950s, the business community would have assumed that in pursuit of the goal of profits, they must avoid, as much as possible, the law (if they could not persuade their friends in the legislature to write it to their prescription), maneuver cleverly through the minefield of ethics, and pass unnoticed in the night beneath the thinly manned battlements of environmental protectors. The 1960s and (especially) the post-Watergate enforcement practices of the 1970s taught a humbler respect for the law: there is no motivation for good citizenship stronger than a visit to a friend in federal prison.

In the late 1970s and early 1980s, the rules of deployment changed again, as the basic tenets of the new field of business ethics became institutionalized. New rules of transparency minimized the possibility of getting through the minefield unscathed. But the result of the new "social contract," the new understanding of how corporations would conduct their business in the larger society, was not at all bad for business. The new "stakeholder" approach to business decision making (originated by R. Edward Freeman et al. at the University of Virginia in the 1980s), which requires that the interests of all with a stake in the outcome be considered in any business decision, turned out not only to avoid certain predictable kinds of trouble from the community – punitive legislation or zoning law, hostile investigations, a bad image for the product – but also to forge partnerships that could lead to new products and new markets. (It must be admitted that even the relatively conservative stakeholder approach is still a minority opinion in many business schools!) In the last quarter of the twentieth century American companies came to realize that values-driven business had strong profit potential, and was worth pursuing for its own sake. The military metaphor was overcome, replaced by a metaphor of cooperation. (The bibliography for this chapter contains a sampling of the literature on this point.)

Now the countryside has changed again, and new strategy is required. The battlements of environmental protection are very well manned indeed, and they have searchlights. The laws protecting the environment, as we saw in the last chapter, have changed only incrementally since the early 1970s, and their interpretation and enforcement follows, like the Supreme Court, the election returns. The price of at least some protection, however, is unclarity and uncertainty. The higher ethical standard of environmental protection is the more worrisome because the science underlying environmental restrictions is often uncertain, the degree of protection demanded is often unclear, and it is enforced, often as not, by self-selected groups that work outside of the accepted political and legal mechanisms (see Chapter 7 on "civil society": the civil society organizations [CSOs], or nongovernmental organizations [NGOs]). Some of the exhausting struggles that companies have experienced with public attacks on environmental grounds are mentioned in this book; there is a large bibliography on the others, for those who would pursue it. Yet there is a good deal of hope amid the questions. US firms face an environmental crisis – a turning point, in which the old ways can no longer be pursued, but in which new ways, uncertain as they are, may prove very profitable. The philosophers remind us that the Chinese character for "crisis" is comprised of two signs, one meaning "danger" and the other meaning "opportunity." Making our way through the new countryside will require a high degree of alertness to both of these. It is not too soon to suggest that we move beyond the metaphor again, and see what "Green strategies" can be most helpful to US business.

The literature on environmental strategy is already launched. My approach in this chapter does not appear elsewhere, but I have borrowed from the best of the work that I have found, primarily *Environmentalism and the New Logic of Business* by Edward Freeman and others, also *Natural Capitalism* by Paul Hawken and Amory and Hunter Lovins, *The Natural Step* by Brian Nattrass and Mary Altomare, and *Cannibals With Forks* (an explanation of the title would take much too long) by John Elkington.[8] We all share one conclusion: the company that pays attention to the Green imperative, the protection of the immediate natural environment and the long-term sustainability of its activities, secures for itself a strong competitive advantage over companies that do not, and positions itself for a century and more of corporate growth.

There is a widely accepted set of measures that will improve competitiveness through Green strategy, which are easy to remember: they follow the acronym **DISCERN**. The Seven Easy Steps to greater competitiveness are Definition (describe carefully your environmental dilemmas), Information (get the facts, the data you need to solve them), Stakeholders (identify the parties whose interests had best be consulted in any decision), compliance (make sure that you are in line with environmental law and regulation), Energy (see where efficiencies can be realized by saving or recycling energy), Resources (see where you can save or recycle the materials that you use), and Niches (see where your products and services can be marketed to environmental niches). At somewhat greater length:

Any strategy requires, first and foremost, a **definition** and prioritization of the dilemmas facing the strategist with regard to the environment. The negative dilemmas – "dangers" – are often, unfortunately, the most immediate: Does this business operation cause harm to the environment that is not acceptable in the current legal and social climate? Does the company have on its premises any waste collection site that may, in some way, affect the health of the neighbors? Do accidents involving the company's products threaten life or health, for humans or others, where they occur, and are they happening too often? Are there waste products discharged from one of the company's factories into the environment that may cause harm to human health or to the health of any species (some of which might be protected by law) in the ecosystem, or to the functioning of the system itself? Do the firm's activities threaten the habitat of any species, or the existence of valued wild land? Whether or not strictly covered by law, these conditions will have to be addressed immediately. After that, the positive dilemmas – "opportunities" – can be considered. The activity of definition should give the decision makers at least a preliminary purchase on the problems and the directions that have to be explored.

The definitional process should also indicate the **information** that needs to be gathered before any action can be taken. The facts should include a reasonably sophisticated appreciation of the ecosystems in question, at least to determine their carrying capacity for the burdens, if any, that are being placed upon them. They should include an understanding of the human ecology of the regions impacted by the firm – for instance, lightly or heavily settled, organized into self-protective organizations or not. The legal department will already have conducted a survey of the history of interpretation of applicable law. The whole process of the activity of the firm, from suppliers twice removed to the ultimate disposal of the product, should be known, for every bit of it will come under scrutiny in the course of the implementation of this strategy. The gathering of information at this point is preliminary. At each stage of the entire journey to environmental stewardship, more information will become useful. But it is important to start.

As is now routine in all analyses of paths to the "triple bottom line" of economics (profits), ethics, and the environment, the third step requires that the firm identify all **stakeholders** in its activities. Stakeholders on the most basic analysis consist of all those affected by the firm's operations, starting with shareholders, employees, and ultimate customers, then extending to suppliers, retailers, and communities. The effect of the firm's actions on the natural environment is included, at this stage, only insofar as other humans are impacted, in health, recreational opportunities, or simple enjoyment of the landscape. Other approaches include at this stage of analysis all those whose actions affect the firm as well as those affected, essentially including all "external factors" with which a firm may have to deal or must take into account. Many of the same parties show up in this list, of course, but some new ones are added – legislators, the media, and any NGOs interested in the company's operations.

These preliminary surveys concluded, the next step, taken in consultation with the legal department, is to ensure that the company is in **compliance** with all applicable law. This step corresponds with Freeman's first "shade of green": *light*, or *legal*, green.[9] The importance of compliance is not seriously debated any more. To be sure, not every regulation can be 100 percent enforced all the time, no matter how regulation-minded the government in power. Like the tax laws and most of the others, law requires a large degree of voluntary compliance. Most of us want to be good citizens, which is fortunate; the day that that is no longer true will be the last day anyone will want to be in business. For a more immediate confirmation of the wisdom of obedience to law, it can be pointed out *first*, that whatever the odds of getting caught, the stakes are too high to trifle with – not just the fines, but the public pillorying that follows an unfavorable verdict can hurt the company's image and profits very seriously. *Second*, the odds of prosecution may be greater than they appear when an anti-regulatory administration is in office (recall that anti-regulatory administrations are usually followed by pro-regulatory administrations with long memories). Further, citizen organizations are perfectly capable of hiring their own biologists to measure environmental damage, and of bringing action against a firm through the civil courts or the media. And *third*, where a judicial verdict happens, civil suits are sure to follow, and the financial damage can get very much worse. But the effect of regulation, even that passed with hostile intent toward the industry, need not be all bad. As Edward Freeman has pointed out, regulation can be a marvelous spur for innovation, which in turn can result in substantial savings for the firm.

So far, the steps toward a more competitive company taken in the environmental path do not differ from any other set of suggestions for a profitable firm: the first two simply require that the company's decision makers understand how the firm works and what problems it faces, the second two ask only that the firm undertake minimal commitments to the law of the land and to those downstream of its work. The next three steps urge the company to become more competitive, through cutting costs and through discovering new markets.

Cutting back on the consumption of (conventional) **energy** is one of the most significant cost-cutting measures a company can undertake. *Natural Capitalism*, following the work of pioneering architect William McDonough, suggests that buildings can be designed to consume almost no energy, simply by good passive solar design (making sure you have sun where you need it and not where you do not) and excellent insulation. A good example is the headquarters of Rocky Mountain Institute, headed up by the Lovins, which maintains comfortable temperatures with the help of two wood stoves alone (no furnace) in a part of the world that regularly hits −47 degrees in winter. It does it with passive solar design, a few photovoltaic (PV) panels, very tight insulation, and well-made windows. Well short of that standard, a company's use of energy can be made much more efficient by careful attention to heat loss from all buildings. We cannot recycle all the energy used in heating buildings (that damnable second law of thermodynamics), but we can collect the heat produced by the manufacturing process, computers, lights, and other machines to help heat the building. We can use fluorescent and other low-energy lighting, and energy-saving appliances generally. Solar panels for the roof in some areas promise to repay the cost of purchase and installation in several years (depending on area and latitude). Academic sources are already talking about the "Negawatt Revolution," or "demand-side management," in which innovative utility companies reward customers for using energy-efficient lights and appliances. They also supply facility energy audits, and lower rates to households or industries meeting energy-efficient standards. (State encouragement is required for these policies, since the major gain for the public is realized in new power plants that do not have to be built, which does not benefit current shareholders.)[10]

Among the famous tales of cost-lowering environmental measures is 3M's success with its Preventing Pollution Pays (3P) program.[11] 3M was really just engaging in good process stewardship, making sure that every bit of material that came into its plants was fully used in its commercial activity. The general objective, that encompasses 3P and all other initiatives to lower the outflow of waste by making sure that all products are used efficiently, is **resource productivity**, and it guarantees more profitable operations not only by staying on the right side of environmental enforcement and public vigilance on the subject of emissions, but by cutting down on the amount of raw materials that are needed to do the same job. Incidentally, in both reduction of energy use and more efficient use of resources, a bonus system for rewarding employee suggestions often results in savings undreamed of by management.

Beyond the cost-cutting measures of energy and resource conservation, the adoption of environmental values allows product innovations to take advantage of societal perceptions of the value of preserving nature. The discovery of environmentally branded **niche marketing** by the Body Shop (soaps, cosmetics, and personal items made from materials from the rainforest), and by Ben & Jerry's (Rainforest Crunch ice cream, made from cashews and Brazil nuts gathered by cooperatives of indigenous peoples in the Amazonian rainforest), has been followed by a large variety of firms. (This step corresponds to Freeman's second shade of green, "market green.") It is now possible to buy "Fair Trade" goods, notably coffee grown in the shade to preserve mountainsides and paying a fair wage to the people who harvest it. An increasing presence in our supermarkets are the products of the entire organic food industry (the most rapidly growing sector of the agricultural market). Consumers often respond to programs that reduce packaging, or make it recyclable, and to programs that invite the consumer to return products (especially computers) for up-to-date replacements.

All seven steps have one attribute in common: they save money and they cost virtually nothing. Even energy and resource conservation, which may require significant re-engineering at the beginning, pay back completely, and then keep paying. All of them, then, are worth doing based on profit-maximization alone; environmental values may drive them, but are not required. Only the fourth (compliance) needs environmental laws to make sense; only the seventh (niche marketing) requires that customers have any sense of the environment at all. These, then, are the no-brainers, the first result of corporate discernment of environmental impacts and requirements. As above, they are easy to remember:

Definition
Information
Stakeholders
Compliance
Energy reduction
Resource conservation
Niche marketing.

We will refer to this process in the parts that follow as **DISCERN**, the approach for the first part of greening a company.

✲ THE NEXT SEVEN STEPS ✲

The last section described the easy part: essentially making the company more competitive by making it more efficient and by taking into account the power of environmental sentiment in selecting marketing strategies. This section describes the next generation's Seven Steps.

Where will the company be at the end of the twenty-first century? American business is notorious for thinking only up to the next quarter, but the future belongs to the companies with vision, who plan now to position themselves for the next 90 years. In that time, energy sources will be lower and more costly (economically or politically); natural capital will be harder to command, and increased popular awareness of environmental stresses will express itself through public (legislative and regulatory) and private (consumer) preferences. Not until that time will the wisdom of frankly environmental additional measures be seen. Yet they should be started now. There is probably an entire alphabet of these more innovative measures, but for now we will confine ourselves to the first seven letters, A, B, C, D, E, F, and G.

First, **alternative energies** for the long term. Included in the Seven Easy Steps above is the suggestion that any company, by use of simple conservation measures like superinsulation and recycling heat, may lower its use of energy, to cut costs and save the environment. All this is well proved. But in the long run, slowing down our use of fossil fuels will not attain the savings the company might want: as the economy expands, even more efficient plants will consume more oil than we can afford, economically or politically. Several long-range strategies are worth thinking about now; the most important of these are *wind power, solar energy*, and *hydrogen cells*.

Wind: Windmills, reminiscent of the Dutch landscape of a few centuries ago except uglier and noisier, had a small following in the US during the twentieth century. With improved technology making quieter, more attractive, and more powerful machines (able to turn out energy in light wind and not stressed beyond capacity in heavy wind), wind "farms," massive plantations of wind turbines, are already economical in Europe. Denmark now gets 15 percent of all its energy from wind turbines, and in parts of northern Germany, 75 percent of the power comes from wind. The prospects look good for expansion in the United States. The proposed farms are not without problems; the Cape Wind proposal, for example, to put a wind farm in Nantucket Sound, which separates Cape Cod from Martha's Vineyard and Nantucket, ran into huge opposition from the neighbors, all those who own property commanding the view. (To the great amusement of the environmental community of the Atlantic Coast, those opposed included environmentalists Robert Kennedy Jr and Walter Cronkite, whose families own property in the area.)[12] As we write, MidAmerican Energy Company, one of Warren Buffett's holdings, has completed plans to build a 310-megawatt (MW) wind farm on 200 acres of farmland in Iowa; it will be the world's largest.[13]

Solar: For years we have expected solar energy to displace oil fuel, and have been disappointed. The disappointment is proportionate to the expectations, perhaps; since there is so much sun, we really expected that all our energy needs could be met effortlessly. Realistically, the prospects are cautiously encouraging. The technology is available to attain enormous savings now, and it is improving; new solar panels can be built into the glass walls of skyscrapers, resulting in a building that can not only supply all its own energy but also feed a large grid. Immediate savings in the use of fossil fuels could be gained simply by plastering our rooftops across the nation with PV cells, now conveniently available as shingles. The PV cells still cost a great deal, in money and resources, to manufacture, but technological advance in PV chemistry should make them more efficient in the near future, and competition should drive down the cost of manufacture. Both trends hold out hope of making solar energy a significant player in the energy game.

Prospects for the growth of these and other alternative energy strategies should not end efforts at conservation. Of course we should conserve energy now. But we must also begin now to invest in the long term, in which independence from oil imports will have become a political necessity and burning coal will be outlawed for health reasons. Geothermal, tidal, and limited hydroelectric sources will help to complete the energy picture. But wind and solar energy are available now and should be part of every re-engineering or expansion plan.[14]

Hydrogen: Hydrogen cells have been announced as the energy source of the future – a clean, abundant source of energy for everything from heating buildings to running our cars. At present, the promise of the hydrogen cell is limited because the only practical way to get the hydrogen is by breaking down petrochemicals. But suppose that skyscraper in the solar energy paragraph had an electrolysis plant in its cellar, so that the extra electrical energy pouring through the building during the day could be used to break up water into oxygen and hydrogen, pack them both in convenient cells, ship the oxygen to hospitals and the hydrogen to fueling stations (bringing back empty containers on the return trip)? In such arrangements we may be able to realize the long-deferred promise of alternative energy production.

Alternative energy is no longer the property of utopian dreamers. In a section of its issue of December 15, 2003, dedicated to "Tech Pioneers," *Time* magazine featured several entrepreneurs heading out into the alternative energy market with every expectation of making a lot of money. Robert Lifton of Medis Technologies, also new enterprises Hydrogenics and Nanosys, are tapping the power of fuel cells and solar panels (which have come a long way technologically since we saw them last) to provide portable energy systems that can serve areas hit by blackouts. Fuel cells are running buses in Tokyo, in nine European cities, and Iceland, which intends to be fossil-fuel-free by 2030.[15] Already they can be miniaturized to be marketed in small "power packs," perfect for recharging the personal digital assistants (PDAs), cell phones, and laptops we insist on carrying with us at all times. Hydrogenics is working on a fuel cell for a new generation of military vehicles, including tanks; both General Motors and Deere are working on hydrogen-powered vehicles. Nanosys is embedding tiny solar cells in sheets of plastic that can be laid over roofs and are easily affordable. All these companies are aware that new technology is not accepted overnight, and that more structural adjustments (inventing the hydrogen filling station, for instance) will be necessary. But the financial backing is there, and they confidently expect to be the leading corporations in the next generation of consumers.

Biomimicry: Nature can be our surest source of innovation. The first bacteria showed up on earth about 3.8 billion years ago, and life has been discovering ways of adapting to this earth (and other life) ever since. What can other life forms teach us? It should be noted that respectful imitation of nature is a radical departure from the usual human attitude of domination and improvement. In "biomimicry,"[16] we look to see not what we can extract from nature, but what we can learn. It is a new approach. Nature manages to manufacture totally biodegradable fibers, foods, and shelters; we ought to be able to do the same. We should model our solar cells on the green leaves, our fiber manufacture on the spider (whose webs are, ounce for ounce, stronger than Kevlar, the strongest material we know how to make. If the spiders can make the strongest substance on earth at room temperature on the strength of a few chewed-up flies and crickets, why cannot we?), our protective materials on the oyster or abalone, our food grains on the renewable and pest-proof prairie, and above all, we should manufacture nothing that cannot, when it is no longer useful, be turned into the raw material for something else. In general, we may ask: If we are trying to develop a product, is there a similar product in nature that we may use or imitate? Also for services: If we want to filter toxins or generally clean up an area, can we use planted wetlands to accomplish the task? Can we grow our food without plowing and weeding (or using herbicides or pesticides) by studying the land from which the ancestors of our plants came? The possibilities are legion. For any problem we have, let us see how nature solves it.

Credit transfers: If we can harness natural services to make industry more environmentally friendly, can we harness the market to the same end? The verdict is mixed. It has been proposed that we can use market forces to (for example) reduce pollution, by creating a market for "pollution credits," based on the current and expected levels of pollution within any industry. On the hypothesized market, a company that decided to invest in pollution-control technology (for example) might quickly recoup its investment by selling permissions to pollute a certain amount (so many tons over such a period of time) to its competitors who had not made the investment. If a power company managed to save enormous amounts of energy by conservation and other economies so that it did not need to build another proposed plant, thereby saving tons of pollution, it would be rewarded by allowances to sell permissions for all the pollution it was not producing by not building the plant.

Such systems are easily implemented, and in some places are in force. Are they a good idea? On the one hand, there are some incentives to reduce pollution, and any reduction is good for the environment. But on the other hand, the system is badly flawed simply because it is so terribly easy to game. For instance, energy companies can make veritable windfalls of profit simply by pleading for permission to build another power plant, and when permission is granted, decide not to build it but sell all its pollution credits. (Many other games are possible.) Further, the system is subject to the primary objection that it is not halting the pollution – it only makes it profitable to make small reductions in the pollution, and that is not the job of government. The credit regimes should be retained as a possibility, if only to lower the net burden of pollution and resource abuse prior to more complete solutions becoming practical.

Downsizing the technology (not the workforce): This step requires some radical rethinking, and some very far-reaching legal/tax encouragement to maintain competitiveness in the companies that adopt it. But it follows logically from the situation as we have described it so far, so it is worth exploring. Start with the history: When our notion of "productivity" was developed, we had more natural resources than we knew what to do with, and too few people. It made sense to develop machines and methods that helped few people do a lot of work. Getting more done with fewer people became the definition of "productivity." Now we have few resources and too many people unemployed. It makes sense to revise our technology to get full employment, substituting people for natural resources, to produce the same product with more people and fewer resources. For instance, cut the tree with an axe and with saws, not a bulldozer-like monster that destroys the fiber of the trees and most of the land around it, operated by one person. That will employ more people to get the same amount of lumber at a time when we are trying to cut down on lumber cutting. The low-technology cutting will also destroy less of the surrounding ecosystem. For another example, the fisheries. If we can restrict the size of the boats, we can employ all the fishermen. We do not have to go back to the sailing schooners (although a sizeable tourist industry lurks in that possibility). But there are many smaller boats that are entirely capable of supporting a few families for the whole year. In combination with the formation of ocean refuges (areas for breeding, temporarily or permanently off limits to fishers), we should be able to keep fishing for generations. The key to this step is to substitute resource productivity for human productivity – to employ the humans, and to reduce the use of natural resources.

Ecotourism: In ecotourism, we find an industry that had no existence 50 years ago, no definition 20 years ago, and is now perhaps the fastest growing industry in the world. People have always been willing to pay for the privilege of enjoyment of places and objects of great value; consider the number of thriving art museums in the world. Traveling to see a wilderness – a rainforest, a tundra (the Arctic National Wildlife Preserve), a redwood forest, even an undersea coral reef – is merely an extension of tourism near and far. Why is it growing so fast? The first objective of environmentalism is teaching the value of nature, for reasons that have little to do with tourism and everything to do with motivating conservation. A corollary of that motivation is the willingness to appreciate nature on nature's own terms; an emerging environmental generation will value wilderness and intact ecosystems generally, and will pay to visit and appreciate them. The enormous benefit of ecotourism for the global environment is that it provides alternative, and very profitable, employment for developing nations that had been confined to environmentally destructive monoculture agriculture.

Farming for the community: Since we are in the mode of radical rethinking, let us consider reconstructing agriculture. City planners have urged for half a century that the pattern of urban/suburban development (or "sprawl") should be changed. Their suggestions, while radical considering our present patterns, deserve consideration. In the community planner's dreams, a tight urban core, to which private motor vehicles would have very limited access, should be surrounded by a broad belt, many miles, of farms. The "suburbs," actually towns and small cities in their own right, should lie beyond that belt. The farms would grow vegetables for the city (although probably not wheat for the city's bread), supply some dairy products, and take in students – city children to spend a semester in the country, learning that food does not grow on supermarket shelves. The farm belt would serve several purposes: to supply fresh local food to areas that do not have it now, to clean the air of the city, to provide esthetic relief from the endless strip malls on the roads leading in and out of the city, and to serve as a regional educational resource. Community Supported Agriculture (CSA) is one movement that thoroughly integrates the agricultural, ecological, and educational goals suggested; it may be the wave of the future.

Green scissors: A creative organization called "Green Scissors" takes aim at the laws that enable the destruction of the land. Chapter 4's assumption that law and regulation inevitably hurt industry to preserve the environment turns out to be wrong; many laws hurt the public, hurt business, and hurt the land all at once. Appropriate targeting of these bad laws can attack the boondoggles of big government, save money, and save the land. One of the more useful paths that the business community can take (harnessing a ready suspicion of government initiatives generally) is to work for changes in laws impacting the environment, to make them more efficient and better adapted to the ends of rewarding efficient and competitive business, saving the green heritage of the United States and saving the tax-payers money all at the same time. Some examples of laws that could use changing, for all reasons:

- The 1872 Mining Law, which permits private companies (many of them not based in the US) to take minerals from the land in US at virtually no cost in royalties, and with no responsibility to clean up the mess. Since they can extract indefinitely with no responsibilities, they never develop the efficiencies of reducing throughput in their operations, and incur enormous amounts of waste. If we made them clean up the mess, that would save the taxpayers between $32 billion and $72 billion per site. If we charged reasonable royalties, or purchase prices for the public lands, that would bring in $519 million per year to the public till.

- The Petroleum Research and Development Program, which does nothing but subsidize research on oil extraction for the big companies. Oil extraction, transportation, and use is an enormous environmental liability, and it is not oriented to the future we will face, which includes greatly reduced use of fossil fuels. Forcing the big oil companies to fund their own research would save $280 million per year.

- Timber Roads Construction: Believe it or not, the US Forest Service actually pays for the construction of the roads that the logging companies use to denude the National Forests. The roads contribute to habitat destruction for bear and elk, and cause erosion and mudslides. This can be stopped; cutting back on roads and subsidies would save taxpayers $311.5 million over five years. Further, it would benefit the lumber companies. They will not build roads unless they intend to use them in the immediate future, so the policy, by reducing the number of roads, will decrease the mudslides that undermine the health of the young trees. The forest will last longer and produce more profits for all its users.

- Then there is the "pork," the special projects to reward special legislators with something for the folks at home, economic benefits that always include jobs. There is no need, for instance, to expand the Savannah Harbor in Georgia; we have enough deepwater ports in the area, and dredging will destroy the freshwater wetlands in the region. We could save $230 million by canceling this project.

- The US Army Corps of Engineers likes to dump sand to "save" popular beaches in fragile areas subject to normal sand flow; they damage the coastal environment and do absolutely no good, since the sand flows around their efforts every time. Meanwhile, the dumping smothers turtle eggs laid along the shore. Canceling this activity would save the turtles and save $3 billion over the next several decades.
- The Corps also wants to pump White River water in a grand irrigation project for rice farmers. What part of the Corps' mission is this? The rice should not be artificially irrigated – it is wrecking the aquifers from which they draw. The subsidies allow the rice farmers to compete successfully with many of the poorest farmers in the world, who cannot participate in global markets because of the subsidized agricultural products from the United States. The subsidies are unfair, and the water should not be used for this purpose; the pumping will damage two national wildlife refuges and harm the ducks which need the river's water. Killing the project would save $319 million.

CONCLUSION

Look to the perspectives on the environment we outlined in Chapter 3. Where is the visionary company on that spectrum of attitudes? It sees past the immediate advantages of wise use of resources – waste not, want not, Gifford Pinchot's original Wise-Use strategy – to the coming restructuring of business enterprise in accordance with the limits presented by the natural world, visible now to those who are paying attention. The endowment represented by nature has been given to us – we inherit it from our parents and hold it in trust for our children – and we are responsible for the stewardship of trillions of dollars of natural resources. When the century closes, we will all be preservationists, whatever other courses the environmental debates have taken.

CASE 5: BEN & JERRY'S[17]

Many companies have attempted "Green strategies" since Earth Day in 1970. Among the most successful, besides those mentioned above, was a small ice cream store-become-MNC, called Ben & Jerry's. Ben & Jerry's was founded in 1978 by Ben Cohen and Jerry Greenfield, childhood friends who thought it would be fun to found a company together. They wanted to start it in Burlington, Vermont, a college town, so considered a pizzeria for their business; when they discovered that Burlington was overstocked with pizza establishments, they decided on homemade ice cream. They set up shop in a reconditioned garage, took a $5 correspondence course on making ice cream from Penn State, and set up shop with a $12,000 investment ($4,000 of which was borrowed). The ice cream was delicious, and they came up with one headline-grabbing publicity initiative after another – free movies, annual free-scoop day, a 14-ton ice cream sundae constructed in St Albans. Five years after starting up, they had multiple franchises and a nationwide marketing scheme. Alarmed by their rapid advance into the Boston market, competitor Häagen-Dasz (H-D) attempted to limit penetration by exclusive contracts; Ben & Jerry's promptly organized a popular campaign, T-shirts and all, to go after H-D's parent company Pillsbury: "What's the Doughboy afraid of?" Graced with an intuitive understanding of effective images – Ben & Jerry's played to the hilt the part of the valiant upstart, and Pillsbury really did not want the public reminded that its elegant-sounding gourmet ice cream was owned by a flour company with a fat little cartoon chef as its logo – Ben & Jerry's won hands down. That year their sales topped $4 million.

In 1984 the company went public, at first only in Vermont. By 1985 they had set up the Ben & Jerry's Foundation, giving it a steady 7.5 percent of sales to fund community-oriented projects. In 1988 they extended the initiative to encourage the United States to spend 1 percent of the defense budget for peace projects, later broadened to include all business and social responsibility; they won the Corporate Giving Award from the Council on Economic Priorities, were named Small Businessmen of the Year by President Reagan, and sponsored the Newport Folk Festival. By now they had 80 stores nationwide and $47 million in sales. In the next year they instituted two of their most famous environmentally oriented policies, announcing that they would buy milk only from cows that had not been given recombinant Bovine Growth Hormone (rBGH), and creating a new flavor of ice cream that drew specifically on products of the Amazon rainforest gathered by indigenous peoples. In 1990 they brought out a new flavor incorporating brownies in the ice cream; the brownies were all bought from Greyston bakery in the Bronx, which employs disadvantaged people from its poorer neighborhoods. Other campaigns that year opposed the Seabrook nuclear power plant and asked for help to support the family farm. To illustrate the point, in the next year they paid a dairy premium of half a million dollars to the small farmers that supply the milk for their ice cream. In 1991 they sponsored a bus tour powered in part by solar energy, held Peace and Crafts festivals in Vermont, Chicago, and San Francisco, and sold $97 million of ice cream. By 1992 they were opening facilities in Russia and spearheading a Children's Needs campaign to get Congress to address particular problems plaguing kids. The millionth visitor toured their factory, and they brought in $132 million in sales.

By 1995 they had brought in a new CEO (after a search including a public contest that drew 22,000 applications), they were selling ice cream in the United Kingdom and in France, soon to be followed by the Benelux countries. Two years later another CEO (different talents) got them into more markets, the two founders crisscrossed the country signing copies of their account of the company (*Ben & Jerry's Double-Dip: How to Run a Values-Led Business and Make Money, Too*) and they won a lawsuit that guaranteed their right to publish on their packaging the fact that the milk they used was free of rBGH. Their new flavor for that year was Phish Food, honoring Phish, the social activist musical group. That year they teamed up with Yahoo!, the search engine company, to promote computer literacy for children. Sales were pushing $175 million. By 1998 they had extended operations to Japan, made a movie about good government for public television, and instituted the practice of using only unbleached paperboard for their ice cream cartons, eliminating a manufacturing process that contributes widely to water pollution. Sales that year were over $200 million. By 1999 they had stores open in Japan, were supporting the YMCA in its efforts to house the homeless, were widely recognized, specifically scoring in the top five in the Harris Interactive poll of corporate reputability, were known as one of the "best companies" in the country, and ranked first in the "social responsibility" category, with 390 million mentions in the media – Ben & Jerry's is by now a household word, standing not only for very good ice cream but for social responsibility in all respects, especially as it affects children and communities, and for the protection of the natural environment. The penchants for wild and weird publicity things continues on, with hot-air balloons, toe-wrestling contests, and flavors honoring TV shows like Seinfeld, while they raise money for local charities across the country and to protect the environment: they donate a portion from the sale of every pint of One Sweet Whirled to research in energy conservation.

Is there a pattern here? From the beginning, Ben & Jerry's was a "value-led business," doing always what they thought was the right thing for the community, the poor, and increasingly, for the preservation of the environment. But they never stopped innovating, they introduced new flavors every year, they modified packaging to make the brand more visible as patterns of preference changed, they introduced yogurt before their competitors, they introduced low-fat products when it was clear that there was a demand for them, followed by low-carb products when Atkins diets became popular, they never overlooked a possibility for profitable expansion, and they ran a very tight and efficient business. They did not hesitate with in-your-face (or possibly, in your pudgy belly) attack campaigns when competitors tried to exclude them from markets; they launched and won lawsuits on occasion. They were good and versatile businessmen. But they found ways to make sure that in the course of doing business, they served the public good and had fun doing it. Can it be that hard?

A cold shiver went up the backs of their large following, and of those interested in corporate social responsibility generally, when Unilever, an Anglo-Dutch conglomerate, launched a takeover attempt for Ben & Jerry's. The only way a takeover attempt on a publicly traded company can be ultimately halted is by a huge infusion of capital – which the target company almost never has. Unilever got the company. But there could be no doubt that a large part of the value of Ben & Jerry's was in the associations with the brand – environmental and corporate social responsibility. The acquirer would not want to risk losing that. So on April 12, 2000, when the deal went down, there were some very special provisions for the management of the company:

> Ben & Jerry's Board of Directors approve Unilever's offer of $326 million ($43.60 per share, for 8.4 million outstanding shares), as well as a unique agreement enabling Ben & Jerry's to join forces with Unilever to create an even more dynamic, socially positive ice cream business with a much more global reach. Under the terms of the agreement, Ben & Jerry's will operate separately from Unilever's current U.S. ice cream business, with an independent Board of Directors to provide leadership for Ben & Jerry's social mission & brand integrity.[18]

There are no guarantees in the corporate world; but the mission of Ben & Jerry's may be safe for now.

Paradise is not without problems, especially in a free-market system. Shortly after Ben & Jerry's announced that they would be buying Brazil nuts at a good price from the tropical rainforests (to make sure that the indigenous tribes, who had always collected the Brazil nuts, could make a good living), entrepreneurial nut-gangs descended upon the undefended rainforests to scoop up as many nuts as they could find; the effort to make sure that the price was high enough to help the indigenous peoples had suddenly made nut-gathering an economic enterprise, and the entrepreneurs had leaped in to soak up the profits. It is not clear that the indigenous peoples were better off for the generosity.

Aside from such inevitable (and often unpredictable) results of market distortions, Ben & Jerry's remains an example of determined businessmen championing their values, and protecting the natural environment insofar as their business impacted it, without losing money – in fact, while making quite a bit of it. We need more such stories, and there does not seem to be any reason why we cannot have them.

Questions for consideration:

- Where do we go from here? Consider the product: Is it part of a class of products that lend themselves easily to the kind of community-oriented business plan that Ben & Jerry's followed? What other products might lend themselves to that particular business model? Or can *any* corporation, or industry, adapt its practices to promote environmental values while increasing its competitiveness?
- Consider further the problems of market distortion by social mission. The sudden opportunity for city exploiters to go out there and gather nuts is not an isolated instance of frustration of good intentions. Can we think of others? What could be done about them?

⊛ NOTES ⊛

1. Lester A. Brown, *Eco-Economy: Building an Economy for the Earth*, New York: W.W. Norton, 2001, p. 7.
2. Costanza et al., *Nature*, May 15, 1997.

3. Janet Abramowitz, "Valuing Nature's Services," *State of the World 1997,* Worldwatch, New York: W.W. Norton, 1997.

4. Abramowitz, op. cit., p. 110, citing Herman E. Daly and John B. Cobb, Jr., *For the Common Good,* Boston: Beacon Press, 1989; also Clifford Cobb et al., "Redefining Progress: the Genuine Progress Indicator, Summary of Data and Methodology," Redefining Progress, San Francisco, CA 1995; Robert Repetto et al., *Wasting Assets: Natural Resources in the National Income Accounts,* Washington, DC: WRI, 1989.

5. See Robert Costanza, a pioneer in the economics of nature, and Dan Janzen, who has put the results to work in Costa Rica, in a study published in *Science* in 2002. They were not alone: Gretchen Daily has written two pathbreaking works, in 1997 *Nature's Services: Societal Dependence on Natural Ecosystems,* and in 2002, with Katherine Ellison, *The New Economy of Nature: The Quest to Make Conservation Profitable* (Washington, DC: Island Press, 2002), calling attention to the numerous ways that nature will provide, free or at reduced prices, the services that cost us dearly to perform ourselves.

6. Abramowitz, op. cit. p. 103.

7. Loc. cit.

8. R. Edward Freeman, Jessica Pierce, and Richard H. Dodd, *Environmentalism and the New Logic of Business: How Firms can be Profitable and Leave Our Children a Living Planet,* New York: Oxford University Press, 2000, and the Harvard Business Review collection *Business and the Environment,* an anthology of eight articles published in the HBR, which appear separately referenced in the bibliography for this chapter; Brian Nattrass and Mary Altomare, *The Natural Step for Business: Wealth, Ecology and the Evolutionary Corporation,* Gabriola Island, BC CA: New Society Publishers, 1999, 2nd edn., 2001; Paul Hawken, Amory Lovins, and Hunter Lovins, *Natural Capitalism: Creating the Next Industrial Revolution,* Boston: Little, Brown & Company, 1999, John Elkington, *Cannibals With Forks: The Triple Bottom Line of 21st Century Business,* Gabriola Island, BC: New Society Publishers, 1998 (first published Oxford, 1997); with extensive debts, of course, to E. F. Schumacher, *Small is Beautiful: Economics As If People Mattered,* Introduction by Theodore Roszak, New York: Harper & Row, 1973.

9. R. Edward Freeman, Jessica Pierce, and Richard H. Dodd, *Environmentalism and the New Logic of Business,* op. cit., p. 39.

10. Miller, op. cit., pp. 400–401.

11. See Elkington's account in *Cannibals With Forks,* supra n. 8, pp. 53–54.

12. Elinor Burkett, "A Mighty Wind," *The New York Times Magazine,* June 15, 2003, pp. 48–51.

13. Anand Rao, "World's Largest Wind Farm Planned for Iowa," World-Watch, July–August 2003, p. 9.

14. See Lester Brown, *Eco-Economy: Building an Economy for the Earth*, New York: W.W. Norton, 2001, especially Chapter 5, "Building the Solar/Hydrogen Economy," 97ff.

15. *Time* magazine, with reporting by Chris Daniels, Unmesh Kher, and Chris Taylor: "More Power to You: Alternative-energy technologies could soon give your phone, your car and your house their own microgenerators," *Time*, December 15, 2003, pp. A10–A12.

16. This account is taken from Janine M. Benyus, *Biomimicry: Innovation Inspired by Nature*, New York: HarperCollins, 1997.

17. This account is taken largely from Ben & Jerry's website, www.benjerry. com, and from the founders' account of the company, *Ben & Jerry's Double-Dip: How to Run a Values-Led Business and Make Money, Too*, by Ben Cohen and Jerry Greenfield, New York: Simon & Schuster (Fire Side Books), 1997.

18. From the Website, http://www.benjerry.com/our_company/about_us/ our_history/timeline/index.cfm.

c h a p t e r   s i x

Globalizing: Environmental Problems Abroad

INTRODUCTION

The subject of our consideration in this work is the interface between the ethical firm and the natural environment – law, ethics, current strategy, and visions for the future. Of necessity, the interface is global. Every business in existence, and hoping to be in existence over the next decade, must consider its international operations – its assembly plants (*maquiladoras*), its offshore manufacturing units (some have called them sweatshops), and more recently, its outsourced communications functions (company switchboards, for instance), as well as all the other relationships it may have with foreign suppliers and customers. The flagship enterprises of the mid- to late twentieth century, the great automobile, steel, and machinery companies that dominated the economic landscape and employed a huge percentage of the middle-class workforce, found their raw materials, their workers, and their markets within the boundaries of the United States. Those days are gone. Any company with more than local appeal must be able to do business abroad, in an age when the Internet has made access to foreign markets available to any private citizen with a computer and a modem.

THE FOUNDATIONS OF THE DISCUSSION

Our first concern (since this is a book about business ethics) is with international obligations generally, whether or not environmental problems are involved. Since there has been a great deal written about the reach of US industry around the world, and the economic, ethical, and policy dimensions of that reach, we will survey that literature very briefly in order to spend the greater part of the chapter on the global interface of multinational corporations (MNCs) and the natural environment of the countries in which they carry on their operations. There are a series of essential questions that we will address in the course of the inquiry: Is the phenomenon we know as "globalization" a good thing for the humans of this earth? Is it good for the earth itself? If those answers might be in the negative, should globalization be reversed? *Can* it be reversed? If globalization of *some* kind is inevitable, must it follow the patterns it has been following? And then we will have to ask, to what extent are US law, institutions, and corporations responsible for directing globalization to be less socially and environmentally responsible than it might be.

In the next section, we will present, very briefly, a description of the process of globalization as it is envisioned by its proponents, followed by a brief survey of the localist, or "anti-globalization" movement, attempting to present both sides as complete worldviews to which we may refer as the argument progresses. The section following it will abstract nine of the challenges, or dilemmas, confronting the globalization process in general and the MNC in particular as it extends its operations into the rest of the world – primarily the developing nations of the South – and see whether the conclusions of the earlier chapters have anything to contribute to a rational approach to those dilemmas. The section "Ten Commandments for Multinational Business" will summarize the literature's consensus on the ethical imperatives (or guidelines) that should govern the policies, internal and external, of MNCs abroad, in a convenient list that can be remembered as *Ten Commandments for Globalization.* The section following it will consider the possible roles of international conventions and agreements to preserve the global environment.

We will be left (the last section) with some questions that cannot be answered, of which the most important is the question of **global stewardship**: to what extent can the citizens of the privileged countries, and especially the profitable MNCs that originate in those countries, be said to have obligations to preserve the natural environment in areas that they deal with in commercial transactions only, regardless of the orientation and policies of the recognized governments of those areas? To what extent must the US, especially in its commercial enterprises, assume the role of the earth's steward, wherever stewardship may be needed? Globalization, in some sense of the word, may be, in fact, inevitable, but many commercial activities lend themselves equally to creative "re-localization" that is in some cases far more protective of humans and the natural environment than practices recommended on economics alone. To what extent are citizens of the US obligated to honor the preferences of peoples to live in traditional ways in traditional places, with their traditional laws protected from economic invasion?

✺ THE CONFLICT AS WE UNDERSTAND IT: ✺ GLOBALIZERS AND THEIR OPPONENTS

In praise of straitjackets: Globalization for the benefit of all

The fundamental argument for economic globalization comes from Adam Smith, and can be derived from the account of Smith in Chapter 2. The principle of division of labor suggests (and has since Plato first formulated it in *The Republic*)[1] that if each person will just specialize in what he or she does best in the market, the result will be much greater efficiency in production (since each person has to accumulate the tools and skills of his or her trade only), much greater quality in product (since each person will perfect the skills for his or her trade only, and will become very good at them), and much better prices (since the overhead will be much lower for the specialist). Smith would add, as Plato did not, that there should be several such specialists in each trade, so that competition will drive down the costs and prices ever further.

So it is among the nations. Especially since nations will differ as to normal soil, sunlight, water resources, metals, sources of energy, and the like, each nation should produce what it produces best and nothing else. International trade should be free and unhindered by any government regulation designed to protect domestic industries; Smith realized that there would be strong domestic pressure to protect the inefficiencies of local industry (by protective tariffs and subsidies, for instance), but insisted it should be resisted. His account of the sources of the products of the workman's life in his own time shows the benefits of international trade even then, over 200 years ago, when transportation of goods was far more expensive and less safe than it is now.

Globalization is more widely praised now, as conducive to freedom, equality, and democracy (since the American employees of the MNCs tend to practice their constitutional freedoms in sight of the locals), conducive to general prosperity (on Smith's model), and the primary engine for equalizing incomes between the North and the South. Thomas Friedman, commentator and columnist on foreign affairs for *The New York Times*, wrote a comprehensive and highly readable defense of the enterprise of globalization (composed mostly of collected columns from the *Times*) entitled *The Lexus and the Olive Tree*, the thesis being that we should welcome the Lexus factory in the developing nation, for the new prosperity and new horizons it brings to that nation's people, but that we must remember to protect the olive tree, the symbol of home, rooted in the land, needed for the happiness of the people.[2] That said, the olive tree tends to get buried under the enthusiasm for global progress. Even the major drawback to economic globalization, the thundering of the anonymous undirected "electronic herd" – the computer-enabled destabilizing rush of "hot" investment capital into nations that seem likely to yield quick profits, followed by (should the returns not suit the investors' desires) the equally rapid and destabilizing withdrawal of the same – Friedman finds acceptable. It is simply the way global capital works now. The only way to avoid disappointing (and losing) that herd is by adopting wholeheartedly all the reforms suggested by the International Monetary Fund (IMF), a "golden straitjacket" that curbs government expenditures, privatizes government enterprises, and opens up all parts of the economy to foreign investment and profit. In line with Smith, market capitalism, and current World Trade Organization (WTO) policy, he argues that globalization unmixed with moral constraints is, in the end, best for the welfare of all people and should be pursued without reservations.

That does not mean that business has to be unethical in order to be competitive. The works of Richard DeGeorge (for example, *Competing With Integrity*)[3] and Thomas Donaldson (for example, *Ethics in International Business*)[4] have provided excellent guidelines for ethical conduct in business abroad. But there is no doubt that the fundamental economic imperatives of business set the path to be taken.

The cry of the olive tree: Alternatives to globalization

Globalization is not playing well in every theater. Protests that cannot be easily dismissed have been launched against it, in general and in particular; most of these will be taken up in the next section, nine dilemmas of globalization. In summary, the opposition to globalization supports local cultures and economies, and claims that (1) The rationale of globalization is a sham – no one believes it – even the United States, defender of free markets worldwide, cannot bring itself to cut its own counterproductive subsidies to powerful political interests (steel today, textiles tomorrow, agriculture always). "Free Trade" is championed only until the next election, and our hypocritical espousal of it does nothing but teach cynicism to those we would convert. (2) Even if it went according to theory, the market is not perfect, and everyone knows that. The IMF was set up at Bretton Woods to *counter* the market in its irrational dips and doozies, and it is not doing it – by insisting on contractionary policy in depression, and encouraging "hot" capital in recoveries, it is pro-cyclic and makes matters worse. (3) Even if the market worked perfectly, there are many other considerations, like the preservation of indigenous cultures and languages, the saving of the dignity of every human (which requires saving his or her job!), and the preservation of local self-sufficiency and pride, which are seriously at risk in the global economy. (4) Then there is the concern for the natural world. Before "globalization," the local methods of farming generally (not always) were adapted to the soil and climate, and could be carried on sustainably – at least, had been carried on for several millennia, supporting whole villages without destroying the natural endowment of the land. What will the new, export-oriented agriculture do? Will the governments of debt-ridden nations in the developing world open up their remaining rainforests to international lumber companies? What will be the consequences of that?

The "dilemmas" of the next section do not constitute a coherent anti-globalization thesis. It is assumed that globalization will continue, and thrive. But ethical challenges will arise in the course of the operations of the global market, many with environmental aspects to them, and we must be aware of them.

An overview of ethical dilemmas of globalization

American businesses have not always felt the need for ethical behavior abroad. Under the general rubric of "When in Rome, do as the Romans do," they merrily bribed, greased, and generally buddied their way through lawless climates, underpaying the workers and bringing home the profits quite without surveillance from any agencies at home or abroad. Those days are gone forever, washed away, in the late 1970s, in the wake of the Watergate.

Let us review some of the major dilemmas – in the traditional form, generally, of indictments of the United States or of one or more of its corporate citizens – that have plagued commercial globalization since its inception. One useful thread to unify the understanding of the problems of globalization is the metaphor of the export trade. America is a land of a multitude of products, many of which are shipped abroad, intentionally or otherwise. Just what is the US exporting? What is it that is packed, materially or metaphorically, into containers and cargo bays for consumption by the rest of the world? For it is the stuff arriving on their shores from America that leaves the first, last and, major indelible footprint of American presence. From the beginnings of business ethics in the 1970s, certain traditional exports have come under severe attack on ethical grounds – pesticides, for instance, pharmaceuticals, easy to misuse in nations without the infrastructure to regulate them; cigarettes, whose markets abroad have expanded vigorously even as the home market has begun to dip; and overwhelmingly, the guns, the trade in arms, which has made the world a much more dangerous place. The first indictment, then, was against the products exported (which did not include, incidentally, infant formula. Nestle USA never made infant formula. All that was done in Switzerland).

The problems raised in the early days of the field have not gone away. Most products exported then are still on the list today, with more added. What unintended consequences dog these products in ordinary use, especially in the developing world (the developed world can take care of itself), and what is the extent of the manufacturer's responsibility to follow these products into the field and ensure the safety of their use? We will call this dilemma – the earliest and still one of the most troubling – **Dilemma I: Product Stewardship**.

Also in those first years of our field, our examination of corporate influence on the developing nations extended to immaterial exports – the dishonesty, for instance, that comes with bribery, in Korea, in Africa, and most spectacularly, in Japan, in the famous Lockheed Case. During 1972 and 1973, pressured by near-bankruptcy and a burdensome loan, A. Carl Kotchian, CEO of Lockheed, paid about $12 million to Japanese partners who, he believed, could persuade Prime Minister Kukeo Tanaka to buy Lockheed's TriStar airplanes for Japan's national airline. Success in the sales could bring the company $400 million, save jobs, save the company, and put Lockheed back in competition. He did bring home the contracts, about $1.3 billion, after paying all the bribes demanded by his contacts. When the whole sorry matter came to light, Kotchian was disgraced and forced to resign, and the contracts were cancelled. But the Japanese officials he had been dealing with, including PM Tanaka and his successor Takeo Miki, were also forced to resign, publicly humiliated, and sent to jail with criminal convictions. Seems the Japanese were more out-raged than the Americans about the seedy aspects of the deal. (Lesson I: when in Rome, make sure you are talking to the right Romans.) In the wake of those scandals, the Foreign Corrupt Practices Act was passed in 1977, since amended. But as the recent Enron case reminds us, the global financial misdoings continue, in a little-examined portion of the globe called the "Money Laundry." Americans, through duly licensed banks and corporations, are not the only ones to use off-shore banking facilities to avoid taxes and to make the tracing of ill-gotten money impossible. The Mafia precedes us by generations. But the Enron scandal, with its "special purpose entities" basking on every Caribbean beach, reminds us that US legitimate operations have done more than most to create fiscal dishonesty abroad. Such cases raise the question: What, really, is for sale in this world? Moral philosophers prefer to believe that integrity is not for sale, but the extravagant means that some commercial entities use to purchase it makes it at least appear that it is worth buying.

There is a murkier problem lurking in the wings. There are places in this world where a great deal is for sale that is not for sale in the US: 10-year-old prostitutes and kidneys, for example. That trade, in which US citizens rarely participate as producers, nevertheless relies on them and the North generally (acting as individuals only) as customers, without which the trade would not continue. Should the citizens of the US, collectively through government or privately through corporations, attempt to do anything about that? Sadly, the corruption in which the North participates tends to discourage the formation of genuinely profitable and sustainable indigenous businesses, since the corrupt practices are so profitable. If bribery (for instance) seems to be the best way to get things done, and often the only way to protect company assets in a foreign land, is it justified for corporate officers to sanction bribery – despite the likelihood that these practices turn the developing world into our partners in lying, cheating, stealing, and in general, commerce that the US electorate would not approve if it were put to a vote? We will call this **Dilemma II: Corruption**.

While we are distributing money around the world, it might be appropriate to note the work of the IMF. Created in July 1944, to assist in the rebuilding of Europe after the war then in progress, it was assigned the task of ensuring global economic stability. Joseph Stiglitz, Nobel Prize–winning economist and author of *Globalization and Its*

Discontents (2002) tells us that the IMF was founded to monitor economic development in nations and to provide loans, from funds supplied by member nations, in case a country did not have the cash to finance the necessary tax cuts and expansion of government expenditures in case of a depression. In its original conception, then, the IMF was based on a recognition that markets often did not work well – that they could result in massive unemployment and might fail to make needed funds available to countries to help them restore their economies. The IMF was founded on the belief that there was a need for *collective action at the global level* for economic stability, just as the United Nations had been founded on the belief that there was a need for collective action at the global level for political stability.[5] Yet virtually all of the actions taken by the IMF since globalization began to affect the developing nations have had the result of impoverishing the poorer countries for the profit of the richer ones and the protection of their banks. The IMF promises to get loans and private investment for development for the South from the North; it does, but the "hot" capital that floods the country does not stay long. It brings waste when it comes, leaves devastation when it leaves, and it is "pro-cyclic": when money is flooding in, more follows, and inflation spirals; when it starts to deflate, capital flees just when it is most needed, and the nation is left with nothing but a huge debt to service.

Within each country, IMF-recommended measures require lowering the cost of government, which amounts to cutting services to the poor while protecting the rich, contributing significantly to global inequality. Its universal remedy for a slack economy in a developing nation, for instance, is to raise interest rates and cut back on government spending – what we call contractionary fiscal policy. Anyone could predict that in a deflationary economy, raising interest rates and cutting government services and employment will only make matters much worse. But the IMF is not apparently interested in making matters better; it is interested in protecting the interests of the banks in the developed countries who made the loans (as recommended by the IMF) to encourage development.[6] Suspicions of a conspiracy to defraud developing nations for the profit of Wall Street deepen, when at the depth of the recession brought on by these policies, the IMF urges the affected nations to sell their government-owned industrial assets at bargain-basement prices to foreign owners who will provide, as they promise, more skilled management.[7]

Stiglitz doubts that all these mistakes are due to conspiracies. He thinks it is just that we have a pack of free-market ideologues – people who are convinced that free markets will solve every problem and that government intervention always does more harm than good – at the helm of the institution created to remedy market failures. The contradiction is amusing, unless you happen to live in a nation at the receiving end of its blunders. (As with many such institutions, the IMF is not "free market" when it comes to protecting its sponsors. In a free market, a bank makes loans at its own risk and takes the loss if the debtor cannot pay it back. In the world of the IMF, the IMF dictates the policies of its client governments to make sure that as long as the current regime survives, the loans will be paid back no matter how much suffering occurs in the rest of the nation. Stiglitz sees in this policy an invitation to riot and revolution, and events tend to reinforce his view.) The United States is one of the strongest supporters of the IMF; those are mostly US banks they are defending. Again, does the US citizenry have a responsibility to do something about the rapid growth of inequality, and the pain imposed upon the poor, by the expansion of Third World debt, and by the misguided policies of the IMF and similar financial institutions? We will call this **Dilemma III: Debt**.

More recently, the list of items on the manifest has expanded enormously, as true globalization has begun. When the export platform was discovered, the first export was, notoriously, jobs. Billionaire Ross Perot, in his brief and colorful run for·the Presidency of the United States, chose as his major campaign issue the opposition to the North American Free Trade Agreement (NAFTA). He argued, cogently, that jobs would be lost to Mexico if the treaty were to be signed, for in Mexico the labor costs were low and the environmental regulations lax. That "great sucking sound" that he called our attention to was Mexico vacuuming up American jobs. Possibly the criticism was overdone; it usually is. But jobs were lost. Every year since NAFTA was put in place, factories have closed in the United States and opened somewhere else. (Since the year 2000, the US has lost jobs at a rate of 70,000 a month, very little of which loss can be attributed to "greater efficiency.") A good deal of the loss is from outsourcing – a company hires another company, based in India for example, to do some job, like answering its phones, that used to be done on site – or "off-shoring," moving operations from a US-based facility to another facility owned by the same company in another country. The pollution problems created by the unregulated *maquiladora* factories, just south of the border with Mexico, are a warning shot across the bow of neighbor globalization; how far down the environmental road should the globalizers be looking for unintended consequences of such global moves? Nor is Mexico the jobs' last stop: Taiwan, Malaysia, and China, possibly using forced labor to keep costs down, now underbid Mexico for the cost of labor. Certainly the US consumer benefits from the lower prices of foreign-produced goods, but that brings out a much more serious dilemma, central to globalization. We will call this **Dilemma IV: Employment** (the producer v. the consumer).

Let us linger with this dilemma for a moment, to consider its foundation and its implications. Who are we, we humans? What part of our selves is important? "Lowering prices for the consumer" is surely not the whole good for humanity; our consuming life is a very small part of our satisfactions. Much more important to us is our working life, our career, vocation, the work that we do to earn the money for our own support, to support our families and give a good start to our children, to give to charity, and to fulfill ourselves. Jobs are much more important than marginally lower prices on sneakers. Nor can a national economy, or polity, survive a rapidly increasing gap between the wealth of the corporate rich and the dwindling savings of the newly unemployed middle class. That is not only economic but political folly. As Sir James Goldsmith, one of the canniest businessmen to grace the twentieth century, put it, "It must surely be a mistake to adopt an economic policy that makes you rich if you eliminate your national workforce and transfer production abroad and that bankrupts you if you continue to employ your own people."[8] Addressing Dilemma IV in its totality is a lot more complicated than that, of course. Political realities may change, depending on the percent unemployed. But the "unemployment" rate is deceptive. It is fairly accurate, and useful, when the major unionized manufacturing jobs disappear, which they did during the 1980s. We sympathized, moralized on the steelworkers' obligation to complete higher levels of education and fit themselves for new jobs in the communications-and-information economy, and forgot about them. Now that the white-collar workers, up to the level of the PhD engineers, are watching their jobs take off for India – where two top-level employees will work for the salary commanded by only one in the United States[9] – how many of the employed are in unrewarding or temporary jobs because their real employment folded up? People are ingenious, after all. Except in highly unionized occupations, they do not all march in a body to the unemployment office when they are laid off. They try to keep working, and find unexpected ways to do it. But their opportunities are painfully contracted, and their life prospects badly diminished, by the economic arrangements corporations have made in the name of profit. (From a whole-world perspective, the great joy felt by the Indian or Chinese middle class at the opening up of opportunities previously out of reach easily balances the sorrow felt by Americans at the permanent loss of good jobs and worthy employment. But we are discussing only the choices that face the American citizen as a political actor; and besides, why should the existence of that equation give the MNCs the right to put the huge profits gained thereby into the corporate pockets? Why should not they be asked to distribute that profit to the disemployed workers?)

To what extent is the private sector, and the economic decisions made by business managers, responsible for this? To what extent is the business community responsible for creating opportunities at home, even if the profit margin is not quite what it would be if the jobs were abroad? Nike shoes are not cheap to make in the US, but they are very cheap to make in Vietnam. There is an enormous profit. To what extent is an American business obligated to attempt to continue work in the United States, even though threatened by competition abroad? Is there such a thing as a moral duty on the American consumer to "buy American?" One major problem is that "made in U.S.A." has no fixed meaning, considering the number of articles that are designed, planned out, parts manufactured, assembled, and shipped from many different locations across the world. It would make little economic sense to launch and implement a "buy American" campaign, unless the definitions were strictly made and enforced, and included the whole nation in the economy – in which case the rule would support American jobs and American prosperity, and would make a good deal of sense. Dilemma IV looks to have a great deal of staying power.

The US also exports food to developing nations, in company with many of our allies in the North, especially Europe. The developing nations do not call it exporting; they call it "dumping." For the food that we export to developing nations is subsidized at this end, in US and in Europe, at the insistence of politically powerful agribusiness or coalitions of small farmers. So much is produced, in order to cash in on the subsidies, that there is no market for it in the producing countries; so as a condition for membership in the WTO the United States insists that developing nations buy the food, which is considerably less expensive than their own non-subsidized food. Now, if we are shipping large amounts of good food to the developing nations, essentially at the expense of the taxpayers who subsidized it, why is it that people in developing nations are starving? It seems that they do not have money to buy the food, because prior to such generosity they made money on the farms that this subsidized competition has put out of business.[10] As those familiar with the hollowed-out economies of the Great Plains will know, once the farmers in an agricultural village are no longer able to support themselves, dozens of small businesses that depended on them will also die, and the unemployed ex-farmers and small business families end up subsisting day-to-day on welfare or on inadequate casual labor based in the cities.

Of course the practice also undermines any effort on the part of the South to use the export of raw commodities to increase its wealth and technological infrastructure to the point where it might compete in fields other than agriculture. One of the major agents of impoverishment in Africa, for instance, is the globalization of purchasing practices for food and other raw commodities. A process that had been essentially a negotiation between cooperatives of local producers in Africa and importers from the North has become an open auction on the websites of the business-to-business (B to B) Internet companies – forcing local producers to compete with overstocks and the dumping of subsidized materials all over the world. Africa's bargaining power has evaporated, and with it all hopes of using the production of raw commodities to pull itself up to a point where it could join the North's high-tech economy.[11] The tenuous economic arrangements that developing nations have made in the attempt to join the valued "free-market" global economy, the creation of viable local economies to deal with the rest of the world, are being wiped out by the intervention of non-free market practices of subsidization. Is this fair? Is it in accord with any pattern of global economy oriented to a viable future of competitive enterprise? This leaves us with **Dilemma V: Dumping**.

The problem does not stop there. When in globalized economies the local economies tend to be wiped out, with them is lost local history, culture, institutions, rivalries, and pride. The personal fulfillment attained in service to one's native community, the holding of local or traditional offices, and the contributions to lasting local monuments for the service of future generations (libraries, schools, museums) is lost. It is a worthwhile question: Do the efficiencies gained in large-scale economic arrangements, realized in exports to developing nations, justify the loss of so much that was valuable to human beings? The US has been grappling with that problem since the middle of the twentieth century, as we lose the small towns of our Middle West; attempts to contemplate the depth of those losses in a traditional economy may be more than we can manage. To the extent that US business is the chief initiator and beneficiary of global business, is there an obligation to consider what these exports do to the large- and small-scale economic and social fabric of developing nations? This question becomes **Dilemma VI: Community**.

What else are we exporting? The fuel consumption patterns in the US, out of proportion to those of the rest of the world, combined with the Bush administration's attitude toward the 2003 Climate Change Treaty (the Kyoto Protocol) for the limitation of emissions of greenhouse gases, has suggested to some that air pollution may be the biggest consumable deposited by the US on foreign shores. Greenhouse emissions are unfortunately not the only contribution from our shores to the world's pollution. Since US landfills, at least in the crowded Northeast, have filled and been closed, simply ridding the streets of garbage has become a major problem. States and municipalities have tried incinerating it, and nearly driven themselves out of town with the dioxin and particulates produced in the process. Transportation is another option; New York City now sends much of its trash in trucks to Virginia. Among the newer projects is to export solid waste to willing areas of the developing world. They have land, the thought seems to be; and the US has money. So contractual arrangements are in progress all over the world, to dump solid waste, and most especially toxic waste (especially the toxic residue from discarded computers and computer monitors), far from where *our* children will have to deal with it (it is fondly hoped). Somehow the United States has become the world center of filth, not only the metaphorical variety, as in corruption, but the real nonmetaphorical stuff. There must be a better solution: That waste will not go away, and may be the major introduction to the US for the next generations of citizens of the developing world. The permanent footprint left by the plastic bottles deposited in the South will be our **Dilemma VII: Garbage**.

Deserts are also on the list of exports. The human contribution to deserts has long been recognized; wherever agriculture is practiced over any length of time (measured in centuries at least, probably millennia), the land becomes salinized, useless, and turns into deserts. (Remember, as per the Introduction to this book, that the Iraqi deserts, splashed over our TVs as battlefields, were once the "Fertile Crescent.") It is possible to farm sustainably, but no one has yet done it on the scale of empire, and this is what is needed.[12] Ironically, now that there is good work available on sustainable agriculture (and significant demonstrations), the trend is toward larger farms more dependent upon non-sustainable practices. For much of the food, which cannot be grown in the US or Europe, is now factory farmed in the developing world. The small, uneconomical, farms of the indigenous people are bought by large MNCs, to grow extensive monocultures of products like cotton or pineapples, which will not feed the people of the area but will bring in payments to the government for the use of the land. The income from the exports is often needed to pay external debt incurred during attempts to industrialize.

The huge factory farms that grow food for export, food too expensive for the local people, take over land that had been used for family vegetable plots. Deforestation is required to get them started, and in operation, they are dependent on pesticides, herbicides, and often genetically modified seed to remain profitable. With constant cropping, they rapidly exhaust the nutrients of the soil, and chemical residues occasionally make it impossible to grow native crops, should the farm be abandoned when it ceases to make money. A host of troublesome consequences follow from these multinational agricultural practices; are they the responsibility of the multinational agribusinesses that profit from the crops? To what extent should a company, or a citizenry, be held responsible for the degradation of the environment of another nation, over which they have no direct control, but to which they knowingly contribute? This is **Dilemma VIII: Environment**.

More recently, the increasing worldwide popularity of the McDonald's hamburger, not to mention the Taco Bell and KFC products, raises the possibility that we may be introducing increasing parts of the world to the pleasures of chronic disease. This dilemma is very different from that posed by our export of pesticides, pharmaceuticals, and tobacco, substances that are clearly and immediately harmful if misused (or used at all, in the case of tobacco), which they probably will be. There is nothing at all wrong or unhealthy or harmful about hamburgers and fried chicken, at least to the majority of the sensible American public. The American-sponsored products are probably less prone to harmful contamination than the native fare. But we know that this kind of good food has played a part in the health problems experienced by many Americans late in life. If people all over the world, at least those who can afford it, choose to join us in our bad eating habits and consequent obesity, heart failure, and Type II diabetes, should our complicity in this choice worry us?

Should it add to our worry that most developing nations do not have the health care infrastructure to care for the sufferers from such debilitating diseases? This is **Dilemma IX: Long-Term Health**.

Consider the situation from the point of view of the US citizen: The history of globalization to this point seems to have a common theme, that we over-privileged Americans are responsible, in the eyes of much of the world, for harmful things that we cannot remember doing. There is an evolution in the dilemmas: it begins with issues that were solved at home (in the US) but then re-created abroad (like the export of pesticides banned, for good reason, in the US); it continues through issues that are controllable on US territory but beyond the capacity of developing nations to control on theirs (the garbage, for instance); and it ends with a problem we are not even sure we recognize at home, although that last problem, chronic disease, may be, by the middle of this century, the most expensive problem facing the American taxpayer.

⊛ TEN COMMANDMENTS FOR ⊛ MULTINATIONAL BUSINESS

Globalization poses problems for business ethics, simply because it is difficult to apply homegrown ethical assumptions to the conditions we find abroad. Within the borders of the US, we may presuppose the inherent goodness of the free-market system, the inviolability of human rights and private property, and the general belief that honesty is the best policy. Not that the effects of the free market are always good, that rights and property are always respected, or that no one is ever dishonest – but discussions of ethical guidelines can at least build upon general agreement that they *should* be. Further, business ethics grew up within the American legal and regulatory framework. This accident of birth is crucial. It means that it contains the rock-bottom assumption that the law will be obeyed, as it generally is in the United States. That includes the assumption that bribery is not condoned and that if you stick to your guns, you will not have to pay a bribe. Further, it means that the government is the most powerful player on the business scene, and will back up its directives with force. That may seem like an irrelevant piece of background, but it is crucially important. It forces management to think "ethically," for whether or not the managers are ethical, they must assume that their critics from the community are ethical, or are aware of ethics, and they know that those critics have access to the government. If they try to make a profit by being very immoral, government will crack down with burdensome regulation, surveillance, and enforcement. You can try, for instance, to exploit your workers with subsistence wages and unsafe working conditions – but you will be found out, and fined; and if the system is working properly (not just with slap-on-the-wrist fines), the last result will be more expensive than the first. If you pollute the stream, the state will make you clean it up. You can try moving to another state to avoid taxes or environmental regulation, or threatening to move in order to get nice deals from state and local government, but the federal government will follow you wherever you go. Once you are dealing with a federal regulation, you cannot play one state off against another to get a better deal on wages or emissions rules.

These are the rules that globalization changes. Abroad, companies are often dealing with people who have got no good out of the free-market system. Their background may be subsistence farming, even foraging, traditional village life, or worse yet, some authoritarian collective system originally identified as "communism." Private property and human rights may be the privilege of the elite. For this reason alone, all business operations in these lands will be charged with complications, some examples of which will be discussed below.

Is honesty the best policy? What if no one else is honest? Should business stick by its American penchant for honest dealings, or should it "do as the Romans do" and pay the necessary bribes? If you will recall the sad tale of CEO Carl Kotchian of Lockheed trying to bribe his way into a major deal for his company in Japan, you will know the problems that arise here: In the wake of this debacle (and others), Congress passed the 1977 Foreign Corrupt Practices Act, modified in 1988, which stands to this day.

Japan, of course, is a civilized nation with law enforcement well in place. But suppose you, managing a division of an agricultural-products company far from home, find yourself in the developing world, in a situation where there is no general government in anything but name. You can make your own arrangements for governing with whatever group you please. More importantly, when it comes to burdensome taxes and regulations, you can, indeed, play countries off against each other, letting them bid for your investment, which they much want. This is more power than you would ever have at home. But how should it be used? Is profit the only object?

Globalization, in short, confronts us with questions that we have not seen since the Wild West of the nineteenth century, and we are not sure how to deal with it. Let us look at a proposed set of guide-lines for global business, and see if they help orient us in a world without too many directions:

Respect for the nation

The first category of rules for global business addresses the problem of interaction with the country itself external to the company, as opposed to the company's employees.

1   *The land*: protect it – Land comes before people: where the land is destroyed, there is no hope for the people.
2   *The law*: obey it – Even if it seems you do not have to. It will help you avoid nasty consequences later.
3   *The culture*: defer to it – American arrogance is most distasteful, and dangerous, if it is read as contempt for the culture of the people. Respect it.
4   *The arts*: support them – This is one of the easiest ways to create positive waves in the community, and the best way to help preserve a culture threatened by the influx of American goods and music.
5   *The public life*: assist in it – Especially if the country is a nascent democracy, model democratic activity. Lobby for what you want openly. If you lose, lose gracefully and do not try illegal means to get around the loss. Respect the system.

Responsibility for the people

The second category of rules for global business has to do with the employees of the company; how you treat them, and what your treatment says about your views of human dignity.

1   Their *physical needs*: pay a sufficient wage – Wages in the developing world are notoriously low. One way or another, make sure the employees and their families have enough to eat and wear, and a roof over their heads.
2   Their *political needs*: observe rights, justice, and honesty – You are in part responsible for educating citizens for democracy; respect rights even if you do not have to, and be honest with them.
3   Their *dignity*: show courtesy and appreciation – Here especially you signal your views on the worth of a human being, and empower them to become responsible.

4   Their *integrity*: prohibit bribery, involvement in dishonesty – And then, do not put pressure on that empowerment by requiring them to act dishonestly on your behalf!

5   Their *potential*: give them education, opportunity, responsibility – It may not be practical to insist that all children go to school from age 6 to 16. But provide education at every opportunity, and promote them wherever possible to positions of responsibility.

This formulation is arguably an improvement on many programs for global business morality, in that it does not pretend that it can be "derived" from some Western idea or another, like "human rights" or "social contract." Where the problem of international morality arises, human rights are very much in dispute and there is no social contract. Nor are the moral guidelines appropriate for international business usefully seen as the result of negotiations among equal parties. There are no equal parties, either. Nor is this some sketch for universal law, on the model of the federal law that makes it impossible to play state off against state within the United States. Global minimum wage legislation is impractical, global environmental legislation is impossible, and right now there is no real and authoritative consensus on ethical guidelines for business among the nations. Each company has to negotiate its own ethical course within itself.

If the guidelines are not an ethical theory, or derived from one, nor a process for reaching fair negotiated solutions, nor the framework of a world government, what justifies them? I suggest two answers to the question: (1) They are good, and (2) they are useful.

The goodness of the guidelines lies in their conformity to general ethical principles (as opposed to strict derivability from ethical theory), on the one hand, and their tendency to make the world a better place, on the other. Whatever your favorite ethical theory, we are enjoined by the principles of ethics to be just and fair to each other, and the guidelines require that in their insistence on obedience to law and respect for the integrity and potential of all who work for us. We are further enjoined to help each other, and to avoid doing harm, and the concern for the welfare of the workers, the community outside the company, and the future of the nation embodies that. We are enjoined also to respect the moral agency and dignity of all the human beings with whom we come in contact, and the guidelines ensure that respect at several points. (Review Chapter 1 if that summary does not seem to be familiar.) New in the guidelines is the high priority placed on the land. We have seen too many projects of "development," home grown or the result of foreign investment, which destroyed the land and rendered it useless for subsequent purposes. If the land is not there – not productive because of overuse, erosion, or pollution, not habitable because of toxins, or not available for the people because of counterproductive allocation arrangements – the people will perish, no matter how well they are treated as the land is degraded.

Beyond the general conformity to morality of the guidelines, they have a single good tendency worth noting: adherence to these guidelines ensures that the presence of the US corporation will do no harm to the country, and indeed may do some good as it draws its profits from the land and from the people. There is no "trade-off" between good for the shareholders and good for the host nation. The corporation must act, as Jim Beré used to insist, as a guest in the community, leaving the room neater than it was when it moved in. The corporation's presence should be not a trade-off but a "win-win" proposition, leaving the country and the world a better place in the long run.

The usefulness of these guidelines, if such there is, lies in the requirement, contained in all of them, that the multinational manager, abroad or at home, stay close to the people affected by the presence of the enterprise in their midst. Acting on these guidelines requires that the manager listen to people, not only to employees (but certainly those) but also the people of the area who see the corporate enterprise as a new crisis in the life of their nation – presenting, as the Chinese character for "crisis" suggests, opportunity laced with danger (or danger within which opportunity may hide). Global capitalism's operations, as Friedman points out so eloquently, intrigue them and frighten them; corporate officers' efforts to participate in community life, through support of the arts, participation in civic organization, and encouragement of education, will bring them in contact with many levels of people in the community, and make them less strange and fearful. There are no guarantees in this area – far fewer guarantees than any company would have a right to expect if its managers participated similarly in a community within the United States. Even though the corporation has *earned* the community's trust, there is no guarantee that it will in fact be trusted. Yet the activities indicated by the guidelines surely give it the best chance of making key friends and contacts in the area of the corporation's enterprise. Setting aside the moral agenda of the guidelines, extensive engagement with the community maximizes the probability that local managers will learn of failures in the other areas of business (for instance, that lower-level managers are in fact paying bribes to local authorities in return for preferential treatment). It also makes it more likely, in this age of terrorism, that they will hear of incipient activity hostile to the corporation and to what it is doing, and more likely that there will be people and institutions that will help them deal with that activity.

ⓐ INTERNATIONAL AGREEMENTS ⓐ

Despite general agreement, based on arguments with a pedigree stretching at least to Adam Smith, that free trade and the bargains freely made among trading partners for the conduct of trade are the best way to carry on international commercial relations, and that government entities are best left out of the equation, the current state of global commercial activity is not well described by those principles. International trade has been supplemented, and modified, by international agreements of all sorts, not just the free-trade agreements, NAFTA, General Agreement on Tariffs and Trade (GATT) and the WTO, which currently dominate economic thinking. As we pointed out in Chapter 4, much of the legal environment of business in the rest of this century, whether or not it directly concerns nature and natural resources, will be an international environment. We will conclude this chapter with a quick consideration of two typical international agreements aimed at protecting the natural environment, to illustrate the possibilities and problems all such agreements contain.

Typical of the international agreements that might be called upon to solve global environmental problems are the Montreal Protocol, designed to halt the destruction of the ozone layer, and the Kyoto Protocol, designed to phase out greenhouse gases. The problems are very similar, on the surface at least – both have to do with climatic and atmospheric changes that are truly global in nature – the documents apparently addressed them sensibly, but one seems to be working and one does not. It is too simple to blame the current administration for refusing to cooperate with Kyoto. Let us take a look at both global initiatives and see what may have determined the difference.[13]

The Montreal Protocol on Substances that Deplete the Ozone Layer took effect on January 1, 1989, after some years of negotiations. It has been amended at least five times since then, to permit inclusion of special circumstances. Essentially, the signatories agreed to limit and then end the manufacture and sale of the chlorofluorocarbons (CFCs) that had been found to cause the deterioration of the ozone layer (with all manner of qualifications to permit small producers to continue manufacture as necessary for development). In general, it worked, although given the uncertainties of data on the ozone layer, we will have to wait for a few more years for the victory party. The protocol had certain things going for it: The CFCs had a few sources, easily identifiable, and their manufacturers were actively seeking (and finding) products that could be substituted for the CFCs. As a result, the Montreal Protocol had little political opposition. The governments were moderately interested in implementing the agreements, and the citizens had no reason or means to oppose. The practice of manufacturing and selling CFCs was modified in the boardroom; the customers had no choice but to accept the substitute.

Greenhouse gases are not like this. The technology of change for greenhouse gases is far more difficult and diffuse, and will be harder to develop. The Kyoto Protocol, developed in early December 1997 pursuant to the Framework Convention on Climate Change constructed in Rio de Janeiro in 1992, attempted to secure agreements to bring the emissions of greenhouse gases back to 1990 levels in the developed nations. Less developed nations were held to a different standard, to allow them to develop their industrial capacity. To cut emissions in this country, we would have to force all our overage coal-burning plants to install new technology or emission-control devices; we would have to cut emissions from our automobiles by 20 percent; we would have to cut back on the use of inefficient diesel engines, which comprise the bulk of our construction equipment. The economic impact would be real, and felt by everyone; sensitive areas, like the make, weight, and use of the family automobile, would be especially heavily affected. Citizens would be directly in the line of its fire. The Kyoto Protocol was a political bombshell the moment it hit the table, and an oil-friendly administration's decision to pretend that it is not there is entirely understandable.

An agreement to decrease the noise, size, and operation of automobiles is unacceptable in the developed world, or at least, citizen acquiescence is going to be problematic. In the developing world, governments profiting hugely from environmentally destructive operations may be disinclined to enforce regimes they see as imposed upon them. Recall that states have power over their citizens only to the extent that they can deliver the goods. Control of distribution of natural resources is part of that power. Agreeing to conserve the resources *or* allowing foreigners to dictate the nature and pace of their distribution, by themselves, will significantly cut that power. Not even the developed nations can institute new systems of property rights, not without a fight, as we saw in the "takings" dispute (Chapter 4).

How, generally, are international agreements supposed to be enforced? There simply are no international law-enforcement mechanisms that can be imposed as a matter of right on unwilling people. We suggested one enforcement mechanism in the last chapter – trade sanctions, which could in theory be spelled out in the original agreement. If all-purpose sanctions can be used against "rogue" states to limit their nuclear capability, surely they can be used to enforce environmental agreements. The rest of the enforcement will probably be carried out by CSOs (civil society organizations, elsewhere NGOs, nongovernmental organizations) by publicity, demonstration, boycott, sit-in, and whatever other means occur. The result can be messy; we turn to these CSOs in the next chapter.

⊛ CASE 6: SHELL OIL IN NIGERIA ⊛

The death of a patriot: The story of Ken Saro-Wiwa[14]

Ike Okonta, Nigerian journalist and environmentalist, and Oronto Douglas, Nigerian environmental human rights lawyer, introduce the story of Ken Saro-Wiwa:

> From the dark days of slavery to the present, the Niger Delta has been ruled by violence, and men of violence have sought to rule her by force. The area's substantial natural and human resources have always proved an irresistible attraction for slave traders, commodity merchants, colonialists, and plain fortune hunters who subjugate the inhabitants through treachery and force of arms and plunder their resources. With the discovery of oil in the area in 1956 by Shell, the oppression and exploitation of the peoples of the Niger Delta entered yet another, and even more insidious, phase. The Movement for the Survival of the Ogoni People (MOSOP) emerged in August 1990 to put to an end this dark chapter in the Niger Delta story.[15]

The movement was the creation of Kenule Beeson Saro-Wiwa, born in Bori, Rivers State, son of Jim Beeson Wiwa, a businessman and community chief. A graduate of the University of Ibadan, he taught at several colleges in Nigeria, administered the oil depot at Bonny

Island, and then served as regional commissioner for education in the Rivers State cabinet. He was a prolific writer, producing at the peak of his career seven books in a year, mostly well-received novels, as well as political essays and poetry. He was active in politics, a journalist, a publicist for his political causes, and was also deeply enamored of English education; he sent all his children to school in England.

As defender of his people, he wrote the Ogoni Bill of Rights, and went to The Hague in July 1992 and registered MOSOP with the Unrepresented Nations and Peoples Organization, pledging his movement to nonviolence. A superb organizer, he supplemented MOSOP with a national youth council, a women's organization, a traditional rulers' conference, a council of churches, a teachers' union, two student unions, and a professional association (all with their own acronyms). He followed up the Hague registration on January 4, 1993, with a massive nonviolent protest against Shell and the government of Nigeria. Around 300,000 Ogoni on the streets told the military junta then in power that the movement had to be taken seriously, and did it with no violence whatsoever.

The shooting started later that year, when police escorting a Shell subcontractor fired on a group of Ogoni protesting the laying of pipe across farmland without notice or compensation. After that, Shell withdrew from Ogoni, citing danger to its workers and to the citizens of Ogoni. Through the summer and fall of 1993, armed gangs from the Rivers State Internal Security, led by one Major (later Lt Colonel) Paul Okuntimo, continued murderous attacks on Ogoni villages. It was not lost on the Ogoni that the boats used by several of the marauding gangs were owned by Shell, and that a Shell helicopter hung in the sky during the September attacks. The terrorist attacks, characterized by random killings, rape, pillage, and burning, continued into 1994, still led by Okuntimo, who by now was openly boasting about them. One of our dilemmas for this case is to characterize these raids: were they, as the central government and Shell observers insisted, primarily the product of ancient tribal rivalries, made more deadly by modern weaponry, where tribal warriors like Paul Okuntimo retaliated against ancient enemies under cover of law? Or were they, as the Nigerian activists contended, deliberately set up by Shell and the government in order to subdue the Ogoni and get the oil flowing again, hiring mercenaries like Paul Okuntimo to do their dirty work for them? Or were they some deadly combination of the two, as thugs like Paul Okuntimo, sensing opportunity in the mutual misunderstandings of Ogoni organizers and foreign multinational companies, used his chance to enrich himself and his thuggish cronies while both sides were helpless to control him? History suggests the validity of all three reads.

By mid-1994, Shell attempted to resume oil operations among the Ogoni on the strength of an "accord" they had drafted, one that Ken Saro-Wiwa had refused to sign. Violence followed; a boy was shot and killed at Korokoro by Okuntimo's men. That time Saro-Wiwa got an audience with Okuntimo's superior, and accused Okuntimo, in front of his superior, of taking "blood money" from Shell.[16] Humiliated, Okuntimo took his revenge by attacking a meeting of Ogoni chiefs on May 21, 1994, at Giokoo, murdering four of the chiefs, and continuing with a night of massacre throughout the surrounding villages.

Later that evening, Ken Saro-Wiwa was arrested for the murders of the chiefs, although he was apparently nowhere in the neighborhood. Other MOSOP leaders followed him to jail. Through most of the summer, the unrestrained massacre and plunder of Ogoniland continued, while Saro-Wiwa and his companions were tortured, starved, and beaten in the jail. The terrorism was no secret; Okuntimo was openly gloating about its effectiveness, even giving detailed instructions on how to carry out his raids.[17] Nor was Saro-Wiwa's condition a secret. Wole Soyinka, a Nobel Laureate (literature) presented an intensely felt, searing description of the miseries of Nigeria and the treatment of Saro-Wiwa, even as it was going on.[18] MOSOP had been founded as a vehicle for communicating the cause of the Ogoni to the world, and it was doing just that. Owens Wiwa, Ken's brother, tried to get Shell to intervene to stop the torture and if possible procure Ken's release, eventually securing three meetings, during the summer of 1995, with Brian Anderson, chief executive of Shell Nigeria.

Anderson insisted that the only condition for his "intercession" with the head of the junta, General Sani Abacha, to set Ken Saro-Wiwa and the other MOSOP activists free was that MOSOP should call off the local and international campaign highlighting Shell and the junta's activities in Ogoni. According to Dr. Wiwa, Anderson also requested that MOSOP put out a press release stating that there was no environmental devastation in Ogoni. Said Owens Wiwa, "Each time I asked him to help get my brother and the others out, he said he would be able to help us get Ken freed if we stopped the protest campaign abroad... Even if I had wanted to, I didn't have the power to control the international environmental protests." Officials of Shell in London later admitted that, indeed, these private meetings took place...

Ken Saro-Wiwa and his colleagues were tried before a military tribunal in October, in a trial that would not meet most civilized standards: evidence that Shell had bribed two of the prosecution witnesses was ignored, and the defense lawyers pulled out of the trial before the end, charging that the kangaroo proceedings were totally unfair. On October 31, nine of the defendants, including Saro-Wiwa, were found guilty; there was no appeal. On November 10, 1995, they were hanged in Port Harcourt prison. A powerful condemnation of Shell and the junta, "Ken Saro-Wiwa's Final Statement to Military Tribunal," was released three days later, denying that he or his organization had any part in violence at all, and suggesting that Shell might try to learn a few lessons from the entire Ogoni affair. He predicted grimly that Shell would be called upon, sooner rather than later, to pay for the environmental damage it had done to Nigeria and for the crimes against the Ogoni people.

What says Shell in its defense? That it was distressed at the arrest of Saro-Wiwa, but that it hoped that the innocent would be promptly released, that all of the defendants would have a fair trial, and that while they were in detention they should be treated humanely. In a statement issued afterward, Shell said:

> The trial and execution of Ken Saro-Wiwa generated worldwide condemnation, because the process itself was seen to be flawed.... trials must be fair, and they must be seen to be fair. The murders, the trial that followed and the execution of Ken Saro-Wiwa and his co-defendants have left deep wounds in the Ogoni community. The best hope for the future must be an openness to dialogue and commitment to reconciliation... It is not for a multinational group of companies such as Shell to interfere in the legal processes of any sovereign nation. But we support, and have publicly reaffirmed our support for, the Universal Declaration of Human Rights. The right to a fair trial is enshrined in the Declaration and in Nigeria's constitution... After the sentence was passed on Ken Saro-Wiwa and his fellow defendants, Shell appealed on humanitarian grounds for clemency to be granted. As we have said before, we will continue

to promote humanitarian values and are ready to intercede either privately or publicly, if this is likely to be helpful ... [19]

Ken Saro-Wiwa, activist, nationalist, and environmentalist, was very sure that Shell Oil's executives were directly responsible for the damage done to his cause and his homeland. Shell's posture is that of a concerned and sympathetic outsider, asking only to continue commercial ventures for the joint good of Shell's shareholders and the people of Nigeria, but quite helpless in the face of the criminal disorders that mar the nation's history, and unjustly singled out as a scapegoat for problems that are not their doing. Consider, in addition to all the other mitigating factors, the fact that Shell Oil Nigeria was not an independent company; like many MNCs, it had been nationalized in 1977, and operated as a joint venture with the government, further restricting its freedom of action. But was it, or its agents on the ground in Nigeria, really reduced to wringing hands while brutality swept back and forth through land they clearly wanted to get back to?

How fares the land?

There can be no truly clean oil exploration and production. The stuff drilled into and brought up from the earth's crust will have devastating effects on any landscape it is poured out on. True, it is not supposed to be poured out. But there are always spills, and sometimes there are devastating fires. The activists claim that the oil operations are causing the spills, the fires, and the devastation of the coastal mangroves on which the fishermen depend for their fish. Shell Oil points out that many of the pipeline breaks are due to sabotage, and are beyond their control. The two explanations are not incompatible.

Meanwhile, the pipelines continue to be laid, an operation that would be no problem in Connecticut, where the soil is firm, but has considerable problematic effect in the essentially swampy land of the Niger Delta. Should the practice be discontinued?

There is no doubt of Shell's commitment to sustainable development and to the protection and remediation of the environment. Multiple statements, and multiple examples of responsible environmental protection and remediation, demonstrate that Shell at the least knows how to formulate the problem and its solutions. But what kind of general company-wide commitments will survive the murky political and economic environment of the developing world? What is a nice multinational corporation like Shell doing in a place like Nigeria?

WWBD?

Was there something more honest, more responsible, about the legitimate colonial empires of the previous century? Upon reaching a foreign shore, Great Britain just assumed that what its explorers saw they claimed, and what they claimed they owned, and therefore, as the superior nation, they were responsible for whatever happened thereafter in that country. When they saw a bad situation, whether or not they actually did anything about it, they recognized a responsibility to act, and refused to be quieted by statements of the form, "this is just our local affair, you stay out of it." Should multinational corporations based in the US or elsewhere, take this approach? We are told that many of our national leaders, confronted with difficult situations, solve them by asking themselves, "What Would Jesus Do?" and emblazon their baseball caps with "WWJD?" Possibly that is the route multinationals should take: ask in every situation, "What Would Britain Do?" and act accordingly. But the developed sophistication of the local and national advocacy groups suggest that the paternalistic era of colonialism is so far past that the moral obligations that pertained to it cannot be revived. We are dealing with a partnership far more complex than any contemplated by the great empires of old, with multiple obligations to stakeholders unforeseen by Victoria Regina, and no clear way that they can all be met.[20]

Consider the following questions: Where do Shell's responsibilities begin and leave off? Should it simply abandon the search for and extraction of oil in Nigeria? What good would that do? The whole world knows the oil is there, and another company would take its place in a heartbeat. Yet as it stands, Shell can be held responsible for a multitude of evil things, with little recourse (remember the fate of Union Carbide when its nationalized plant blew up in Bhopal, India – it had very little power to influence matters in India, but it for sure took the blame.) Maybe it should involve itself more thoroughly with Nigerian affairs, in an attempt to establish greater control to match its liability. Or is that possible?

 NOTES

1. Plato, *The Republic*.
2. Thomas L. Friedman, *The Lexus and the Olive Tree*, New York: Farrar, Straus and Giroux, 1999.

3. Richard DeGeorge, *Competing With Integrity in International Business*, New York: Oxford University Press, 1993.

4. Thomas Donaldson, *Ethics in International Business (Ruffin Series in Business Ethics)*, New York: Oxford University Press, 1989.

5. Joseph E. Stiglitz, *Globalization and Its Discontents*, New York: W.W. Norton, 2002, p. 12.

6. Stiglitz, op. cit., p. 129.

7. Loc. cit.

8. Sir James Goldsmith, "The Winners and the Losers," in Mander and E. Goldsmith, eds., *The Case Against the Global Economy*, San Francisco, CA: Sierra Club Books, 1996, p. 173.

9. Bob Herbert wrote some trenchant columns on this new development for *The New York Times*: "Bracing for the Blow," December 26, 2003, on IBM's "global sourcing" of thousands of its high-paying jobs, and "The White-Collar Blues" December 29, 2003, reflecting on the nation's obligation to structure trade agreements to promote the long-term well-being of the citizens, not the corporations. Op-ed.

10. Documentation of this process is amply provided in a *New York Times* editorial series, "Harvesting Poverty." See editorials (and associated news articles), July 20, 2003, "The Rigged Trade Game," July 22, 2003, "The Great Catfish War," July 25, 2003, "The 'Free Trade' Fix is In," August 5, 2003, "The Long Reach of King Cotton," September 10, 2003, "Showdown in Cancun," Elizabeth Becker and Ginger Thompson, "Poorer Nations Plead Farmers' Case at Trade Talks," *The New York Times*, September 11, 2003, A3; September 16, 2003, "The Cancun Failure," Elizabeth Becker, "Poorer Countries Pull Out of Talks Over World Trade: Farm Subsidies at Issue," *The New York Times*, September 15, 2003, A1, James Brooke, "Farming is Korean's Life and He Ends It in Despair," *The New York Times*, September 16, 2003, A6.

11. Anver Versi, Tom Nevin and Milan Vesely, "A U.S. Perspective on Globalisation," *African Business*, October 2000.

12. This is the thesis – amply proved – of Clive Ponting's *A Green History of the World: The Environment and the Collapse of Great Civilizations*, New York: Penguin Books, 1991.

13. The sources for this discussion are United Nations documents, primarily from the United Nations Environment Programme.

14. The source for this part of the case is, unless otherwise noted, Ike Okonta and Oronto Douglas, *Where Vultures Feast: Shell, Human Rights, and Oil in the Niger Delta*, San Francisco: Sierra Club Books, 2001. The work is not (in case the title and the publisher did not register) particularly favorable to Shell Oil. The central source for the background to the incident here described is Ken Saro-Wiwa, "My Story," full text of Saro-Wiwa's statement to the Ogoni Civil Disturbances Tribunal, in

Ogoni: Trials and Travails, Lagos: Civil Liberties Organization, 1996. The sources for the murder itself are contemporary accounts.

15. Okonta and Douglas, op. cit, p. 116.
16. Ibid., p. 128.
17. Ibid., p. 132.
18. Wole Soyinka, *The Open Sore of a Continent: A Personal Narrative of the Nigerian Crisis*, New York: Oxford University Press, 1996.
19. Shell Nigeria website: www.shell.com/home/Framework?siteld=nigeria& FC2=/nigeria/html/iwgen/news/updates.
20. Other sources, drawn on variously for the latter part of the case, include: www.moles.org/ProjectUnderground/drillbits/6_07/3.html and www.kirjasto.sci.fi/saro.htm. For Ken Saro-Wiwa's Final Statement to Military Tribunal, www.hartford-hwp.com/archives/34a/020.html. For Shell Nigeria's position, www.shell.com/home/Framework?siteld=nigeria which has a rich array of issues to follow up.

chapter seven

The Role of Civil Society Organizations

INTRODUCTION: HOW BRENT SPAR CHANGED THE RULES

One of the most cited examples of watersheds in the business climate is the strange story of the Brent Spar. "Brent Spar Rewrote the Rules," proclaimed a prescient article after Greenpeace and a Greenpeace-forged coalition of environmental and citizen activist groups had forced Shell Oil to withdraw its plan – approved by all relevant government agencies – to sink an obsolete oil buoy at sea.[1] Finding the buoy, the Brent Spar, to be past its period of usefulness, Shell decided (after many discussions with government agencies and environmental groups) that the safest way to dispose of it would be to scuttle it in a deep ocean canyon. Everyone agreed, and the appropriate permits were issued to tow it out into the ocean and sink it. But Greenpeace did not agree, holding that any disposal at sea would poison the ocean and hurt sea life; it would be environmentally safer to dispose of the buoy on land somehow. When the tug, buoy in tow, started down the passage to the sea, a flotilla of boats showed up to block its path. Greenpeace had sent them. The disposal could not continue. Everybody had to back off, the talks resumed, and eventually the buoy was cut up to make a pier.

This was a revelation to the business world (not to mention the government world, that had issued all those permits). All the stakeholders had been consulted, all the powers had agreed, but some other power emerged from the woodwork, vetoed the decision, and prevailed. Who are these people, it might be nice to know, and why are they gumming up the works?

✦ THE BRENT SPAR WAS NOT ALONE: ✦ TWO SENTINEL CASES

Of the ethical challenges that face global businesses, the most immediate and the most troubling deal with the interface between the (apparently) clear ethical demands of the situation at hand and the persuasive claims of values taken for granted at home – especially when those claims are presented by civil society organizations (CSOs), also known as nongovernmental organizations (NGOs),[2] with strong ties at home and a global reach equaling that of business. These dilemmas occasionally hit the headlines – for instance, when a major television personality discovers that a line of clothing bearing her name pays workers abominably low wages, or a star basketball player discovers that the annual endorsement fees he gets from a major line of athletic shoes would pay all the workers in the Southeast Asian factories where they are made for two years and more. But they are faced on the ground in the developing world on a daily basis. On the one hand, it would be nice, as the "No Sweats" anti-sweatshop movement demands, to give all workers at least the US minimum wage, plus life and health insurance and a variety of educational benefits, which their US counterparts enjoy. On the other hand, such largess would dis-tort the economy of the nation, with unpredictable results, and incidentally make it impossible for the company to compete. Further, dreadful as the wage structure is, it is better than the nation enjoyed before and is genuinely appreciated by the workers in those developing lands. Meanwhile, many American workers are in the unemployment office collecting their first checks, while the Asians manufacture the clothes sold at Wal-mart. There is no clear right answer to the dilemma in any case; the unrelenting hail of hostile publicity provided by the No Sweats campaign may not be helpful in the long run. On the other hand, it may be; there will never be an answer if we simply forget the problem, which we probably will if the CSOs go away. Recall the major role of the "enviros" provided in the introduction to Chapter 4: their weapon is not votes, not money, but publicity.

One of the first cases that attained renown – or notoriety – among business ethicists became known as the "Nestlé Case," although many other corporations, including Abbott Laboratories and Bristol Myers, were caught up in it. When the baby boom ended in the North, the manufacturers of infant feeding formula turned their attention to the new professional class in the developing world in the South. Finding a good market, they expanded their marketing initiatives, recruited nurses for their sales representatives and trained them (or had Derek Jelliffe, of the Caribbean Institute for Infant Nutrition, train them) to help out in the hospitals while they gave away samples of formula. Sales were going briskly when Jelliffe changed his mind, and started accusing infant-formula companies of contributing to infant death, according to an intriguing scenario that rapidly captured the popular imagination. According to Jelliffe's scenario, the marketing practices of infant-formula companies – the posters of fat and happy babies sitting beside cans of formula, the seductions of the "milk nurses" (or "mothercraft nurses") in the hospitals – lured new mothers into abandoning the traditional practice of nursing their babies, choosing instead the "modern, Western" way of feeding, that is, formula. When the mothers got home from the hospital, of course, their breast milk having dried up by now, they found they could not afford the formula, so tried to stretch it with water; the water was contaminated, and they did not know enough to boil it to make it sterile; so the infant got diarrhea, in addition to the malnutrition from the inadequate diluted formula, and died. The syndrome was called "bottle illness" in the developing countries, and wherever formula was introduced, it was firmly believed, infant mortality increased. The marketing practices of the formula companies, especially Nestlé, which held most of the market, were to blame for the deaths; or as one German pamphlet put it, "Nestlé Kills Babies." The outrage against Nestlé and similar companies was unbounded; the Infant Formula Action Committee (INFACT) declared a boycott against Nestlé products, and paraded with baby coffins and giant baby bottles with skull and crossbones painted on them.

When the UN eventually commissioned anthropological research on the matter, it turned out that the whole Jelliffe scenario was (as far as research could ascertain) false. Where infant formula use was increasing, primarily among a Westernized professional class in the cities, infant mortality was decreasing. In most rural areas, where most families could not afford to use infant formula regularly, it was not used at all (despite occasionally vigorous marketing) unless a child became too ill to nurse and a physician suggested its use. In most of the reported instances of "bottle illness," infants who sickened while being fed from bottles, it was impossible to tell whether infant formula or goat's milk or bush tea was in the bottles (or if the infants had been put on bottles only after they were too sick and weak to nurse). Most interesting from the perspective of social action was the pattern of women's work requirements in parts of the developing world – where traditional peoples had been pushed off their land, their women had no choice but to work in the rapidly growing cities, and whatever their income, they could not afford to miss work to nurse a child. These comprised a steady clientele for the sick-baby clinics. For what it was worth, they could not afford to buy the formula, either, and the infant had to make do with gruel and goat's milk. But the single study, commissioned by USAID (United States Agency for International Development) in the late 1970s, that brought these results to the fore had no effect whatsoever on INFACT's campaign. The results, to the extent they were known, were shrugged off, and the anthropologist who had assembled them, Dana Raphael of the Human Lactation Institute, was discredited as an industry stooge. The boycott continued until 1984, and there have been periodic attempts to revive it since.

Nuclear energy is another industry blindsided by activist groups. The promise of nuclear energy in the 1950s was enormous – tiny amounts of long-lived fuel, pouring out electricity "too cheap to meter" for the new all-electric America, clean, safe, and inexhaustible. Then a funny thing happened on the way to Energy Utopia. The "anti-Nuke" activism that has shut down the nuclear energy industry entirely in Germany and threatens to do the same in the US came originally from a combination of the anti-nuclear weapons organizations of the 1950s and 1960s (like SANE: the Society to Abolish Nuclear Explosions) and the anti-Vietnam War activism of the 1960s and 1970s; when the testing was stopped and the Vietnam conflict abandoned, the activists went right on demonstrating, this time against nuclear power plants. There was an attenuated association with the anti-war movement – some nuclear by-products could be used for weapons – but there was also a strong element of the growing environmental movement. Nuclear waste was difficult to dispose of, and hazardous; the activists urged that we ought to be using only non-hazardous renewable energy; therefore nuclear power plants should be abolished. Again, the scientific basis of the activists' claims was suspect. The nuclear industry has an admirable record (compared, say, to the oil extraction industry) of worker and community safety. In France, most of the country has been powered by nuclear energy for years without serious incident. In the US, we have to search for combinations of human error that actually result in an accident; the most famous, at Three Mile Island, caused no discernible injury whatsoever. Even in the ill-constructed Soviet plants at Chernobyl, the engineers carrying out the ill-advised experiment that resulted in the meltdown of the main reactor had to overcome 14 separate safety systems, any one of which would have shut down the reaction if not manually disabled. And what are the alternatives to nuclear power plants? Coal burning? But where does coal stand with regard to safety and environmental protection? Not very well: almost every coal miner dies of his trade, as far as safety goes, and burning coal puts acid in the sky and mercury in the water. Yet it is in the nature of activism that it need not come up with viable solutions. Even with California going into periodic energy tailspins, it is politically impossible to build a nuclear plant in the United States. We are not sure where to go next, but nuclear energy is not the direction we will take.

⊛ WHAT IS GOING ON? THE POWER SHIFT ⊛

Jessica Tuchman Mathews was among the first to comment on the new sources of global political power, in her groundbreaking article, "Power Shift," in *Foreign Affairs*, 1997. The article gathers, for the first time at this level of reflection, the evidence that the 1648 Westphalian Settlement – the outcome of the Peace Congress that ended the 100 Years' War, essentially dividing the world into nation-states – had broken down. As states "failed," a new term in the very late twentieth century, or became unable to counter the global forces within their borders, new international enterprises had emerged, dedicated to causes that until then had survived, if they survived at all, only under the protection of government. Human rights organizations like Amnesty International and environmental organizations like Greenpeace, confrontational in philosophy and tactics, joined venerable charitable organizations like Save the Children and the Red Cross in gathering resources at home to gather power globally. As Mathews points out, in many cases they now have more recognition, resources, and influence than government organizations with the same general charge, or the corresponding agencies of the United Nations. Amnesty International, for instance, now has more money (and better fund-raising mechanisms) than the United Nations Commission on Human Rights; it is better informed than any nation-states on human rights violations within their borders and all over the world, it has ready access to news media to publicize them, and it has the political clout to get something done about them. In short, the CSOs are a force to be reckoned with, and global business enterprises will have to reckon with them.[3]

The history of global civil society, the network of not-for-profit projects that now form part of most of the governing regimes of the world, can be traced back to the international labor movement of the nineteenth century, with its immediate legitimation coming from the founding of the United Nations in 1945 which from its inception included international charitable and other CSOs in its list of consultants. Perhaps 50 CSOs consulted with the UN at its beginning; by 1998 the Economic and Social Council recognized over 1,000 of them, and according to one source, the total number of CSOs now working with the UN is in the tens of thousands.[4] The 1990s saw the rapid growth of the sector, most visible in the 1992 Earth Summit in Rio de Janeiro, Brazil. There, an apparent attempt to sideline the CSOs by placing them in a single area outside of the main operations of the conference served only to emphasize their strength (approximately 2,400 representatives of CSOs showed up to lobby the national delegates), and provide an excellent and well-used opportunity for networking. It could be argued that as far as the natural environment is concerned, global civil society was forged at Rio. These CSOs were given a central role in the Committee on Sustainable Development that followed up on the Sustainability Agenda of that gathering. CSOs went on to play a central role in the 1994 Cairo World Population Conference and the 1995 World Conference on Women in Beijing.[5]

Their work has borne some fruit: when several global CSOs set out to ban the production, storage, and use of landmines, they succeeded magnificently: "...not only was the treaty to ban landmines signed in 1997, but the International Campaign to Ban Landmines and its representative Jody Williams were awarded the Nobel Peace Prize."[6]

How on earth did they get that done?

> The most powerful engine of change in the relative decline of states and the rise of nonstate actors is the computer and telecommunications revolution, whose deep political and social consequences have been almost completely ignored. Widely accessible and affordable technology has broken governments' monopoly on the collection and management of large amounts of information and deprived governments of the deference they enjoyed because of it....In drastically lowering the costs of communication, consultation, and coordination, [the information technologies] favor decentralized networks over other modes of organization...Businesses, citizens organizations, ethnic groups and crime cartels have all readily adopted the network model.[7]

In short, the Web. The secret is the Internet, that worldwide communication mechanism that can rouse thousands and tens of thousands of participants overnight for public rallies, fund-raising drives, or information campaigns. The Internet has already shown its peculiar power. One highly visible triumph was the worldwide march in protest against the proposed US military expedition against Iraq on February 15, 2003. One estimate had one person of every thousand worldwide on that march: six million in the streets in a world population of six billion.[8] That is power. The danger, of course, is that it will be used for evil, or at least, for less than good. We will come back to this point.

⊛ THIRD SECTOR, GLOBAL CIVIL SOCIETY ⊛

What is this new "third sector," civil society? Its definition is in part political; its partisans define it as broadly as possible, other analysts bound it more narrowly. The International Forum on Globalization, a group allied with many CSOs, describes it as follows:

> The evolving alliance of civil society organizations brings together union members, farmers, landless peasants, people of faith, women's organizations, youth organizations, small business owners, artisanal producers, economic justice organizers, prison reform advocates, environmentalists, AIDS and other health activists, politicians, independent media organizations, civil servants, the homeless, peace and human rights organizations, gay and lesbian groups, intellectuals, consumer advocates, and even a few corporate CEOs of every age, religion, race, and nationality. It is the product of a largely spontaneous awakening of millions of people to the reality that their future and the future of their children depends on exercising their democratic right to participate in the decisions that shape their future.[9]

This description can be characterized as romantic (We Are the World), political (aimed to gather, rather than to describe, support) and not a little self-serving. CSOs are in fact self-selected, self-appointed, have nothing to do with democracy, and most of the groups mentioned above are inadequately represented by any CSO (or anything else, for that matter). But the sense of their own power is certainly well conveyed.

Civil society designates that part of society which is not part of the formal apparatus of government, but governs nonetheless: the churches, trade associations, fraternal organizations, social and charitable societies, neighborhood and interest groups of all kinds, organizations for the relief of distress or for the advancement of some good cause – schools, garden clubs, and the Sailors' Relief Fund. It has a political side, just not a state office; it has traditionally encompassed

> not only political representation and participation, privacy and the autonomy of association and private institutions, but also the free formation of all sorts of movements and parties, whether socialist, liberal, conservative, feminist, environmentalist, or of any other kind...a historically evolved sphere of individual rights, freedom and voluntary associations whose politically undisturbed private concerns, interests, preferences and intensions is guaranteed by...the state.[10]

This is precisely the part of human life most impacted by the advent of "modernization," the industrialization and commercialization of all parts of life, since this aspect of collective life was most closely tied to the village, or local community. Yet here it is again, only globalized. Globalization has been accompanied by the creation of new institutions that have joined with existing ones to work across borders. In the arena of international civil society, new groups, like the Jubilee movement pushing for debt reduction for the poorest countries, have joined long-established organizations like the International Red Cross.[11]

The movement to form CSOs began as scattered protests from organizations with no knowledge of each other, but rapidly developed into an anonymous but global alliance. Consider the following statement from the organizers of the 2001 Harvard workshops on Practice-Research Engagement and Building Transnational Civil Society:

> Behind the concept of these workshops is the belief that much can be gained from contacts among "activist scholars" and "reflective activists" in the service of better understanding complex political, economic and social problems. *These workshops sought to foster relationships and organizational arrangements that would allow members to learn from each other's perspectives and advance both theory and practice on issues of global concern.* We hoped to learn more about circumstances under which contacts between practitioners and researchers produce outcomes of value to both

groups, and to encourage continuing contacts focused on specific topics in the future.[12]

The anti-corporate, anti-government bias in most CSO work follows in part from their origins. Note the time of origin of the two cases cited above, the assault on the nuclear power industry and the infant formula campaign. CSO activism, boycotts, and campaigns started right after the conflict in Vietnam, whose end released a generation of seasoned activists, already well equipped with a hearty distrust of government and a well-founded conviction that large corporations exist in symbiosis with large governments. That bias will be difficult to break.

International, transnational, or global civil society, a power to be reckoned with, is a grand union of CSOs of all political stripes, able to unite behind dozens of causes toward basically the same ends, primarily regional and local preservation with a very strong preferential option for the poor. On those grounds, it reflexively opposes globalization – multinational companies and all the trade structures that support them (the World Bank, International Monetary Fund, above all the World Trade Organization). It tends to be very suspicious of the corporate world, no matter in what manifestation, and the governments of nation-states. That disposition can make it unreasonably difficult for governments and corporations to operate, even in missions designed to solve social and environmental problems; for structural reasons, as will become clear below, CSOs are rarely in a position to reward responsible corporations for responsible action.

Yet CSOs may have a crucial role to play in a globalized future. In strategies to maintain competitiveness in an increasingly watchful world, many corporations have adopted forward-looking and innovative codes of social and environmental conduct, designed to protect them against the financial exposure that comes from blatant ethical misconduct and egregious damage to the environment. Some of these industrial codes, for example Responsible Care® for the American Chemistry Council (ACC), are excellent blueprints for a responsible future for a competitive industry. That Code in particular provides for third-party monitoring of industry compliance to the code. Like it or not, the CSOs will be the monitors of any international agreements to preserve human rights and the natural environment. In any system of global accountability, run by any international agency, the freestanding CSOs collected under the heading of civil society would be the watchdogs, the communicators and complainants, and the administrators of the ultimate sanctions of the process.

⊛ DEALING WITH ATTACKS FROM CSOs ⊛

Consider again our sentinel cases. Here we have two industries, the **infant formula** industry and the **nuclear power** industry (to be joined later by a third, the case of Monsanto and the **Genetically Modified Organisms**, as the case for this chapter), with enormous promise for the world – to feed the starving babies of the developing world, and to provide an endless source of energy for us all – stopped in their tracks by organized groups playing on nameless popular fears. How did this happen? How come no one ever asked us, when our interests were being represented by these groups? How come the claims of these groups so easily overwhelm the evidence available? And since we approach this topic from the perspective of the global business manager, how can a global industry deal with them?

Three comments might be worthwhile at this point. First, we must start with the assumption, not far-fetched in any of these cases, that the general claims advanced by the CSOs have merit. Globalization (see Chapter 6) threatens a great deal that we hold to be valuable. By its substitution of distance factory farming for the family farm, for example, it effectively removes from the human experience the environmental context in which we evolved, and there is no surer recipe for general anxiety. In the US, the family farm is essentially gone; in Europe, farmers continue to insist on their viability, and make alliance with any CSO that can possibly help them (Greenpeace, for instance). In its insistence on the destruction of trade barriers that protected traditional industries, globalization wrecked livelihoods generations in the making, for instance in the steel industry. At every level it threatens local and regional industries and the communities that depend on them. Those who fight to defend communities that have sheltered their families for a century and more are not hopelessly irrational, and it is not a foregone conclusion that the fight will fail. There is genuine opposition to economic globalization, and those who carry on the battle are, almost by definition, not the corporations (the private sector) that expect to benefit from globalization, nor the governments (the public sector) that are its chief sponsor. That leaves the CSOs to defend community values.

Second, the sentinel cases are perfectly plausible, before we realize that what the advocates claimed was simply not true. There is no question that inexperienced mothers in the developing world, now separated from the network of traditional wisdom and experience that would have guided them in the displaced village, may make mistakes about the best way to feed their children; education and aid (of the sort provided by the US Women, Infants and Children [WIC] Program) are surely called for. It is certain that nuclear energy has downsides – in extreme circumstances, the reactor can melt down, and the disposal of waste is a problem not yet solved. So far so good, or at least understandable. But even contemporary surveys of the safety of these products or methods showed them to be at least as safe, for human use and consumption, as any available alternatives. The available alternative to infant formula was, in most cases, not breast milk but indigestible goat's milk; and the alternative to nuclear energy most likely to be adopted is not solar energy, whose technology is not yet sufficient for most purposes, but coal. Whatever plausibility the claims may have had on first presentation, further study showed them to be misplaced apprehension – the products or methods that they replaced held more real danger to the consumers.

The third comment is that as in so many similar cases, the industries attacked by the CSOs responded in all the wrong ways, at least at first. Years ago, Elisabeth Kubler-Ross wrote a groundbreaking essay on the "stages" of dying – the mental and emotional steps a person goes through from first diagnosis of a terminal illness to the end of life. They are much like the stages that any person, real or, like a corporation, fictive, goes through in response to any piece of bad news. They start with denial – it simply cannot be happening. Both industries, especially the flagship corporations identified by the NGOs for special treatment, were completely blindsided by the attacks. They ignored the protests and accusations until far too late. When they finally noticed them, they went on mis-reacting. After denial comes anger – a counterattack on the evil ones who are bringing the bad news. Nestlé, for instance, brought a full-scale lawsuit against a tiny group that had "libeled" it with a nasty pamphlet, winning the suit but suffering a devastating loss in public relations. Later, Oswald Ballarin, speaking on behalf of Nestlé South America before Edward Kennedy's Senate Subcommittee on Infant Nutrition, labeled the accusing NGOs (including several religious orders of nuns) "communists," and rapidly lost the sympathy of the US Senate. Similarly, the nuclear industry kept having the anti-nuke protestors arrested, losing public approval every time.

After anger comes bargaining – an attempt to deal with the situation by rational means that have worked before. For a beleaguered industry, that usually means a public relations campaign, reasonably explaining their position, persuasive arguments and friendly faces presented on slick brochures and prominent paid advertising. It never works. Every effort to court the public after the original public relations disaster simply turns more people against the company.

Then what *does* work? Nestlé eventually tried one enormously effective mode of combat: it set up a corporation (the Nestlé Conference on Children's Nutrition, NCCN), staffed by its most personable and articulate young executives, whose sole job was to listen to complaints about its products, talk respectfully to the complainers, and travel anywhere to talk to people, talk, but mostly to listen. Nestlé discovered that where dealing with a fearful or angry public is concerned, people do not want to be *told*. People want to be *heard*. If the people can be convinced that you have heard what they are saying, that you understand what they are afraid of, what their concerns are, then they are much more likely to trust you to determine whether or not there is a real danger present. NCCN worked; the boycott rapidly ran out of steam, supporting groups started to withdraw their support, and a newly chastened Nestlé S. A. pledged to follow new "breastmilk substitute marketing guidelines" and to continue dialog with any groups that wanted to talk to them. Then, inexplicably but all too typically, as soon as the tumult and the shouting died, Nestlé disbanded NCCN – as too expensive to keep up. The campaign against Nestlé began again almost immediately, and the expenses have not gone away.

What characterized these industries (and so many more!) was arrogance, the conviction that they could determine their own modes of operating without consulting anyone outside of their usual lines of authority – without having to put an ear to the ground and listen. They were wrong. The lines of communication, and the avenues of power, have irrevocably changed. No longer can arrangements that impact the natural environment or human rights be quietly negotiated between corporations and governments. CSOs concerned with these issues continue to force open issues considered closed, simply by using their vast (and inexpensive) network of international contacts, connected by the World Wide Web, to rally public support, in terms of money and bodies for rallies, in crucial nations.

Governments, with whom all these industries had very cordial relationships, were no help at all. Actually, Mathews suggests, hierarchically structured governments may be in the worst position to negotiate with the CSOs. Governments continue to operate on the basis of authority and legal empowerment. All the other players in these dramas – corporations, the CSOs, even ethnic societies and crime cartels and especially terrorist organizations, are way ahead of government in the decentralized, node-centered, multi-interaction world of the website, the network, and the chatroom.[13] The power is now with the people, represented by CSOs for better or for worse, linked together by means of communication that make the slick promotional brochures of the large corporations look terminally silly.

To deal with this new power structure, this formless web of comment and criticism, crystallizing in rallies, boycotts, and campaigns, global industry has to learn to listen – not just to its shareholders, nor even to its customers, but to a vast public that may be forming opinions and impressions, and preparing to act on them. The impressions may seem ludicrously inaccurate, and the opinions disgracefully uninformed, but they must be respected – not just refuted or contradicted, but listened to and addressed.

✆ CHALLENGES FOR THE CSOs ✆

We know the origins of the movement that we now call "global civil society." The possibility of going global – of ignoring national boundaries and spreading rapidly across an unresisting world – had tempted corporations to become multinationals, and in the name of profit they did so. The success of those very corporations has forced their traditional critics to do the same, and in the process of organizing to combat very specific threats, they have created a new vision of society, beyond Locke, beyond the Westphalian system, beyond any political arrangements with which we are familiar.

Somewhere along the line, for starters, the CSOs are going to have to define their claim to legitimacy. There is no doubt that they have power. But that power is what in philosophy we call "normative power," or the power of the conscience. Referring back to Chapter 4 and the Clean Air hearings that introduced it, we may note that the threat from the "enviros" was not violence, not an opposing campaign waged with lots of money, or even lawsuits. All they threatened to do was to tell the newspapers, and the prospect of seeing their conduct of the public business on the front pages of the leading newspapers was enough to stop the senators in their tracks. But the power of such appeals must lie in the righteousness, the justice, of the CSOs' cause – if they wield moral power, they must be morally right. How would they establish that, in any given case?

How can the CSOs meet the test of accountability? Who would ever be in a position to hold them accountable? The rank and file of the CSOs are generally unaware of the details of the actions taken in their name. Only the committed few have the time to dedicate to their international campaign. They cannot be fired, at least not by anyone we might be able to identify, and they do not compete fairly. This general lack of accountability is, as far as we can see, intractable. Governments can be called to account by the citizens, and corporations by the investors, but the amorphous CSOs seem to report only to God. They can be sued, but (see the Nestlé case) the suit usually does the plaintiff more harm than it does the CSO, no matter how the case comes out.

Central to the problems that CSOs have to address in any future operations is their relation to the media, since large-scale publicity is essential to their survival. They have often been accused of manipulating the press – using the press to create a promotional scene out of an event with no "news" value at all. CSOs, recall, have agendas too. They must meet payrolls and fund operations to keep them in existence. Their only source of funds is an aroused public. In order to get resources – contributions from that public – they need to stay in the public eye, especially, if they can manage it, with grandstand plays on the front pages of the newspapers. That means that they must find matters to outrage them (and us), they need *not to find out* that things are going well. They cannot afford to become irrelevant.

The communications requirements of the type of actions CSOs need in order to survive inevitably result in distortion of the truth. Whatever legitimate message may be buried in their actions, the message gets dumbed down for the media, since only simple messages will get across. Subtleties that might discourage quick assent and quick action tend to be suppressed, and we may end up with only a tag end of the truth.

The need for publicity requires ever more unorthodox (and frankly unacceptable) means to their ends. If picketing the factory or the Pentagon gets little done, many organizations have taken to picketing the homes of CEOs of targeted corporations; animal rights organizations have recently taken to picketing the homes and neighborhoods of middle- and low-level employees, who are less likely to shrug off the attacks.[14] Usually these methods are legal, but are they right?

Sometimes the methods are not legal; drawing on traditions that include Henry David Thoreau, Mohandas Gandhi, and the US Civil Rights Movement, many political CSOs have endorsed selective breach of the law. (Most CSOs, on the model of the Red Cross, do nothing of the kind.) Unjust laws, of course, deserve to be broken, but the usual targets of demonstration-bred lawbreaking are the inoffensive prohibitions against entering upon or damaging property, or breaching police lines. To enhance the drama of their confrontations (and secure that front-page spot) the demonstration leaders break the law somehow, draw the police into arresting them, and that gets the vans and the handcuffs on the front page. The lawbreaking disposition has the desired consequences – they get the headlines – but several undesirable ones as well. It may, probably will, smear the target of their protest with the label of brutality, even when that target has done nothing at all to deserve it; it may, on the other hand, alienate a good portion of the citizenry from the cause the CSO espouses, which may, after all, be a good one; and it always distracts, and lowers respect for, the police who have better things to do than fill the front pages with these planned arrests.

The structure of CSO action also makes it difficult for it to compromise. If many CSOs are involved in the same general advocacy, the CSO that cooperates with the target – individual, business, or government – tends to be marginalized among the CSOs, and rendered ineffective. In some campaigns, CSOs with different characters and histories can divide the campaign labor between an "outside" CSO (like Greenpeace) that demands total victory, and an "inside" CSO (like the National Wildlife Federation) that quietly works with corporations for politically achievable ends.

And finally, on the other side of the equation, they themselves can be manipulated, especially the best of them. Note the history of the humanitarian organizations trying to help refugees from civil wars, from Burundi in the course of the Rwanda conflicts to Thailand in the wake of the genocidal slaughters of Pol Pot in Cambodia. It is impossible to distinguish a frightened civilian refugee, who wants only to live in peace, from a soldier out of uniform, entering the refugee camps to form and maintain a resistance movement against the victorious party in the fighting that drove the civilians to the camp. Left to their own devices, the soldiers will take over the camps, set up a mob-style government, tax the refugees (for the goods distributed by the CSOs or for goods the refugees may have brought with them), assemble weapons, and start to mount guerrilla raids across the border on the country they left behind. The CSOs, meanwhile, have committed themselves to helping all indigenous people displaced by the war. Hoist on their own commitments, they dare not back off and say, "this enterprise is corrupt."[15]

⊕ THE ULTIMATE HOPE FOR THE CSOs ⊕

In the end, the CSOs may be our best hope for the future of the land and environmental protection. Consider the limitations of the other sectors for that role:

(a) *Business* has its own imperatives. Any publicly traded corporation has to work to increase the wealth of its shareholders; any corporation at all has to advance the interests of its stakeholders; there are times when these commitments can be reconciled with saving the land (see Chapter 5) but there are other times when they cannot. Simple survival reinforces what fiduciary duty demands, that the investors who hold the right and the power in the corporation shall be served.

(b) *Government* is duty bound, whether or not democratically elected, to advance the welfare of the people. That means living people, not future generations. In a democracy, representatives that cannot advance the economic interests of their constituents will not survive the next election; dictators who leave their people in poverty will not survive the next revolution. So for government, economic growth is an absolute imperative, and growth very often entails assaults on the environment.

The result of the above is that the powers that are, those legitimately empowered by charter and office to act on behalf of people in some respect, often have little choice but to accept an environmental assault if it promises to advance economic welfare. The role, therefore, of the third sector, is to speak for that which is voiceless in the normal distribution of power: to speak for the trees, and for the indigenous peoples who live among them and protect them. The CSO, unlike corporation or government, can make a direct appeal to the conscience of the world, and that appeal, ultimately, is the only hope for the protection of the natural environment.

Then how can we put together an agenda of cooperation for the multinational corporations (MNCs) and the CSOs whose mission is the protection of the environment? There are obvious problems. The first task must be to replace opposition with a concept of Arms-Length Cooperation: the mutual adoption of parallel agendas. Such cooperation would have to begin with the search for common values, which may not be as difficult as it sounds; both sides generally know at least that all-out war will harm them both. The next move must be to find a common validation – some audience, body of constituents, or polity, that acknowledges them both as legitimate and would like to see them abide by certain rules of engagement (for instance, nonviolent protests in the US, under the watchful eye of generally friendly police, can often accomplish their purposes without damaging the target or scarring the society). At that point the creation of a system, a framework for ongoing coordination, may be possible, always subject to the limitations noted above: that the appearance of close cooperation between a corporation and a professedly hostile CSO will draw credibility from both sides.

The goal of these arms-length negotiations is finally the development of a set of dovetailed standards for working together, rather along the lines of the labor compacts of the 1930s and the more effective of the international treaties now in effect. A major condition for the success of that effort, as well as a significant product of it, will be the muting, defusing, of the ideology on both sides. In preparation for that time, the MNCs might consider avoiding the rhetoric of business ideology as much as possible in any dealings abroad, especially those that have anything to do with the natural environment.

In the end, global environmental governance will be carried on by shifting alliances of CSOs, MNCs, and governments, whose major tasks will be interpreting and enforcing global environmental covenants. The result may be a new level of peace, a Hegelian synthesis of the profit-oriented expansion of the free market in economic globalization and the localist and environmentalist opposition that it called forth in the course of its operations. What shape that peace may take will probably surprise us.

The peace probably cannot be permanent. The competitive scene is constantly changing, and the MNCs will be required by economic imperatives to move into new areas that evade whatever agreements have governed the previous peace. CSOs, in their turn, have a finally prophetic role in the pursuit of their mission. They have the irreducible and unavoidable task of observing, reporting, and opposing environmental degradation, whatever the previous engagements. Agreements simply cannot change the fundamental obligations of either institution.

In the end, the environmental CSO speaks for a constituency that by definition cannot speak for itself – generations yet unborn, and the land itself. For this reason there is no way to a negotiated permanent peace. If the natural world is threatened, the environmental CSO cannot be quiet.

⊛ CASE 7: MONSANTO AND THE ⊛ GENETICALLY MODIFIED ORGANISMS

The puzzling case of Monsanto and the genetically engineered plants began in the early 1980s, with the development of a tomato, the Flavr Savr, engineered to stay fresh in the refrigerator longer than most tomatoes. Engineered? Yes, new genetic material had been placed in the seed to create different qualities. In itself, the fact that the tomato had slightly different genetic material should have caused no problems for anyone. Plants mutate, undergo random changes in their genetic makeup that are passed on to their offspring, all the time, even as other organisms do in this diversified life. It is not unheard of for creatures to change by incorporating parts of very different organisms in their genetic endowment; they think, for instance, that our cellular mitochondria started as parasites. Since the beginnings of scientific agriculture, genetic changes in plants have been deliberately accelerated by selection of favorable mutations for seeds for the next crop, and by hybridization that will produce at least one generation of improved crops. When the techniques of recombinant DNA came along, the agricultural scientists immediately adopted them. Hence the Flavr Savr, and all similar modifications since that time.

The advances made in genetically modifying organisms for desirable traits are truly amazing. Careful research isolated the genetic material that helps a flounder resist frost; transplanted into strawberries, it helps the strawberries do the same. Monsanto, a chemicals company that got into the seed business to join it (as a "life sciences" project) with its pharmaceutical business, managed to engineer into soybeans a resistance to its own powerful herbicide, Roundup, so that a soybean grower can save most of the labor from weeding and applying herbicides between the rows in his or her fields; one solid spray across the whole field, and the weeds are gone and the soybeans are fine. There is a naturally occurring pesticide, *Bacillus thuringiensis* (Bt), that organic farmers have used for decades to kill insects without leaving chemical residues in the soil; Monsanto managed to engineer Bt into corn (maize) to kill off the larvae that feed on the roots and seeds of the corn. Farmers with this type of genetically modified corn do not have to use pesticides, so the farmer's labor and other costs are reduced, and the environment is protected from the barrels of harmful chemicals that used to be part of every growing year. Who could possibly object? When Monsanto put Roundup Ready soybeans and Bt-engineered corn on the market, farmers snapped them up, and by the end of the 1990s large percentages of the corn and soybeans sold were genetically modified organisms (GMOs). One of the largest successes was Bt-engineered cotton; cotton notoriously requires huge inputs of pesticides, and the engineering reduced them almost to zero. (*Forbes* magazine, recognizing the controversy over the use of GMOs, nevertheless confidently pronounced the adoption of engineered cotton as good, being "the lesser of two weevils.")[16]

There was opposition from the likes of Jeremy Rifkin, anti-science activist for all purposes, who identified the GMOs as a plot by corporations to poison our food for profit, and then Greenpeace, a major player on the environmental CSO scene, joined a crusade to have the GMOs removed from the market. To the amazement of Monsanto and most other observers, the campaigns found an audience, and at last tally, had managed to have GMOs banned from most European and all Japanese markets – on grounds of safety. To date, there has never been any evidence at all that corn or beans modified in these ways differ in safety in any way at all from those not so modified, except that the corn does not have borer tracks. After all, on any scale larger than an organic garden, the alternative to corn genetically engineered to repel corn borers is corn marinated in insecticide, and that is not very safe, either.

The campaign against the GMOs originated abroad, but had its devotees in the US also. In June 1999, a study emerged from Cornell[17] purporting to show that Bt-engineered corn was dangerous for the environment; the experiment had consisted in capturing many Monarch butterfly larvae (caterpillars), feeding them Bt-containing pollen from corn, and seeing if they died. Many, indeed, did. The claim was that the study had proved that planting Bt-engineered corn could kill Monarch butterflies since the pollen might blow over to the milkweed on which (exclusively) the Monarchs feed, and obviously such pollen kills Monarch larvae. The problems with the study are too extensive to list: most Monarch caterpillars die no matter what, so there is no way to establish significance; most milkweed do not grow near cornfields, most Bt-engineered pollen does not blow on milkweed, and the Monarch are in any case not anything like endangered, at least in their Northern range. But the anti-GMOs advocacy seized on the study as evidence for their cause, and it has been hard to make this particular myth die. Why is that, do you think?

Eventually, the burden of the anti-GMO case was carried by the farmers of the European Union (EU), who argued that there was no proof of the safety of GMOs and more to the point, no way that anyone could use the GMO seed profitably without being a very large monoculture farm like those in the United States, when European farmers, traditionally committed to small multi-product farms, had no intention of adopting that model. The small farmers have tremendous political power in the EU, so their argument prevailed. Is this a good way to decide environmental policy?

Why did Greenpeace join the fight against the GMOs? There was no claim that GMOs hurt the land. Indeed, compared to the herbicide and pesticide cycles that had gone before, it could be argued that GMOs are the best thing that ever happened to the land. They are certainly not the best thing that ever happened to the small farmer; as a matter of fact, widespread adoption of GMOs would put the small farmers out of business. It is possible that the Greenpeace opposition to biotechnology is an example of the co-optation of CSOs mentioned above. The protesters are not obviously protecting the environment, but they are serving well the interests of the small farmers and their defenders in government. It could be that country environmentalists are just as capable of hijacking the agenda of a liberal cause as anyone else.

Consider the questions that arise from this case:

1 How much science do we have to know in order to determine whether GMOs are "safe"? Or will we never know enough science to be certain of that?
2 What lies behind the opposition to GMOs? Can you diagram the forces whose convergence resulted in the success of the campaign?
3 What should Monsanto do to get rid of the objections to GMOs? Or should it do anything?
4 GMOs do not arise in nature. For that reason, should we reject them as unnatural? Why or why not?

❦ NOTES ❦

1. R. Grove White, "Brent Spar Rewrote the Rules," *New Statesman*, July 20, 1997.
2. Civil society itself is in rapid evolution, and its nomenclature seems to be, too. Some sources still refer to these organizations collectively as "NGOs" (the older terminology), others prefer the more recent "CSOs," others (for instance, Neera Chandhoke, "The Limits of Global Civil Society," in *Global Civil Society 2002*, Oxford: Oxford University Press, 2002, pp. 35–53), distinguish between them in ways not altogether clear, while acknowledging that NGOs make up the greatest part of the CSOs.
3. Jessica Tuchman Mathews, "Power Shift," *Foreign Affairs*, 76(1): 50–66 (January–February 1997).
4. William Korey, *NGOs and the Universal Declaration of Human Rights*, New York: St Martin's Press, 1998.
5. Helmut Anheier, Marlies Glasius, and Mary Kaldor, eds, *Global Civil Society 2001*, Oxford, 2001.
6. Neera Chandhoke, op. cit., pp. 38–39.
7. Jessica Tuchman Mathews, op. cit. As to the importance of the Internet in coordinating the activities of the NGOs, see also Ross Irvine, "Netwarriors' fight way to top in corporate PR," *O'Dwyer's PR Services Report*, May 2000.
8. Patrick E. Tyler, "A New Power in the Streets: A Message to Bush Not to Rush to War," *The New York Times*, February 17, 2003, A1, A9–11.
9. *Alternatives to Economic Globalization*, San Francisco: Berrett-Koehler, 2002, pp. 11–12.
10. Salvador Giner, "Civil Society and Its Future," in *Civil Society*, ed. John Hall, Cambridge: Polity Press, 1995.
11. Stiglitz, op. cit., pp. 9–10.
12. L. David Brown, Angela Johnson, and Sarah Titus, "Practice-Research Engagement and Building Transnational Civil Society: Two Connected Workshops," in *Practice-Research Engagement and Civil Society in a Globalizing World*, Cambridge, MA: The Hauser Center, 2001.
13. Jessica Tuchman Mathews, "Power Shift," op. cit.
14. Alex Markels, "Protesters Carry the Fight to Executives' Homes," *The New York Times*, December 7, 2003, BU 4. In the lead case for the story, protesters had sent a hearse to an employee's home – with her name on the coffin.
15. See Fiona Terry, *Condemned to Repeat? The Paradox of Humanitarian Action*, Ithaca: Cornell University Press, 2002.
16. Gary Slutsker, "The lesser of two weevils," *Forbes*, October 15, 1990, pp. 202–203.
17. *Nature*, June 1999.

chapter eight

Sustainability: The New Directions for Business

⊛ INTRODUCTION ⊛

A century ago, we thought the natural world was limitless, infinite in its possibilities for our use, there to be conquered and enjoyed by us and by endless generations of our children and grandchildren. We do not think that any more. As a people, we have grown into a position of responsibility, in our recognition that the natural world is limited and vulnerable, and that the actions taken by humans in our generation can seriously affect its future as well as our own. Maybe previous generations did more preventable damage to the earth than we do, but that is beside the point. It is a very different thing to choose a course of action ignorant of the harm it does, and to choose that same course after you know what it does to the natural environment and to the options that will be available to your grandchildren. A certain bru-tish innocence has been lost. We and the world are no doubt the better for this loss of innocence, but it surely makes our choices more painful.

We are embarked upon a new project – the first century in the history of the species that we have entered in the knowledge that we are responsible for the future of the natural world on which we depend. We may think of it as a journey, clearly burdened and not a little frightening, into the future. The first section will talk about some of the fears and burdens we carry on the journey. But in what we have seen already in the previous chapters, there are good reasons to believe that the worst scenarios are not inevitable, and that there is a good deal we can do to make sure that they do not happen. The second section will review some of those reasons. And if those reasons prevail, and we settle into the habit of squaring economic decisions with environmental laws, we have an excellent chance of creating a society that our children can be proud of and in which our great-great-grandchildren will enjoy a more satisfying life than we can imagine. The third section will attempt to sketch some of the possibilities.

⊛ LOOKING INTO THE ABYSS ⊛

Business people, more than others, are asked to develop certain virtues, of integrity, caution, patience, and perseverance; willingness to inquire in depth, examine options thoroughly; and from these develop the overarching business virtues of prudence and responsibility. The intersection of the integrity they must have and the prudence, foresight, that they are required to develop is the virtue of honesty – the ability to face the facts, as they have been discovered, without fear and without requiring that they be chocolate-coated before they can be presented to the corporate leaders. The present facts, and probable future conditions, of the natural environment are not the stuff of feel-good promotions. Without indulging in doomsday scenarios, any sober assessment of the state of the global natural environment reveals many areas of very serious concern. The business leaders who will assume responsibility for corporate enterprise in this century will have to have the courage to look the facts in the face and deal with the situations that they find. The future is not for sissies.

Let us review. The major challenges, or problem areas, that we identified in Chapter 3 projected the image of the natural world as a **CORPSE**, collapsed and dead from the ravages of Climate change, Overpopulation, Resource depletion, Pollution, Species extinction, and Energy waste. What is the worst-case scenario for the development of these processes into full-scale crises? We see an Easter Island world, its resources gone, its soil poisoned, its species reduced to humans, rats, and lizards, and overrun with hungry humans who end their days in cannibalism.[1]

Faced with such a scenario, what would be recommended by the environmental reactionary as the measures that have to be adopted immediately to reverse the processes and restore the natural world? The best way to describe the world preferred by the environmental reactionary is one that **CRAMPPs** our style, by taking away six freedoms that we have come to value: freedom of Consumption, Reproduction, Affluence, Mobility, Pollution, and Property (in land). Let us take those one at a time, and briefly, since they are not pleasant to think about.

Consumption

The supermarket bins are piled with every kind of fruit or vegetable, regardless of season or latitude of origin; we assume that any food we can imagine will be available where and when we want it, at whatever cost in transportation or, more to the point, in the depletion of the soil and other resources where they were grown. Much of that abundance is thrown away at the end of the day. The shelves at Wal-Mart, again, overflow with goods from all over the world, available to us at very low cost because little care was taken to provide just compensation for their makers or to preserve the natural environment in the country they came from. All that is going to have to come to an end. Either we must insist that all environmental and social safeguards attend the production of this abundance, in which case the prices will rise very significantly, or we will have to ban these products from the market. A frugal life, which never did anyone any harm, will have to replace this pattern of unlimited consumption.

Reproduction

The major environmental problem is overpopulation. If there were few enough of us, it really would not matter how we chose to live; the earth would recover. But we already have more people than we can sustain, and the population keeps growing. We will have to license the right to have children. Though the measure sounds draconian, we know that it will work: China, the most populous nation in the world, significantly reduced its population growth through promulgation of a "One-Child Contract," an agreement signed by a family and by a township that no more than one child would be born to that family. Incentives were necessary to persuade families to sign the contract, and corresponding penalties attended its breach; strong social pressure helped to keep families in line. Anti-fertility measures have not been popular in any nation where they have been tried, but they are clearly possible, and necessary.

Affluence

Our affluent lifestyle, which we enjoy at the expense of the poor of the world and of the natural environment, will have to go. The affluence is a corollary of the level of consumption – we enjoy goods and foods from all over the world at such low cost that we have resources left over to invest in yet further material ventures, investment, or new levels of consumption. Affluence is a serious affront to justice. The poor of the world are suffering, from hunger and sickness, on a daily basis while Americans have more money, literally, than they know what to do with – so they buy All-Terrain Vehicles and Ski Mobiles, used for recreational purposes only, which destroy the land where they are used. Here we can kill two birds with one stone: by redirecting that wealth to take care of the poor across the globe, we also help preserve the environment.

Mobility

Transportation is taking up far too many resources, much of it needless. Personal automobiles are the worst offenders, as far as the environment is concerned. It is not just the fuel consumption, nor the emissions that contribute to the greenhouse effect, nor the debilitating effect on our lives of the endless traffic jams. The car has shaped our landscape in an environmentally devastating way, flinging houses and shopping malls (totally dependent on cars) across the country, spreading us further and further apart until we now need at least two cars per family and build our houses with three bays in the garage, whether or not we can afford them. Each expansion of our population spreads people further and further from where they work, requiring more paved roads, more gas stations, and more polluting hours on the road. Worse, the trend in cars is to become larger, less fuel efficient, and more dangerous. We will have to reshape our townships, to cluster in small areas, preserving large areas of farms and open space between them. Such clustering will make possible the restriction, also shown by the Chinese to be effective, of personal transportation to the bicycle. Incidentally, this contraction of the construction footprint, houses and roads, would also be a boost for local agriculture, which we will need, for the terrible environmental cost of trucking goods all over the country, just in terms of air pollution and the paving of the greenfields, is more than can be borne. We are going to have to restructure our work, recreation, and community life around our local centers, and use some form of public transportation – buses or trains – to travel between them.

Pollution

We may not think of "pollution" as one of the freedoms we value as Americans, but it is a freedom we have fought hard to retain, canceling our recycling programs and expanding the production of materials that will not biodegrade. With our current population, we cannot place more permanent waste on the earth. Strict laws, strictly enforced, will be necessary to make sure that all waste is recycled. Along with these new provisions will have to come renewed efforts to clean up the messes that are already there.

Property

Come to think of it, why did we ever think we could *own* land, or the natural cover of the land (forests, for instance), let alone what lies beneath the land? We did not create it, and we cannot replace it, yet it is as essential to the survival of people seven generations from now as it is to us. As a natural species, we may presumably enjoy the use of the land, and take from it what we need to live. Hunting and foraging rights certainly make sense, as does a commonwealth ownership and supervision of the extraction of minerals. But private ownership – as in, "it's mine, I can do what I like with it" – makes no sense at all. Privatization of land amounts to giving away the capital in the endowment with which we have been entrusted.[2]

The rapid adoption of all measures recommended above – reducing consumption to the level necessary to live frugally, limiting each family on earth to one child, redirecting the resources of the earth from the too-rich to the too-poor, clustering human habitations in self-contained townships and banning automobiles except for emergency purposes, insisting on 100 percent recycling, and abolishing private property in land, lakes, forests, and mines, would indeed improve the condition of the natural environment. Nor would it be fatal to business; entrepreneurs would be able to adjust their practices to this new world with no trouble at all. But it may not all be necessary. Let us review some of the more hopeful trends we found in previous chapters.

CLIMBING OUT OF THE ABYSS

Well short of such drastic measures, we found that there have been, and continue to be, fine examples of how industry and the market can work with the requirements of the natural environment for profit and protection at the same time. As Paul Hawken and Amory and Hunter Lovins pointed out in *Natural Capitalism*, we have the technology now to recycle a factory's heat to reduce the power needs of the building, to use solar power to make electricity, to the point where every manufacturing plant could produce more energy than it uses. We can make "hypercars," comfortable and fuel efficient; we can make hydrogen cells to run our buildings or our transportation. Whole cities have been laid out on environmental principles, and they work – in the poorest parts of the world. We also have the knowledge to grow all the food we need without large chemical inputs and without destroying all the woodlands and prairies from which farmland is taken. Most of the environmentally friendly technology we have is transplantable, as usable in the developing world as it is in the developed; for the developing world, meanwhile, a variety of "appropriate technologies" (essentially, agriculture that does not depend on subsoil nutrients and lower technologies that consume much less fossil fuel) could lower the cost of development. Fabric free of all harmful chemicals is now available for upholstery and carpeting; recycling technologies hold out the possibility of small profit, or at least of drastic reduction of loss in the disposal of wastes.

Natural Capitalism focuses on the basic physical needs of humans: for shelter, food, and transportation. Some of the companies mentioned in previous chapters show that in areas not basic to human survival, entrepreneurs can find markets that no one knew were there, tied to environmental awareness, and collect a very satisfying return on investment in the process of promoting ethical practices friendly to the natural environment. Ben & Jerry's is everyone's favorite example, simply because its founders, still very active on the political scene, tell everyone who will listen how they did it (and where to buy the book they wrote that tells how they did it). Equally well known, for another example, is Anita Roddick's The Body Shop, which guarantees that its products are all natural, for the most part purchased from indigenous growers in the developing world, and which uses its revenues to support a large number of charities.[3] The pioneer in the field of environmental protection, the Minnesota-based 3M company, was one of the first to discover that the costs of managing wastes can be turned into profit by careful monitoring of the manufacturing processes.[4]

Meanwhile, industry-wide initiatives, like Responsible Care® for the American Chemistry Council, the association of chemicals manufacturers, force companies not traditionally associated with environmental awareness (to put it mildly) to hold themselves to a higher standard of protection of the natural environment and sign off on their efforts on a yearly basis, or lose membership in their effective trade association.

In short, the technology is available – not the best technology we will ever have for protecting the natural environment while remaining competitive in a market system, but certainly the technology to improve on where we are. Profitable companies have showed us how to use it, and make use of it for purposes ranging from pulling the teeth of environmental regulation to marketing purposes. So the CRAMPP scenario is not the necessary end of all economic endeavor. That abyss is there, but we can avoid it.[5]

But is it enough to avoid catastrophe? Can we not do better than that? The promise of economic life lived in cooperation with the processes of nature is of a life infinitely richer for human beings than an economic life not so lived. Let us turn, finally, to the Land Ethic as a guide for long-range thinking in business.

⊛ ON THE HORIZON: ADOPTING A REALISTIC ⊛ AGENDA FOR THE CENTURY

Suppose we consider Aldo Leopold's brief statement of the Land Ethic as a guide for the development of technology and method in pursuit of return on investment – as a management creed for the competitive company in the future. The statement, as we recall, is that "A thing is right when it tends to preserve the integrity, stability and beauty of the biotic community. It is wrong when it tends otherwise." Note that the "biotic community" includes human beings. Our health, integrity, stability, and beauty is just as important as anything else's. What can we do to preserve and enhance the biotic stability of the world? Beyond mere survival, can we envision a better world in a possible future?

Let us take Leopold's standards one at a time. **Integrity** designates the wholeness of nature, the incredibly complex thoroughgoing interdependence of all its parts. No organism, in fact no stone, stands aloof from the action of a whole ecosystem, and each ecosystem is an integrated part of the biosphere as a whole. It is folly to think we can disrupt one part of the ecosystem for our profit without causing disruptions in the rest of it. Prudent managers will wonder just what disruptions will result from any action of theirs, and how they should be handled. (Remember the case of the Bangladeshi farmers who slaughtered frogs in order to export their legs, and found themselves paying twice as much as they were earning in order to buy the pesticides to do the job the frogs had done.) But here we want to go beyond the prudent manager casting up the chances every single time any action is contemplated that may affect the environment. Here we want to project a time when the cost–benefit analysis does not have to be done every time because the company, the industry, and the nation (and the world) will have adopted a simple principle: each ecosystem, and the biosphere as a whole, shall be treated as a whole being, worthy of respect, and all initiatives taken within the natural environment shall be done with sensitive awareness of the possibilities of damage to the ecosystem. The honoring of integrity, then, requires the acquisition of sensitivity to interdependence, a curiously ecological virtue that we might hope will carry over to other human affairs as well. In its ecological context alone, it is a virtue of holistic perception, of the ability to see and respect the whole as it is.

Stability is a political value, demanding that we respect a central structure of the thing whose stability we intend to maintain. (Integrity designates a unity of parts negotiated by the parts themselves at the micro level; stability designates a visible, cognizable structure, like a legal system, which orders the system at the macro level.) Ecology provides a variety of such law-like structures for ecosystems, from the most general designation of the natural biome (tropical rainforest, tundra) to the detailed descriptions of the flora and fauna of the area. Experience tells us that removal of one of the species, or intro-duction of a new one, will destroy the stability of an ecosystem, and on occasion send it on a course to destruction. The effort to preserve stability, then, requires the moral virtue of respect for the laws of the system that happen to be there in nature.

While the integrity and stability of the system may be difficult to distinguish theoretically, one from another, the third criterion of beauty seems to stand apart. Is not beauty in the eye of the beholder, totally subjective and beyond the purview of business? But the evidence suggests that perception of beauty starts at a far deeper level than the individual or cultural attributions of "beauty," which vary from place to place. First of all, the bats and insects seem to agree with us. The flowers, known to be beautiful as long as people have been people (or before people were people: flowers have been found to be included in Neanderthal gravesites) attract us as they attract the insects, not for the same reason (we share *very* little DNA with the insects) but with the same power. The perception of beauty in our own species is known to be a product of natural selection: we choose as mates the members of the opposite sex that we find beautiful, and our understanding of physical beauty correlates highly with youth and good health (and therefore with the ability to bear many healthy offspring). It is likely, then, that our decision that a natural spot is "beautiful," agreeable, has something to do with the experience of the species, that such places are fruitful places to live, well watered, with abundant fruits, grain, and game. The development, then, of the esthetic virtue of appreciation of beauty may be more closely related to survival than we might imagine. Beauty does more for us than amuse, by the way. There is evidence that allowing sick people to be surrounded by plants helps them recover faster, and much evidence that people are physically and mentally more stable when in an environment rich with pets and other living things.

What can the corporate manager be expected to do in defense of the land ethic? First, the manager can *recognize the convergence of interests*: for reasons that can be drawn from every chapter so far, it should be clear that the protection of the natural environment will be in the interests of the corporation. Second, the manager can employ every strategy for environmental enhancement of competitiveness, rather along lines laid down in previous chapters. Third, to make sure that the next generation of employees and customers understands and supports the company's strategy, the company should support environmental education, and the efforts made by the town fathers to come to grips with environmental projects at the town level.

The reward for all this effort may not be immediately evident. The development of an environmental consciousness across the company that renders unnecessary the "environmental impact" thinking that is done for legal purposes only may indeed spare the company legal troubles; the acknowledgement of the moral right of the ecosystem to its own stability may prevent unwise actions that will cost the company in the long run; and the recognition and support of the beauty of nature, at least at the local level, may earn the company goodwill that will carry through a series of crises. But that is not the point. In the long run, in the seventh generation from now, the business community has to live in the same world that we all inhabit, and the preservation of the biosphere is the major obligation we have to that generation, to live well and make us proud of them – and vice versa.

☙ CASE 8: THE BRONX COMMUNITY ☙
PAPER COMPANY

The Bronx Community Paper Company (hereinafter BCPC) was a project from heaven.[6] The City of New York and New York State would assist a major paper company to acquire a parcel of land designated "brownfields" – land so polluted by prior industrial activity that it could no longer be rehabilitated for agriculture or residential use – build a recycling plant, wastepaper de-inking plant, and finished paper factory there, directing New York City's (NYC's) huge waste stream of paper into the plant and producing office-grade recycled paper for the huge NYC market. Everything about the idea was good. New York City had run out of landfill for its waste; at enormous expense, an enormous volume of city waste was being trucked to Virginia for disposal on a daily basis. About 12,600 tons of that daily waste was paper, especially newsprint; the BCPC would be a less expensive way of getting rid of it. Meanwhile, in the far reaches of Canada, forests hundreds of years in the making fell before the chainsaws of the paper industry to supply paper for the law firms, financial industry, and publishing houses of the city that does not sleep. (1.5 million tons of newsprint alone is consumed in the city each year, 12 percent of the consumption of the nation as a whole.) Could the excess and the lack, the supply and the customer, be brought together? Why not? Here was a chance to minimize waste disposal and save the forests at the same time. Further, the South Bronx, where the factory was planned, is one of the poorest places in the world, largely because of the exodus of manufacturing jobs from northeastern United States during the last half of the twentieth century. While unemployment nationwide was about 4 percent (in 1990, the date when the planning started), unemployment in NYC was about 6 percent, and in the South Bronx, about 20 percent, finding labor for the project would thus be no problem at all. The BCPC would have provided 2,200 jobs during construction and over 400 permanent jobs when the plant was operating, and made a major contribution to the economy of the South Bronx. The entrepreneur for the project was Allen Hershkowitz, a brilliant lawyer from the Natural Resources Defense Council (NRDC), a man of tireless energy, with a talent for getting people to work together. From the beginning, he recognized the need to get the civil society organizations (CSOs) of the area – notably Banana Kelly, a powerful

Bronx neighborhood association – not only on board with the project, but involved as active partners in development. All they needed was capital, and they had assurances that if they could get certain government grants, grants specifically aimed at enterprises like this one, the private sector would step in and back them. The plant itself was designed to be environmentally beneficial, complete with solar energy and recycled heat, and beautiful: it was designed by Maya Lin, designer of the Vietnamese War Memorial, and it won a special exhibit all to itself in 1997, when it was made the centerpiece of the Municipal Art Society's show, *Designing Industrial Ecology: The Bronx Community Paper Company*, in the main gallery of Rockefeller Center at Christmastime. Everything was done right. But it was never built. Why not? What happened?

The tale is a heartbreaker, because the idea was so logical, because so much good would have been done, because it would have stood as a beacon of the possible in the murk of accepted impossibilities, and because it almost happened. Much of it will have to be foreshortened in this account – the tale reads like Tolstoy's *War and Peace*, with a huge cast of characters and rich, emotional action, and we simply have no space to capture the spirit of it. For the whole story, we may read with profit two excellent accounts of the attempt. Allen Hershkowitz himself wrote one of them, *Bronx Ecology: Blueprint for a New Environmentalism*; the other by a journalist who accompanied the project throughout, Lis Harris, *Tilting at Mills: Green Dreams, Dirty Dealings, and the Corporate Squeeze.*[7] The telling that follows is taken, without special attribution, from those two books, especially the latter.

A brief chronology

The story begins in 1992, when Hershkowitz realized that the huge waste-paper stream from NYC could be recycled into office-grade paper and sold back to New York, the largest market for such paper in the world. He had found a company in Sweden, MoDo, that had figured out a bleach-free process for the production of paper, avoiding the worst of the pollutants usually associated with making paper. Along the way he found out that most paper companies were not interested in such a project: they hated the NRDC with which he was associated, they hated New York, and when he told the paper executives that he intended to recruit community activists to help develop the project, they rejected it without further discussion. But MoDo was interested, so Hershkowitz recruited Yolanda Rivera, of the Bronx nonprofit Banana Kelly, to help direct the project toward the needs of the community, and Anita Miller, head of the Comprehensive Community Revitalization Program, to help put together the capital that would be needed.

In January 1993, Hershkowitz took Rivera and several others, including Fred Ferrer, borough president of the Bronx, to Sweden to visit MoDo executives and to see the paper mills. City officials concerned with waste paper disposal and consumer affairs were enthusiastic, and S. D. Warren, a subsidiary of Scott Paper Company, seemed interested in buying the paper they produced. A flurry of meetings over the next few months confirmed everyone's enthusiasm; building sites were scouted, and the project acquired a name, the BCPC. By the end of the year, Maya Lin, designer of the Vietnam War Memorial, had agreed to design the buildings. Trouble had begun to surface: it was clear that Rivera and Fred Ferrer, aligned as their interests might be, saw each other as political rivals. Ferrer kept pushing Hershkowitz to include other groups in the coalition, Rivera kept insisting that her group would put together any community advisory group that was necessary. Also, a group called the South Bronx Clean Air Coalition showed up, asking for money, and threatening opposition on environmental grounds. Hershkowitz could do nothing about political rivalries, but assumed that Ferrer and Rivera would cooperate eventually; and since the project would produce no significant emissions at all, he was not worried about the clean-air group.

All through 1994 momentum for the project grew, but so did political opposition. Suddenly Anita Miller turned against the project, arguing that it would hurt the interests of the community. The South Bronx Clean Air Coalition brought a lawsuit, ignoring Hershkowitz's pleas to meet with a panel of distinguished Puerto Rican scientists that had been assembled to review the data on emissions. Their most important industry partners, MoDo and Scott Paper, backed out of the arrangement discouraged by the lawsuit, the apparent local turmoil, and the lack of progress on securing a site. At the end of the summer of 1995, the lawsuit was finally resolved, but precious time and alliances had been lost. Dealings with state officials, in their attempts to get development grants from state funds, had mixed results; Republican Governor George Pataki was enthusiastically supportive of the project, but Charles Gargano, head of the Empire State Development Corporation, through whose office all such grants had to pass, was quietly opposed; most of the community leaders were involved with Democratic politics, and Gargano, a Republican, did not want them to get any funds. About that time they found out that a competitor, Visy, who would also want some of the paper flow from NYC, had arrived on Staten Island backed by private money, had obtained the required environmental permits in record time, and set up in business. There were apparently strong political ties to Rudolph Giuliani's mayoral office; their existence complicated the prospects for the BCPC.

By the beginning of 1996, they were reasonably confident that they had a new paper company committed to the project, Stone Consolidated of Montreal; a site had been settled on, most of the permissions to build had been obtained, and the Governor's office was encouraging about state grants. The city, however, in the office of the NYC Economic Development Corporation, was dragging its feet on the $250 million needed in financial backing before private investors would sign on. Dealings with the Department of Sanitation (which would have to transport their waste paper) and with private carting companies were difficult; with Rudolph Giuliani's ascent to the mayoralty of NYC, the department heads had lost much of their independence; Giuliani was not favorable to the project, and the private carters all turned out to be involved with racketeering. Relations with Yolanda Rivera had soured, and become complicated with other players; Hershkowitz still thought that all these mini-storms could be weathered. Then, in March, Stone Consolidated voted to expand its operations in South Korea rather than work with the BCPC. They were out looking for a new paper company again. In that same month, an environmental justice conference held at the Rutgers Law School in Newark, New Jersey, featured presentation after presentation that accused the NRDC of disrespect for communities of color. Apparently the South Bronx Clean Air Coalition, after losing the lawsuit, had spread the accusation to stop the project, and their word, backed up by their history as a neighborhood advocacy group, had been taken as gospel. A lawyer from the NRDC who attended the conference, having no previous knowledge of the project, wrote a letter to its Board suggesting that the project might be harming NRDC's reputation as scrupulously careful on all issues of justice – a reputation on which their success in all their other endeavors depended. Others in the organization who knew the project defended it, but the seeds of suspicion had been planted, and now Hershkowitz had the NRDC's commitment in doubt. By the fall of the year, the team had acquired another interested backer, a construction company, Morse Diesel, that seemed to be interested in engineering and building the project with no payment until the end. Efforts to put together a consortium of newspapers to be both supplier and customer for the plant had failed, but they did have some agreements with newspapers and magazines to purchase the finished product. But by the end of 1996, they still had no owner – Morse Diesel had not finally signed on (it was in the process of negotiations with other companies), and no other company seemed to be interested in owning and running the paper plant.

In March 1997, despite strong opposition from the Empire State Development Corporation, New York State agreed to award them the development seed money they asked for, which they hoped would encourage private investors. To reach those investors, Hershkowitz then went to a private fund, the New York City Partnership, which might be able to make them a $2 million bridge loan. The Partnership commissioned a feasibility study from Salomon Brothers Smith Barney, which was simple and negative – there was too much capacity in the paper industry, and therefore it would be inadvisable to put the mill in New York. Other consultants had disagreed, but the Salomon Brothers report was widely circulated, and cast doubt on the project in the investment community. Nevertheless – incredibly – the planning process went on, changing the wastewater disposal system in the new plant, negotiating new water rates for the water that they would be taking on, spending long nights trying to figure out how to cut construction costs. In late spring of 1997, Hershkowitz had worked out the structure for a contract with NYC to have the Department of Sanitation bring the waste paper to the plant – but NYC was evincing great hesitation about signing that contract. In July 1997, an advisor to the project came up with one last paper company that might qualify as owner, Joseph Kruger, in business as a supplier of low-end paper, primarily toilet paper. A meeting with Kruger was set up for September, five days after Hershkowitz had closed on the state's revolving fund advance (in a meeting to which Yolanda Rivera, again, did not show up). Kruger turned out to be a minimal investor, not willing to put in enough money to reassure Wall Street, and demanded his full investment back in one year. They went forward with Kruger anyway, and seemed to be about to build and produce, when in October, a small player, who had been talking with them about participating some years back, suddenly showed up and announced he was suing everyone in sight, including the NRDC, for "tortious interference," claiming that he had a right to the company and everyone else was taking it away from him. He had no case, but the NRDC's Board thought the lawsuit a good occasion for getting out of a project that had gone on far too long without getting anything done, and decided to terminate its – and Hershkowitz's – connections to it. While they were figuring out how to do that, the consortium got its first real agreement with a paper company, Kruger, signed by all parties. (The last party to sign, Yolanda Rivera, signed her name on February 27, 1998, one day before the city's environmental permits expired.)

Through most of 1998, Hershkowitz was prohibited, because of the lawsuit, from talking to most of the principals in the project. In the maneuvering that followed, the parties that were still standing for the project at the end were Morse-Diesel and the owner of the land, Galesi. They inherited the project. By the fall of 1998, the state was out of the project, unwilling to give it any more money; Banana Kelly had effectively imploded, dictatorial and corrupt, while it continued with an ownership interest in the project. Morse-Diesel and Galesi sent Kruger packing, because of the bad deal he had attempted to foist on them, but in the end, they were not able to find another paper company. Banana Kelly sent new people to represent them on the Board, but all they did was obstruct whatever else was happening and ask for money for Banana Kelly. Finally, as the century drew to a close, the city withdrew its cooperation on the water projects, Morse-Diesel refused to put up any further money, the award-winning design for the building was scrapped as too expensive, and the project died. Fingers were pointing in all directions (still are), attributing blame to various parties. A strong cause is possibly simple "project fatigue": it had been going on so long, there had been so many setbacks, and no one was willing to spend any more effort on it. Whatever the cause, the project will not go forward, at least not now.

A preliminary analysis

What went wrong? There was nothing wrong with the project. The problem was, somehow, with the human beings that the project encountered. There are weak and unreliable people everywhere, and the project met its share. But the dynamic went well beyond weakness, ignorance, or failure of attention.

This book is a work in environmental philosophy, environmental economics, and economic and business ethics. None of those fields have the analytic machinery to handle what went wrong in the

BCPC. Economically, the project made sense; it would have been a good investment from any standpoint. "Excess capacity in the paper industry," as one participant pointed out, is a very relative term; the industry goes through wild cycles, and in the down cycles the inefficient plants drop off the edge. This plant would have made money in a reasonable time. Why did the Wall Street-NYC partnership not only accept a report from Salomon Brothers Smith Barney that had been put together with virtually no research, but go to extra lengths to spread the report as widely as possible in the investment community, to make sure that private investors would not consider the project? Had the investors wanted more reassurance, there were a number of government grants earmarked for just such projects, from the city through the state to the federal government; why was there such foot-dragging in every office approached? The project would have involved some new technology, and a bit of conceptual rethinking, but it was largely a conventional paper plant, and a good one; why did the paper companies avoid it? Are they that encrusted in their standard ways of operating? The project would have provided jobs in construction, manufacturing, trucking, and maintenance, all readily handled by the Bronx workforce; why did the community groups suddenly turn against it? The project was specifically designed for environmental enhancement, down to requiring that the trucks to and from the plant operate on natural gas. Where did the "Clean Air" protests come from? Above all, the project would have had a ripple effect all through the Bronx – creating an area of genuine beauty (Maya Lin's design was not only environmentally innovative, but startlingly beautiful) and economic prosperity would make the adjacent areas much more attractive to future investors. Why were the politicians so cool to a project that would have helped their constituents? Nor will the old participatory democracy explanation help us out here – people do not want to be "done for," they want to be empowered to do for themselves, so the project failed because it was being *imposed* on the community. Hershkowitz knew participatory democracy well enough; indeed, the NRDC is famous for it. He built participation by community groups in from the start. Essentially, all the stakeholders failed to support, and largely opposed, a project in which they all had a hand and was clearly in all their interests. Why?

The assumption with which we began this book, and which has informed it throughout, is that most of economic/ethical/environmental life is a non-zero-sum game; that is, solutions to many problems can be found where everyone comes out ahead. (In the jargon of the time, we seek and expect "win-win" resolutions.) Further, it is our duty as citizens and as moral people, on a variety of grounds, to seek those solutions wherever possible, even in areas where we think we can with impunity have our interests prevail to the detriment of the other parties to the transaction. (That is, in areas where we can turn the situation into a win-lose game, and win it.) But not every part of human activity conforms to that duty. When we play true games, for instance, like football, the point is that one side wins and the other side loses. Part of us likes this aspect of games a lot; strict rules are necessary in many games to make sure that winning does not turn into an orgy of the deliberate humiliation of the losing team. We have been working, through this book, to move as many fields of human activity as possible into areas of mutual benefit and away from formula adversarialism and resource-consuming contests. Some fields are seen here to be intractable to that effort. To understand the BCPC, we will have to consider two concepts that do not fit into the frameworks that we have been using: **power** and **fear**.

"Power" in the human sense has multiple definitions; the simplest is the ability to make people do what you want whether or not they like it. Power, political, economic, social power, is like real games. If I have it, you do not. If you have it, I do not. Power is a fact, not a norm – unlike "authority," you can have power even if, by all the rules, you should not. Power is singular. There are of course schemes we can call "shared power," but all such schemes involve normative elements. The simple belief that "power should be shared," for instance, is a normative belief; any arrangement for sharing power must appeal to some notion of "justice." Without normative elements, power over some area of human activity is held by one entity alone; typically, it is jealously guarded. Power is a good, from the perspective of its seeker and its wielder; the root of power-seeking is "envy," the apprehension that others may have more power than you have. A power struggle, fueled by envy, is a struggle to get power away from someone else. It is a quintessential zero-sum game; and the story of the BCPC is the story of power struggles.

"Fear" is also a factual term, ordinarily evident on the social scene as "mistrust," or lack of trust. Either you (individually or collectively) do or you do not trust another party (individual or collective), as a matter of fact. Maybe you *should* trust that party, in that the party is trustworthy, and your trust in that party will lead to good results

for you. (In the recent past, for instance, NYC public health administrators had a difficult time persuading African American men
with AIDS to seek treatment, because they did not trust the white
physicians – or African American physicians either. But the doctors
were in fact trustworthy, the mistrust was not justified, and their
health might have been much improved if they had sought and
accepted medical treatment.) Mistrust is easy to create; anyone
wishing to make some people distrust others has only to tell them
that the others threaten them in some significant way, thereby producing fear. Trust, however, is less easy to establish, and cannot be
legislated or brought about in any reliable way. The BCPC story is
a story of distrust, of fear, of something, usually of the unknown.

It is fear that makes people decide to turn what could be a win-win
situation into a win-lose game, and occasionally, as in this case, into
a lose-lose proposition. The obstacle that Hershkowitz found most
difficult to understand and accept – and which he was never able to
overcome – was the distrust of the small community advocacy
groups for *each other*. Each group saw, no doubt clearly, that if the
project went through their group would benefit. The question was,
would other groups benefit *more*, or new groups come in, so that at
the end of the day other groups would have more power than their
own? It seems a silly question to ask, but it was decisive. In the end,
the leaders of the coalitions were better off keeping the political
alliances with the opponents of the project than risking radical
changes in the power structure that might result from its success.

Fear, distrust, runs through the chronicle of the BCPC. From the
beginning, paper companies would not join the project because
paper company executives feared the community groups that were
helping in the development, because such groups ordinarily
opposed paper companies and their polluting plants. They feared
the NRDC even more, because the NRDC ordinarily advocated for
those groups, and for the environment, against paper companies.
Paper companies tend to locate in rural areas; Hershkowitz was
amused at their fear of NYC. They did not trust the new technology; would it work? (They did not trust the engineers who said it
would.) Hershkowitz assumed, as would most of us, that for
a project clearly in their interests, they would overcome their fears.
They did not.

The same distrust is seen in the investment community. The
analysts from Salomon Brothers Smith Barney did not think they
needed to talk to the consultants for the project. All they needed

to know was that it was headed up by a lawyer from a "Greenie" organization and incorporated the insights of street groups. Both of those features, central to the project, placed it outside the ken of the money men, so they feared it and rejected it.

The public servants, elected or appointed, also failed the project. A particular aspect of "power struggle" recurs throughout the BCPC story, which will have to be taken into account by any future project of this sort. Among the community leaders, legislators, and presidents, there was a strong perception that jobs were what was needed for the area, and that any enterprise that promised jobs was good. So far, so predictable. But central to any public participant's understanding is that the jobs had to come from and through *their own* organization, office, or administration, and that they had to be *perceived* as coming from them – for on that perception their power depended. Not only must my constituent benefit, the reasoning went, but he must be indebted to *me*, and only me, for that benefit, and he must clearly see that. Hershkowitz did not fully understand this during the life of the project; he kept assuming that ultimately the plain interests of their constituents would bring them to set their "differences" aside and work together. But power does not work like that.

So Anita Miller turned against the project, in the middle of a public workshop, with no warning, after some activists from her district had opposed it on (completely unwarranted) environmental grounds. Why? Well, the project had picked up opponents, as from the "Clean Air" coalition, and as another participant suggested, "the enemies of the project were more important to her as a constituency than its friends."[8]

In the end, the opposition was devastatingly simple: If my group does not run the project – distribute the jobs, disburse the money, make the decisions – then no one is going to, because I cannot afford to let any entity, no matter how goodhearted, gain in power while I do not. (Elsewhere, this phenomenon is known as the "crab in a bucket" syndrome: if crabs are kept in a bucket, when one tries to crawl out up the side, the others will immediately try to crawl up over it, trying to get out themselves, but succeeding only in pulling it down and ensuring that none of them escape. You are not going anywhere unless you take us all with you.) As the project began to disintegrate, Hershkowitz asked every stakeholder, "What more do you want?" One Latino politician summarized the answer: "*Quitate tu, ponerme yo*," "You get out of the way so that I can take your place."[9]

Strike me blind in one eye

People are irredeemably perverse. It is not just that they are selfish. They can want all the goods in the world for themselves, and collective schemes will find ways to channel that selfishness into increasing the availability of goods for everyone. (The free market, as described by Adam Smith, is such a collective scheme.) It is not just that they demand justice, fairness, in their social relations. If it is just equality they want, we can structure our laws to guarantee equality, especially equality before the law and an equal right to participate in the political arena. It is not even that they demand freedom, respect, and the opportunity to make moral choices on their own. They can enjoy all the liberty they like, compatible with a like liberty for all. To bring us back to our classical philosophers from Chapter 1, we can realize all the social goods advanced by the philosopher John Rawls in *A Theory of Justice*, and we can advance human happiness in all the ways suggested by the utilitarian philosopher Jeremy Bentham and all his school (including Adam Smith, along with John Stuart Mill and the legal philosopher John Austin). But both schemes require rationality of their human participants. People must (eventually, after education) recognize their own real interests, and act on them; people must be free of irrational envy.

What is irrational envy? There is a folk tale about a man who was told by God that he could have anything he wanted, on the condition that his neighbor receive twice as much. His first request: "O God, strike me blind in one eye!" The overwhelming impression left by the BCPC story is that most of the players would be willing, under those conditions, to be struck blind in one eye: the paper companies, to judge from their reactions, would be willing to see their taxes raised if they could be sure the money was going to crush the CSOs like NRDC and Banana Kelly; several of the neighborhood advocacy groups were willing to kill any project as long as it defeated the white people who were running it; and all groups were willing to scuttle any initiative that did not leave them in visible control of the goods to be distributed – even if scuttling it would mean there would be no goods at all. None of our ethical theories can order human conduct toward human happiness in the presence of irrational fear or envy, the basis of the power struggle.

For political theory, the BCPC story sends us back, past John Rawls, J. S. Mill, Jeremy Bentham, and John Locke, to Thomas Hobbes (whose major work, *Leviathan*, appeared in 1651),[10] an acute observer of human nature, who held that the reason we need government is that people are motivated, not by simple survival needs alone, but by "diffidence," fear, worry that the stranger approaching may be contemplating violence of some kind, and by "vainglory," pride, the desire for eminence and for the ability to exercise power (as defined above). Since the way to achieve "eminence" is to cause others to fear you and acknowledge your power, the fear felt when the stranger approaches is actually rational: since you know full well that you would cause that stranger to fear you, if only you could figure out how, your best bet is that you should fear him. The sovereign, who is so strong that he can cause you both to fear him more than anything else, and to fear his anger if you fight with each other when told not to, represents the only possibility for peace. Since without peace you will (famously) achieve nothing else, but live a life poor, mean, nasty, brutish, and short, you are strongly advised to submit to the sovereign. That of course is the answer to the problems faced by the BCPC; when the forces at play in the society include fear and envy at the top of the list, only a very strong government (or other overwhelming force, like the entrance of a private developer with truly awesome amounts of capital to spend on buying a site, erecting the building, and buying off community groups) has any hope of getting the job done.

In conclusion, then, the BCPC, a project sent from heaven, is the necessary reminder that all our ideas for achieving social, economic, and environmental goals all at once depend ultimately on the human factor. People have to want to change, to achieve any progress at all, and that desire can only be cultivated by long and patient public education. It is to be hoped that corporate America, just in its own best interest, will elect to take a leading role in that education.

⊛ NOTES ⊛

1. The story of Easter Island – how its people mindlessly consumed the resources on which they depended, overpopulated their tiny home, and turned to cannibalism – has been told many times, most beautifully by Jared Diamond, *Discover Magazine*, August 1995, and also by Clive Ponting, *A Green History of the World*, London: Penguin Books, 1992, pp. 168–170. Incidentally, scenarios along this line, applied to this century, have been presented by Robert Kaplan, among others; see "The Coming Anarchy," *Atlantic Monthly*, February 1994, pp. 44–76.

2. As Kristin Schrader-Frechette has pointed out, we are no longer able to use a Lockean justification for private property in land. Locke justifies private property only for the object that results from one's own labor, and allows private property in natural objects only if the appropriation leaves "enough and as good" for the next person. There is no way that Shell Oil (to cite the case for Chapter 6) leaves "enough and as good" when it takes the oil from Nigeria; it could be argued that "it is not clear that it is ethical for humans to claim to have Lockean property rights over land, water, air, minerals, and other natural resources" at all in this over-crowded world. From "Property Rights in Natural Resources," *The Global Possible: Resources, Development, and the New Century,* ed. Robert Repetto, New Haven: Yale University Press, 1985, pp. 115–116. See also Larry Becker, *Property Rights,* London: Routledge & Kegan Paul, 1977, p. 109.

3. Material from The Body Shop website (http://www.thebodyshop.com/web/tbsgl/values.jsp) includes commitments to sell no products and use no ingredients tested on animals, to support small producer communities around the world by purchasing natural ingredients from them, to give active support to human rights, especially for those for whom rights are not assured, and to protect the environment, locally and globally.

4. 3M reports, for the period 2000–2002, a 10 percent improvement in energy efficiency, a 12 percent reduction in waste, 25 percent reduction in volatile organic air emissions (pointing out that they reduced those emissions 93 percent from the time the program started in 1990 to the year 2000!) and a 38 percent reduction in US EPA Toxic Release Inventory (TRI), also on top of a 93 percent reduction in the same for the decade preceding.

5. We will still have a problem with the human factor, of course. The technologies we have in place right now are not adequate to preserve the natural environment. We have too many vehicles consuming too much oil, for starters. In many cases alternative technologies are available, as we pointed out in Chapter 5, but there are many obstacles – legal and bureaucratic as well as economic – to getting them adopted. Essentially, all citizens of the developed world would have to agree at the same time that sensible technologies shall be adopted immediately for houses, cars, waste disposal, water use, electricity generation, agriculture, fishing, logging, and mining, that no concessions at all shall be made to mollify those who are enriching themselves under the present regime, but that all shall march in step toward environmental sustainability. It is technically possible that this can happen – one recalls the onset of World War II – but how likely is it?

6. The material in this introductory paragraph is drawn from Allen Hershkowitz, *Bronx Ecology: Blueprint for a New Environmentalism,* Washington DC: Island Press, 2002, Foreword by Maya Lin and Introduction

by Allen Hershkowitz, pp. 1–17. A centerfold has a beautiful rendering of the proposed plant.

7. Allen Hershkowitz, op. cit.; Lis Harris, *Tilting at Mills*, Boston & New York: Houghton Mifflin, 2003. To get us through the ever-changing plot, Harris has a list of the *dramatis personae* at the end of the book. I could have used a timeline and a few maps, too.

8. Harris, p. 59.

9. Ibid., p. 86.

10. Thomas Hobbes, *Leviathan* (1651: reprinted), London: Penguin Books, 1981.

Bibli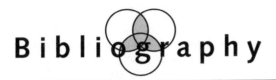aphy

The bibliography is picked with the beginning instructor and the student in mind: what books are readily available to continue reading on the subject of each chapter?

❀ USEFUL ANTHOLOGIES ❀

Annual Editions: Developing World 03/04, ed. Robert J. Griffiths, Guilford, CT: McGraw-Hill/Dushkin, 2003. ISBN 0-07-283855-8.

Annual Editions: Global Issues 02/03, ed. Robert M. Jackson, Guilford, CT: McGraw-Hill/Dushkin, 2002.

Annual Editions: Global Issues 03/04, ed. Robert M. Jackson, Guilford, CT: McGraw-Hill/Dushkin, 2003. ISBN 0-07-283857-4.

Global Civil Society 2002, ed. Glasius, Marlies, Mary Kaldor and Helmut Anheier, New York: Oxford University Press, 2002. ISBN 019-925168-1.

Practice-Research Engagement and Civil Society in a Globalizing World, ed. L. David Brown, Cambridge, MA: Hauser Center for Nonprofit Organizations, Harvard University, 2001.

Rooted in the Land: Essays on Community and Place, ed. William Vitek and Wes Jackson, New Haven: Yale University Press, 1996.

State of the World 2003, ed. Gary Gardner et al., New York: W.W. Norton & Co., 2003.

State of the World 2004, New York: W.W. Norton, 2004.

The Case Against the Global Economy and for a Turn Toward the Local, ed. Jerry Mander and Edward Goldsmith, San Francisco: Sierra Club Books, 1996.

The Environmental Ethics and Policy Book, ed. Donald VanDeVeer and Christine Pierce, Belmont, CA: Wadsworth, 3rd edn., 2003. ISBN 0-534-56188-8.

❀ INTRODUCTION ❀

Ponting, Clive, *A Green History of the World: The Environment and the Collapse of Great Civilizations*, New York: Penguin Books, 1991. ISBN 0140176608.

✤ 1 ETHICS: TERMS AND FORMS OF ✤
REASONING

Aristotle, *Nicomachean Ethics*, New York: Viking Penguin, 2004. ISBN 0-14-044949.

Aquinas, Thomas, *Treatise on Law*, Washington, DC: Regnery Gateway, 1988. ISBN 0-89526-918-X.

Augustine, *On Free Choice of the Will*, Indianapolis: Hackett Pub. Co., 1993. ISBN 0-87220-188-0.

Bentham, Jeremy and John Stuart Mill, *The Classical Utilitarians: Bentham and Mill*, Indianapolis: Hackett Pub. Co. 2003. ISBN 0-87220-649-1.

Kant, Immanual, *Groundwork for the Metaphysics of Morals*, New York: Oxford University Press, 2003. ISBN 0-19-875180-X.

Kant, Immanual, *Foundations of the Metaphysics of Morals*, New York: Library of Liberal Arts, [1785] 1959.

MacIntyre, Alasdair, *After Virtue: A Study in Moral Theory*, South Bend, IN: Notre Dame University Press, 1984. ISBN 0268-00611-3.

MacIntyre, Alasdair, *A Short History of Ethics*, South Bend, IN: Notre Dame Press, 1997. ISBN 0268-01759-X.

Mill, John Stuart, *On Liberty*, New Haven: Yale University Press, 2003.

Mill, John Stuart, *Utilitarianism*, Indianapolis, IN: Hackett Pub. Co. [1859] 2002. ISBN 0-87220-605-X.

Rachels, James, *The Elements of Moral Philosophy*, New York: McGraw-Hill, 2003. ISBN 0-07-119876-8.

Rawls, John, *Justice as Fairness: A Restatement*, Cambridge: Harvard University Press, 2001. ISBN 0-674-00511-2.

Rawls, John, *A Theory of Justice*, Cambridge: Harvard University Press, [1970] 1999. ISBN 0-674-00078-1.

Case 1: New England fisheries

Blueplanet Quarterly, Summer 2003, "Cod Overfishing Highlights Need for New Management Approach," p. 17.

Broad, William J. and Andrew C. Revkin, "Has the Sea Given Up Its Bounty? Overfishing Imposes a Heavy Toll," *The New York Times*, July 29, 2003, F1.

Pohl, Otto, "Challenge to Fishing: Keep the Wrong Species Out of Its Huge Nets," *The New York Times*, July 29, 2003, F3.

Revkin, Andrew C. "Under the Sea: Conservation as the Catch of the Day for Trawlnets," *The New York Times*, July 29, 2003, F3.

Weber, Peter, *Net Loss: Fish, Jobs, and the Marine Environment*, Worldwatch Paper 120, Washington, DC: Worldwatch Institute, July 1994.

World-Watch 16(5), September/October 2003, "Populations of large ocean fish decimated," p. 9.

Broad, William J. and Andrew C. Revkin, "Has the Sea Given Up Its Bounty? Overfishing Imposes a Heavy Toll," *The New York Times*, July 29, 2003 F1 (Science Times).

Nierenberg, Danielle, "Populations of large ocean fish decimated," *World-Watch*, September–October 2003, p. 9.

Williams, Ted, "The Exhausted Sea: Good Fish Managers, Like Good Parents, Eventually Learn that One of the Kindest Words They Can Utter is 'No.'" *Audubon*, September 2003, pp. 42–48.

⊛ 2 FROM ETHICS TO BUSINESS ETHICS ⊛

Boatright, John Raymond, *Ethics and the Conduct of Business*, Upper Saddle River, NJ: Prentice-Hall, 2002. ISBN 0-13-099159-7.

Boatright, John R., ed., *Ethics in Finance*, Boston: Blackwell Publishing, 1999.

Bowie, Norman and Patricia H. Werhane, *Management Ethics*, Boston: Blackwell Publishing, 2004. ISBN 0-631-21473-9.

Brenkert, George G., ed., *Corporate Integrity and Accountability*, Washington, DC: Sage Publications, 2004. ISBN 0-7619-2955-X.

Callahan, David, *The Cheating Culture: Why More Americans Are Doing Wrong to Get Ahead*, New York: Harcourt Brace, 2004. ISBN 0-15-101018–8.

Damon, William, *The Moral Advantage: How to Succeed in Business by Doing the Right Thing*, New York: Berrett-Koehler Publishers, 2004. ISBN 1-57675-206-2.

DesJardins, Joseph R. and John J. McCall, *Contemporary Issues in Business Ethics*, Belmont, CA: Wadsworth, 2004. ISBN 0-534-58464-0.

Ehrenreich, Barbara, *Nickel and Dimed: On (Not) Getting By in America*, New York: Henry Holt, 2001. ISBN 0-8050-6389-7.

Gini, Al, *Case Studies in Business Ethics*, Upper Saddle River, NJ: Prentice-Hall, 2004. ISBN 0-13-112746-2.

Hartley, Robert F., *Business Ethics: Violations of the Public Trust*, New York: John Wiley & Sons, 1993. ISBN 0-471-54591-0.

Hartman, Laura Pincus, *Perspectives in Business Ethics*, New York: McGraw-Hill, 2004. ISBN 0-07-288146-1.

Huffington, Arriana, *Pigs at the Trough: How Corporate Greed and Political Corruption Are Undermining America*, London: Crown Publishing Group, 2004. ISBN 1-4000-5126-6.

Kidder, Rushworth, *How Good People Make Tough Choices: Resolving the Dilemmas of Ethical Living*, New York: Harper, 2003. ISBN 0-688-17590-2.

Machan, Tibor R. and James E. Chesher, *A Primer on Business Ethics*, Lanham: Rowman and Littlefield, 2002. ISBN 0-7425-1389-0.

Newton, Lisa and Maureen Ford, *Taking Sides: Clashing Views on Controversial Issues in Business Ethics and Society*, Guilford, CT: Dushkin Publishers, McGraw-Hill, 2003. ISBN 0-07-291719-9.

Newton, Lisa and David P. Schmidt, *Wake-Up Calls: Classic Cases in Business Ethics*, Natorp, Ohio: South-Western (Thomson), 2004. ISBN 0-324-26152-7.

Pfeiffer, Raymond S. and Ralph P. Forsberg, *Ethics on the Job: Cases and Strategies*, Belmont, CA: Wadsworth, 2004. ISBN 0-534-61981-9.

Shaw, William H., *Business Ethics*, Belmont, CA: Wadsworth, 2004, ISBN 0-534-61972-X.

✪ 3 FROM ETHICS TO ENVIRONMENTAL ✪
ETHICS

Armstrong, Susan J. and Richard G. Botzler, *Environmental Ethics: Divergence and Convergence*, New York: McGraw-Hill, 2003. ISBN 0-07-283845-0.

Berry, Thomas, *The Dream of the Earth*, San Francisco: Sierra Club Books, 1988.

Brown, Lester R., *Who Will Feed China? Wake-Up Call for a Small Planet*, New York: Norton, 1995.

Burch, Mark A., *Stepping Lightly: Simplicity for People and the Planet*, Gabriola Island, BC: New Society Publishers, 2000. ISBN 0-86571-423-1.

Callicott, J. Baird and Michael Nelson, *American Indian Environmental Ethics: An Ojibwa Case Study*, Upper Saddle River, NJ: Prentice-Hall, 2003. ISBN 0-13-043121-4.

Callicott, J. Baird, *Beyond the Land Ethic*, Albany: SUNY Press, 1999. ISBN 0-7914-4084-2.

Callicott, J. Baird, *In Defense of the Land Ethic*, Albany: SUNY Press, 1989. ISBN 0-88706-900-2.

Carson, Rachel, *Silent Spring*, Boston: Houghton Mifflin, 1962, special edition with Introduction by Al Gore, 1994.

Dallmeyer, Dorinda, ed., *Values at Sea: Ethics for the Marine Environment*, Atlanta: University of Georgia Press, 2003. ISBN 0-8203-2470-1.

Deane-Drummond, Celia, *The Ethics of Nature*, Oxford: Blackwell Publishing, 2003. ISBN 0-631-22937-X.

Des Jardins, Joseph, *Environmental Ethics: Concepts, Policy, Theory*, Mountain View CA: Mayfield Publishing Co., 1999. ISBN 1-55934-986-7.

Des Jardins, Joseph R., *Environmental Ethics: An Introduction to Environmental Philosophy*, Belmont, CA: Wadsworth, 2nd edn., 1997. ISBN 0-534-50508-2.

Diamond, Jared, "The Last Americans: Environmental Collapse and the End of Civilization," *Harper's Magazine*, June, 2003, pp. 43–51.

Glick, Daniel, "GeoSigns," *National Geographic*, special issue on global warming, vol. 206 #3, September 2004, pp. 12–33.

Gudorf, Christine E. and James Edward Huchingson, *Boundaries: A Casebook in Environmental Ethics*, Washington, DC: Georgetown University Press, 2003. ISBN 0-87840-134-2.

Hardin, Garrett, "The Tragedy of the Commons," *Science* 162: 1243-1248 (1968).

Hargrove, Eugene C., *The Animal Rights/Environmental Ethics Debate*, Albany: SUNY Press, 1992. ISBN 0-7914-0934-1.

Leopold, Aldo, *A Sand County Almanac and Sketches Here and There*, New York: Oxford University Press, 1949, Commemorative Edition 1987.

List, Peter C., ed., *Radical Environmentalism: Philosophy and Tactics*, Belmont, CA: Wadsworth, 1993.

Martin-Schramm, James B. and Robert L. Stivers, *Christian Environmental Ethics: A Case Method Approach*, Orbis Books, 2003. ISBN 1-57075-499-3.

McKibben, Bill, *Enough: Staying Human in an Engineered Age*, New York: Henry Holt, 2003.

McKibben, Bill, *The End of Nature*, New York: Random House, 1989. ISBN 0-394-57601-2.

Miller, G. Tyler, Jr., *Living in the Environment*, Belmont, CA: Wadsworth Brooks Cole, 11th edn., 2000.

Montaigne, Fen, "EcoSigns," *National Geographic*, special issue on global warming, vol. 206 #3, September 2004, pp. 34–55.

Morell, Virginia, "TimeSigns," *National Geographic* special issue on global warming, vol. 206 #3, September 2004, pp. 56–74.

Pojman, Louis P., *Environmental Ethics: Theory and Practice*, Belmont, CA: Wadsworth, 2004. ISBN 0-534-63971-2.

Rolston, Holmes III, *Environmental Ethics: Duties to and Values in the Natural World*, Philadelphia: Temple University Press, 1988, 2003. ISBN 0-87722-628-8.

Schumacher, E. F., *Small Is Beautiful: Economics As If People Mattered*, New York: Harper & Row, 1973.

Sideris, Lisa H., *Environmental Ethics, Ecological Theology, and Natural Selection*, New York: Columbia University Press, 2003. ISBN 0-231-12660-3.

Speth, James Gustave, *Red Sky at Morning: America and the Crisis of the Global Environment*, New Haven: Yale University Press, 2004. ISBN 0-300-10232-1.

Sterba, James P., *Earth Ethics: Environmental Ethics, Animal Rights, and Practical Applications*, Englewood Cliffs, NJ: Prentice-Hall, 1995. ISBN 0-02-417102-6.

Sutton, Phillip W., *Nature, Environment and Society*, New York: Palgrave MacMillan, 2004. ISBN 0-333-99568-6.

Taylor, Paul W., *Respect for Nature: A Theory of Environmental Ethics*, Princeton: Princeton University Press, 1986. ISBN 0-691-02250-X.

Wilson, Edward O., *The Diversity of Life*, Cambridge, MA: Harvard University Press, 1992. ISBN 0-674-21298-3.

4 THE LAW AND THE NATURAL ENVIRONMENT

Hoban, Thomas More and Richard Oliver Brooks, *Green Justice: The Environment and the Courts*, Boulder CO: Westview Press, 2nd edn., 1996.

Kubasek, Nancy K. and Gary S. Silverman, *Environmental Law*, Englewood Cliffs, NJ: Prentice-Hall, 1994.

Plater, Zygmunt J. B., Robert H. Abrams and William Goldfarb, *Environmental Law and Policy: Nature, Law and Society*, St Paul, MN: West Publishing Co., 1992.

Salzman, James and Barton H. Thompson, Jr., *Environmental Law and Policy*, New York: Foundation Press, 2003.

Steinzor, Rena I., "Toward Better Bubbles and Future Lives: A Progressive Response to the Conservative Agenda for Reforming Environmental Law," 32 ELR [*Environmental Law Reporter*] 11421 (December 2002).

5 GREEN STRATEGIES AND NEW OPPORTUNITIES

Benyus, Janine M., *Biomimicry: Innovation Inspired by Nature*, New York: HarperCollins, 1997. ISBN 0-06-053322-6.

Brown, Lester R., *Plan B: Rescuing a Planet under Stress and a Civilization in Trouble*, New York: W.W. Norton, 2003. ISBN 0-393-32523-7.

Costanza, Robert, et al., "The Value of the World's Ecosystem Services and Natural Capital," *Nature* 387: 253–260 (May 15, 1997).

Costanza, Robert, Herman E. Daly and Joy A. Bartholomew, "Goals, Agenda and Policy Recommendations for Ecological Economics," in Costanza, ed., *Ecological Economics: The Science and Management of Sustainability*, New York: Columbia University Press, 1991.

Daily, Gretchen, ed., *Nature's Services: Societal Dependence on Natural Ecosystems*, Washington, DC: Island Press, 1997. ISBN 1-55963-475-8.

Daily, Gretchen and Katherine Ellison, *The New Economy of Nature: The Quest to Make Conservation Profitable*, Washington, DC: Island Press, 2002.

Elkington, John, *Cannibals With Forks: The Triple Bottom Line of 21st Century Business*, Gabriola Island, BC, Canada: New Society Publishers, 1998. ISBN 0865713928.

Freeman, R. Edward, Jessica Pierce and Richard H. Dodd, *Environmentalism and the New Logic of Business: How Firms Can be Profitable and Leave Our Children a Living Planet*, New York: Oxford University Press, 2000. ISBN 0-19-508093-9.

Greider, William, "The Greening of American Capitalism," *Onearth* (Natural Resources Defense Council publication), Fall 2003, pp. 20–22.

Hawken, Paul, Amory Lovins and L. Hunter Lovins, *Natural Capitalism: Creating the Next Industrial Revolution*, Boston: Little Brown, 1999.

Henderson, Hazel, *Creating Alternative Futures: The End of Economics*, Kumarian Press, 1996. ISBN 1565490606.

Nattrass, Brian and Mary Altomare, *The Natural Step for Business: Wealth, Ecology and the Evolutionary Corporation*, Gabriola Island, BC: New Society Publishers, 1999. ISBN 0865713847.

Pearce, David, *Economic Values and the Natural World*, London: Earthscan, 1993.

Pimm, Stuart L., "The Value of Everything," *Nature* 387: (May 15, 1997).

Roodman, David Malin, *The Natural Wealth of Nations: Harnessing the Market for the Environment*, New York: W.W. Norton, 1998. ISBN 0393318524.

Rowe, Jonathan, "Accounting for the Commons: Accounting must move common assets from the invisible to the visible," *Business Ethics*, Winter 2003, p. 4.

Sagoff, Mark, "Can We Put a Price on Nature's Services?" ISEE Forum, http://csf.colorado.edu/ISEE/ecovalue/proceedings/0046.html.

Sagoff, Mark, *The Economy of the Earth: Philosophy, Law, and the Environment*, New York: Cambridge University Press, 1988. ISBN 0-521-34113-2.

Sawin, Janet, "Charting a New Energy Future," *State of the World 2003*, pp. 85–109.

Stevens, William K., "How Much is Nature Worth? For You, $33 Trillion," *The New York Times*, May 20, 1997.

Timmons, Heather, "British Plan Major 'Wind Farm' to Generate Power Along Coasts," *The New York Times*, Friday, December 19, 2003, p. A6.

Wall Street Journal, Science Journal, "Furry Math? Market Has Failed to Capture True Value of Nature," *The Wall Street Journal Online*, August 9, 2002.

⊛ 6 GLOBALIZING: ENVIRONMENTAL ⊛ PROBLEMS ABROAD

Alternatives to Economic Globalization: A Better World is Possible, a report of The International Forum on Globalization, San Francisco: Berrett-Koehler Publishers, 2002. ISBN 1-57675-204-6.

Armstrong, Jeannette, " 'Sharing One Skin': Okanagan Community," *Case Against the Global Economy*, pp. 460–470.

Berry, Wendell, "Conserving Communities," *Case Against the Global Economy*, pp. 407–417.

Browne, John, "Beyond Kyoto," *Foreign Affairs*, 83(4): 20–32 (July/August 2004).

DeGeorge, Richard, *Competing With Integrity in International Business*, New York: Oxford University Press, 1993.

Donaldson, Thomas, *Ethics in International Business* (Ruffin Series in Business Ethics), New York: Oxford University Press, 1989.

French, Hilary, *Vanishing Borders: Protecting the Planet in the Age of Globalization*, New York: W.W. Norton, 2000. ISBN 0393320049.

Friedman, Thomas L., *The Lexus and the Olive Tree*, New York: Farrar, Straus and Giroux, 1999.

Goldsmith, Edward, "Global Trade and the Environment," *Case Against the Global Economy*, pp. 78–91.

Goldsmith, Edward, "The Last Word: Family, Community, Democracy," *Case Against the Global Economy*, pp. 501–514.

Goldsmith, James, "The Winners and the Losers," *Case Against the Global Economy*, pp. 171–182.

Hines, Colin and Tim Lang, "In Favor of a New Protectionism," *Case Against the Global Economy* pp. 485–493.

Huntington, Samuel P., *The Clash of Civilizations and the Remaking of the World Order*, New York: Simon & Schuster, 1996.

Imhoff, Daniel, "Community Supported Agriculture: Farming with a Face on It," *Case Against the Global Economy*, pp. 425–433.

Ignatieff, Michael, *Empire Lite: Nation-Building in Bosnia, Kosovo and Afghanistan*, London: Random House, 2003.

Irvine, Ross S., " 'Netwarriors' fight way to top in corporate PR," *O'Dwyer's PR Services Report*, May 2000.

Jensen, Derrick, Simon Retallack, Paul Kingsnorth, Matilda Lee and Mark Lynas, "Global Trade: A Special Report," *The Ecologist*, June 2003, pp. 27–40.

Johnson, Chalmers, *Blowback: The Costs and Consequences of American Empire*, New York: Henry Holt and Co., 2000.

Kaplan, Robert D., "Supremacy by Stealth: Ten Rules for Managing the World," *The Atlantic Monthly*, July–August 2003, pp. 65–83.

Kimbrell, Andrew, "Biocolonization: The Patenting of Life and the Global Market in Body Parts," *Case Against the Global Economy*, pp. 131–145.

Khor, Martin, "Global Economy and the Third World," *Case Against the Global Economy*, pp. 47–59.

Korten, David C., "The Mythic Victory of Market Capitalism," *Case Against the Global Economy*, pp. 183–191.

Korten, David C., *When Corporations Rule the World*, West Hartford, CT: Kumarian Press, 1995.

Krugman, Paul, *The Great Unraveling: Losing Our Way in the New Century*, New York: Norton, 2003. ISBN 0-393-05850-6.

Lindsey, Brink, *Against the Dead Hand: The Uncertain Struggle for Global Capitalism*, New York: John Wiley & Sons, 2002.

MacDonald, Mia and Danielle Nierenberg, "Linking Population, Women, and Biodiversity," *State of the World 2003*, pp. 38–61.

Mabogunje, Akin L., "Poverty and Environmental Degradation: Challenges Within the Global Economy," in Robert Griffiths, ed., *Developing World 03/04*, p. 167.

Mathews, Jessica Tuchman, "Power Shift," *Foreign Affairs*, 76(1): 50–66 (January–February 1997).

McMurtry, John, "Why The Protestors Are Against Corporate Globalization," *Journal of Business Ethics*, 40(3): 201–205 (October (II) 2002).

Morris, David, "Communities: Building Authority, Responsibility, and Capacity," *Case Against the Global Economy*, pp. 434–445.

Norberg-Hodge, Helena, "Shifting Direction: From Global Dependence to Local Interdependence," *Case Against the Global Economy*, pp. 393–406.

Okonta, Ike and Oronto Douglas, *Where Vultures Feast: Shell, Human Rights, and Oil in the Niger Delta*, San Francisco: Sierra Club, 2001. ISBN 1-57805-046-4.

Palast, Greg, *The Best Democracy Money Can Buy*, New York: Penguin (Plume), 2003.

Ponting, Clive, *A Green History of the World: The Environment and the Collapse of Civilizations*, New York: Penguin Books, 1991. ISBN 0140176608

Postel, Sandra, *Pillar of Sand: Can the Irrigation Miracle Last?* New York: W.W. Norton, 1999 (Worldwatch series).

Reinicke, Wolfgang H., *Global Public Policy*, Washington DC: Brookings Institution Press, 1998.

Sale, Kirkpatrick, "Principles of Bioregionalism," in *Case Against the Global Economy*, pp. 471–484.

Schumacher, E. F., *Small Is Beautiful: Economics As If People Mattered*, New York: Harper & Row, 1973. 1989 edition with prefaces by John McClaughry and Kirkpatrick Sale; HarperPerennial. ISBN 0-06-091630-3.

Shuman, Michael, *Going Local: Creating Self-Reliant Communities in a Global Age*, Free Press, 1998. ISBN 0684830124.

Singer, Peter, *One World: The Ethics of Globalization*, New Haven: Yale University Press, 2002. ISBN 0300096860.

Soros, George, *The Crisis of Global Capitalism*, New York: Public Affairs, 1998.

Stiglitz, Joseph E. *Globalization and Its Discontents*, New York: W.W. Norton & Co., 2002. ISBN 0393051242.

Toffler, Alvin, *Powershift: Knowledge, Wealth and Violence at the Edge of the 21st Century*, New York: Bantam Books, 1990. ISBN 0553292153.

Vallely, Paul, *Bad Samaritans: First World Ethics and Third World Debt*, Maryknoll, NY: Orbis Books, 1990. ISBN 0-88344-668-5.

Victor, David G., *Climate Change: Debating America's Policy Options*, Council on Foreign Relations 2004. ISBN 0-87609-343-8.

⊛ 7 THE ROLE OF CIVIL SOCIETY ⊛ ORGANIZATIONS

Brown, L. David, Angela Johnson and Sara Titus, "Practice-Research Engagement and Building Transnational Civil Society: Two Connected Workshops," *Practice-Research Engagement*, pp. 9–30.

Keane, John, *Global Civil Society?*, New York: Cambridge University Press, 2003.

Lipschutz, Ronnie D. with Judith Mayer, *Global Civil Society and Global Environmental Governance*, Albany, NY: SUNY Press, 1996.

Ritchie, Mark, "Cross-Border Organizing," *Case Against the Global Economy*, pp. 494–500.

⊛ 8 SUSTAINABILITY: THE NEW DIRECTIONS ⊛ FOR BUSINESS

Berry, Wendell, *The Unsettling of America: Culture and Agriculture*, Sierra Club Books, 1996 (reprint). ISBN 0871568772.

Ehrenfeld, David, *Beginning Again: People and Nature in the New Millennium*, New York: Oxford University Press, 1995. ISBN 0195096371.

Harris, Lis, *Tilting at Mills: Green Dreams, Dirty Dealings, and the Corporate Squeeze*, Boston: Houghton Mifflin, 2003.

Hershkowitz, Allen, *Bronx Ecology: Blueprint for a New Environmentalism*, Washington, DC: Island Press, 2002.

Laszlo, Chris, *The Sustainable Company: How to Create Lasting Value Through Social and Environmental Performance*, Washington, DC: Island Press, 2003.

Newton, Lisa, *Ethics and Sustainability*, Upper Saddle River, NJ: Prentice-Hall, 2003.

Thornton, Joe, *Pandora's Poison: Chlorine, Health, and a New Environmental Strategy*, Cambridge: MIT Press, 2000.

I n d e x

tragedy of the commons, 27, 125
transparency, 131
triple bottom line, 152
tropical rainforests, deforestation
    in, 99
truth-telling, duty of, 23

United States Agency for
    International Development
    (USAID), 202
United States Army Corps of
    Engineers, 163
unlimited exploitation, 84
unrealized assets, 146
usury, 51, 64
utilitarianism, 16, 48, 55, 68, 82,
    88, 129

values, 12, 20
Venn diagram of Environmental
    Studies, viii
veracity, duty of, 23
virtues, 13, 56, 58, 68, 71, 221
    defined, 13
vocabulary of ethics, 12
vocation, 52

Watergate, 174
Wealth of Nations, 54
welfare (as a value), 16–20
wetlands, 147
Wilderness Act of 1964, 121
Wilderness Areas, 87–8
wilderness, x, 120–1
Wildlife Conservation Society
    (WCS), 104
Wilson, Edward O., 81, 90
wind power, 156
"windfall," 117
"wipeout," 117
Wise Use, 85–6
Women, Infants and Children
    (WIC), 209
work ethic, 51–2
World Bank, 207
World Resources Institute, 99
World Trade Organization (WTO),
    173, 189, 207
World Wide Fund for Nature, 104

Yale School of Forestry, 121
Yerkes Regional Primate Research
    Center, 109